Detonate

A whole year's worth of teaching materials for 5–11s

- Useful Insights Into Reaching A Totally New Generation
- Over 100 Games
- 52 Unique Stories, Bible Texts And Bible Lessons
- Step-by-step Curriculum Guide
- Over 150 Illustrations
- Major Format Ideas
- Contemporary Magazine-style Presentation
- The Curriculum That Really Works

Mark Griffiths

MONARCH
BOOKS

Oxford, UK & Grand Rapids, Michigan, USA

First published in the UK in 2005 by Monarch Books
(a publishing imprint of Lion Hudson plc),
Mayfield House, 256 Banbury Road, Oxford OX2 7DH
Tel: +44 (0) 1865 302750 Fax: +44 (0) 1865 302757
Email: monarch@lionhudson.com
www.lionhudson.com

Distributed by:
UK: Marston Book Services Ltd, PO Box 269,
Abingdon, Oxon OX14 4YN

ISBN 1 85424 679 8

British Library Cataloguing Data
A catalogue record for this book is available
from the British Library.

Printed in Malta.

Detonate (det'onate),
v. to cause an explosive event

There are three types of people in our world:
those who watch history taking place,
those who record history and – the final
category – those who make history.
At this point in time our churches need
people who make things happen,
those who will be part of this explosive
event that will once again see thousands of
boys and girls coming to know Jesus.

FOREWORD

Mark Griffiths has gone and done it again! *Fusion* was good; *Impact* better. But *Detonate* could cause the explosion so desperately needed in children's evangelism. If you want loads of the best ideas currently available on offer today for your curriculum and programmes with children then look no further - *Detonate* is definitely for you!

Detonate, grasped properly, is not just a programme or curriculum; it's a vision. It's a dangerous training manual to change tomorrow. Mark has put something in all our hands that can help us be those people who live in the "make history" category.

This curriculum will inspire and resonate with young heart and minds. His story-based stuff is fantastic. Children are copy cats: they are looking for heroes they can follow and model their lives on. Mark goes deeper. He challenges us to be those heroes the children copy. We are the visual aids in the end.

Mark's passion is for a new "sunday school movement" to explode through us that will bring good news and transformation to our society today - the section on Robert Raikes is very inspiring and provocative.

Detonate is a wake-up call to the church.

Wake Up, Church, before it's too late!

Andy Kennedy
King's Kids International
A ministry of Youth With a Mission (YWAM)

A FEW WORDS FROM THE AUTHOR

The story of Samson has a wider application than the one we tell in our children's groups. It shows us something very prophetic about the church of Jesus Christ. Through living a life of compromise and focusing on things that he should not be focusing on, Samson reaches the point where the Philistines capture him, tear out his eyes, lead him in front of their gods and begin to mock him.

Samson is in effect left visionless (he doesn't know where he is going) and wounded (he's been hurt). Samson is a very real type of the church at the start of the 21st century. Through our propensity to major on the minors, and our constant desire to compromise (we don't like this word "compromise" so we use the word "toleration" in completely the wrong way), we have become hurt and visionless. We have been paraded in front of a mocking world who have taken to worshipping very different gods.

This is not the most positive picture. But Samson cries out to his God again. Having been brought to a place of desperation, he calls out to God. The Bible says he then accomplishes more at the end than he did during his whole life up to this point.

The picture of a glorious, triumphant church is exciting indeed. But it is also realisable. God will build his church, and the gates of hell will not prevail against it. It is an absolute fact. And as a passing comment (because scripture doesn't allow much more room than to make this a passing comment), in the biblical story it is a young man – some versions render it "a child" – that leads Samson. Likewise, a passing comment: maybe through the work that you do with boys and girls the church can be led back to glory.

When a person is immunised against smallpox, doctors inject the patient with a small amount of cowpox. The virus isn't dangerous, but it is something like the dangerous virus, and it allows our body to develop the immunity to combat the real thing. When we present the Bible without proper application we give the children *something like* the word of God, and it has the terrifying effect of immunising them against the real word of God – that's why children from church backgrounds can often be the hardest to minister to at conferences and camps. They have been exposed to something like it, but not it – not the life-changing Spirit of Jesus who so desperately wants to invade your children's gathering.

This curriculum presents the word of God with clear application. It is not written by a theorist. This material has been refined in the fire. For that reason you have in your hands a curriculum that will work. The material looks at heroes of faith, those who have taken their faith to foreign nations, who on the whole heard their call from God as children themselves, and also includes a sprinkling of new stories such as the Pirate King and MacTavish. Themes such as salvation, perseverance, and the love of God are returned to again and again. There is also a series on the Nicene Creed which is used to form a basic systematic theology for children. Again, Disney movies prove a useful reference point; specifically we draw on the modernised story of *Treasure Island* in Disney's *Treasure Planet*.

The need for us to do this work is great. But it can be done. With our shoulders to the plough we can truly make a difference in this nation and in the nations of our world.

Section 1 is there to motivate and enthuse you afresh; it also highlights the process of starting new children's provisions. Section 2 describes how to outwork the material and of course is packed with the 52 weeks of resource material designed to change the lives of the boys and girls you will minister to.

Mark Griffiths
May 2005

CONTENTS

If you are new to
children's ministry or
need some enthusing,
then please spend some
time in Section 1. If you
are eager to get started
and/or you are familiar
with the previous books
in this series (*Fusion* and
Impact), then feel free to
jump straight into
Section 2.

SECTION 1

Why start an outreach children's club? And how!

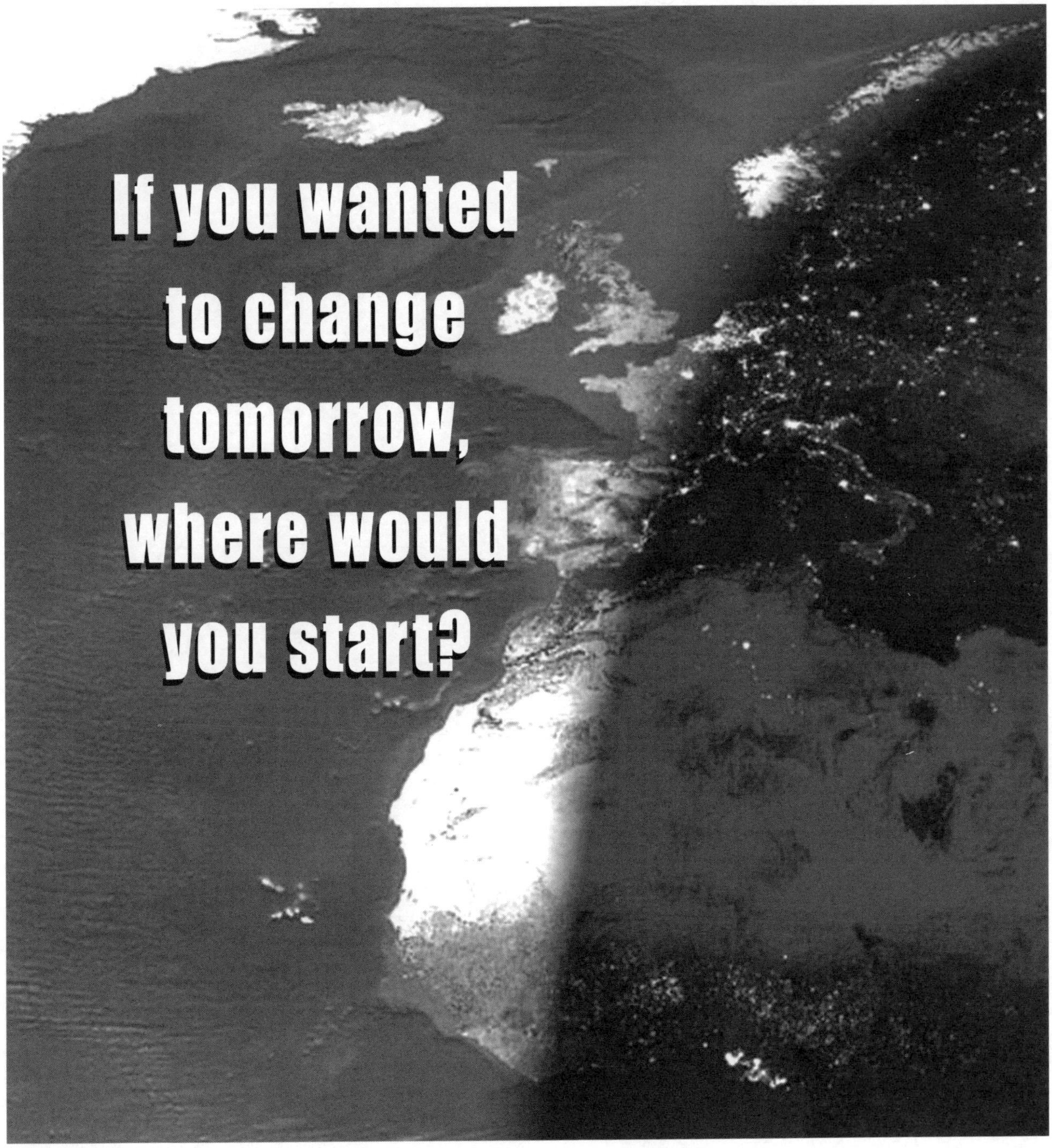

If you wanted
to change
tomorrow,
where would
you start?

WHY START AN OUTREACH CHILDREN'S CLUB?

The basic question we are trying to answer was articulated by Rob Bradbury of Kidsrus Australia: "If you wanted to change tomorrow, where would you start?" Before we can begin to answer this question we will need to be clear in our own minds that tomorrow needs to be different from today. We need to look no further than the 1998 church attendance survey for our motivation. The first and most alarming feature of the survey is that it presents in factual form what we had long suspected: the church is losing contact with children. Even when we take mid-week attendance figures into account[1] it doesn't change the reality that the church is losing contact with children. Even in situations where mid-week outreach clubs are working well, the link between them and Sunday church is often non-existent. The church is only ever one generation away from extinction.

For the first time in several centuries we find ourselves seriously having to swim upstream – please hold that thought: "It has been worse than this before." We are confident that God continues to build his church and we are confident that the gates of hell will never prevail against it. But it is also clear that we need to ensure that our sleeves are well and truly rolled up and we are working our proverbial socks off to turn this thing around.

So how did we end up at this point and "How do we change tomorrow"?

In the beginning...

The communication of a generation's belief system to the next generation has always been of vital importance. If the present generation fails to communicate its belief system to the next, then the survival of the belief system itself is jeopardised. Judaism understands this; the instructions from the early parts of the Old Testament are that the present generation must pass on their beliefs to the next generation. Deuteronomy chapters 6 and 11 explain the pattern. Not only are the children to be taught God's laws at home, not only are they to learn about them every day, but they are also to be made aware of them in their daily lives, when they walk along the road, when they go to bed at night. These verses, along with verses in Joshua 4 and Exodus 4, also show who is responsible for the teaching or communication of the law: teaching and instruction is based within the "family".

This has long been an argument against the establishment of children's projects that communicate the Christian message to children from families where this belief system is not present. "The place for teaching Christianity to children is in the home, and by parents" is the usual articulation of this particular view. However, the word most commonly translated as "family" in Hebrew is מִשְׁפָּחָה (pronounced "mish-paw-khaw"), which means much more than mother, father and children. It carries with it the sense of clan or community. It is clear from scripture that the whole community had a shared responsibility for communicating the faith to the next generation. This was about the shared responsibility of ensuring that the next generation had grasped God's life-changing message, although it is also clear from scripture that the immediate family and particularly the father had a specific role to play in communicating the world view.

This is the biblical ideal. It is a model of the immediate family with the support and input of the wider community communicating God's truth in both word and action to the next generation. When Christianity became the prevailing religion in the fourth century, the ideal came into its own. Now every family was free to communicate the Christian faith to its children. Christendom had arrived and Christianity thrived.

1. The 1998 church attendance survey only looks at children's attendance on Sundays. It doesn't consider the vast number of mid-week clubs that are now regularly presenting solid biblical teaching to our children.

A brief history

While Christianity continued to be the prevailing religion, and the churches of the day were able to support and nurture these faith communities, all was well. But the overwhelming social changes of the 18th century began to erode these systems. In Britain, rapid population growth meant that a smaller percentage of the population was attending church.[2] The widespread movement of people from rural areas to the more urban, rapidly growing people-centres was to cause the established church major difficulty. There were no mechanisms within English law to establish new parishes, with the result that the church became dysfunctional; it was not able to change and adjust to meet its new environment.

The Christian faith was no longer being passed from generation to generation. The 59th Canon of the Church of England, which requires all clergymen to instruct children and young people in religious teaching, was on the whole ignored. Many children simply had no religious knowledge or understanding. This was a church (not unlike today's church) where traditionalism was hindering its ability to react appropriately to meet the changing needs of society. This was a church that was proving irrelevant in the face of sociological developments. All looked hopeless, all looked lost...

Then onto the stage of history marched the legends: John Wesley and George Whitefield preached a message of repentance and of hope, a message of responsibility and grace, a life-changing message. They invited a response and many lives were changed. Against this background Robert Raikes would begin his experiment: a plan to change the lives of boys and girls.

If you wanted to change tomorrow, where would you start? Raikes started today and he started with the child.

Against the background of a dysfunctional church and enormous sociological changes, Raikes would become known as the father of the Sunday school. It is a deserved title if it can be understood what Raikes developed in the latter part of the 18th century. What Raikes developed here mustn't be confused with the outdated, dull and dreary Sunday-school institution that may have done more harm than good. The last sentence almost certainly needs to be qualified: when church-based children's work is done well, it communicates a living and active faith to the next generation of churchgoers; when it is done badly, it reinforces in the minds of the children the commonly held view that Christianity is irrelevant and outdated. Therefore the only conclusion is that the only thing worse than not running church-based children's work is running it badly.

To understand what Raikes developed will necessitate breaking down the elements that made up the original Sunday schools, namely professional teachers, reinforcement of good behaviour through prizes and trinkets, connections between Sunday school and church, connections between Sunday school and community (home visits), hymn-singing and prayer, and meeting a clear social need – in this case, literary skills. It is worth re-emphasising that this is 1780!

	Elements present in the birth of Sunday schools (1780–1800)
1	Professional teachers
2	Reinforcement of good behaviour through prizes and trinkets
3	Connections between Sunday school and church
4	Connections between Sunday school and community (home visits)
5	Hymn-singing and prayer
6	Meeting a clear social need – in this case, literary skills

The initial Sunday school paradigm (circa 1780)

2. It's worth re-emphasising that church attendance hadn't really dropped at this point. It was the rapid increase in population and the lack of increase in the church that meant that church attendance involved a smaller percentage of the overall population.

I will explain more fully the background and development of the initial Sunday-school paradigm in my book *One Generation From Extinction: the Raikes Paradigm in the 21st Century*,[3] but the elements will be touched on below.

PROFESSIONAL TEACHERS

From the very start Raikes recruited competent teachers, not simply those who were willing to do the job. They had the ability to communicate, but what is more clear is that Raikes chose those who could also keep order and discipline. Creating an environment and atmosphere in which teaching can take place is often as important as what is taught. When children will not sit still to listen, an ability to assert control becomes more important than what is taught – if nobody is listening, what does it matter what is being said?

We need to continue to recruit teachers who have the right heart and aptitude, we need teachers with a sense of calling and who love kids, but we must also train our teams, develop people, and enable them to be professional in what they do.

REINFORCEMENT OF GOOD BEHAVIOUR THROUGH PRIZES AND TRINKETS

It is comforting to know that over 200 years ago the concept of reinforcing positive behaviour was already in place. Some still see this as bribing kids to be quiet – such critics fail to understand that all of life works on this mechanism. If we do a good job we get extra pay/promotion/job satisfaction/bonuses. We are all motivated by reward sometimes – we don't always do things out of the goodness of our heart. Sometimes we do things when the reward is simply the ability to put food on the table.

CONNECTIONS BETWEEN SUNDAY SCHOOL AND CHURCH

This is so important, and in many ways became one of the primary mistakes of the Sunday-school institution. The Sunday school, with its superintendents, its own financing systems, its own summer trips and its Christmas prize-giving, became distinct from the church. Very often, Sunday-school teachers didn't go to church, and clergy never went near the Sunday school. In the church I recently ministered, a previous rector had deliberately had the Sunday school built as far away from the main church (and his house) as possible; he didn't want church "spoiled" by lots of children. Sunday schools didn't want to lose their autonomy to church oversight, and so the division was made. And then critics comment that children never graduated from Sunday school to church!

We must keep the link strong. All-age services may be difficult to do well, but we must do them well and we must do them. Regular events for families are essential to keep the links strong. There are various opinions regarding how children's work should develop and be "the church" itself, without the necessity of becoming part of the "adult church". I don't subscribe to this viewpoint – 200 years of Sunday-school history has proved this doesn't work.

CONNECTIONS BETWEEN SUNDAY SCHOOL AND COMMUNITY

Raikes refused to let the walls of his church isolate him from his community. He was determined to be a positive force in his community, even amongst those who never came to church. He would visit the homes of the children who attended Sunday school. He would make the link with the parents; he would ensure that if a child missed he would know why. And when he was told that a child didn't have suitable clothes for Sunday school he remarked that "as long as soap and water have been applied to the child the child is suitable".

We need community figures who understand how to join up all the pieces. This is about changing our world, not about filling our churches. Children's works that genuinely don't have the time or personnel to visit the homes of the children must maintain contact in other ways, such as e-mails to the parents with colouring competitions for the following week and general information (note: e-mail

---

3 To be published in 2009. The book will also include discussion of our understanding of conversion amongst children, a look at the sociological climate in which our message of love and hope must be communicated and also case studies showing the work of some of the most successful children's ministries throughout the UK.

the parent, not the child – we must guard ourselves against allegation always). If people don't have e-mail, then the good old post office will have to help! But contact must be maintained.

HYMN-SINGING AND PRAYER

We mustn't forget the foundation of all that we do. Somewhere at the heart of this are the basic building blocks for developing spiritual giants: prayer, praise and preaching. Don't neglect them for a strictly social programme.

MEETING A CLEAR SOCIAL NEED – IN THIS CASE, LITERARY SKILLS

Having said the above, don't be afraid of the social programme. This is where so many analysts of Raikes' work misunderstand. They suggest that he was interested in teaching children to read and write, and therefore couldn't be involved in spiritual activity. They forget that worship is a lifestyle and not just singing songs.

Meeting social needs is perfectly acceptable and should be encouraged. As well as providing spiritual input, why shouldn't we provide safe and secure play environments for our children? If they are not safe to be left to play by themselves outside any more, then let's provide a safe alternative – let's bless our communities. If we become aware that children are staying at home alone until their parents finish work, then let's provide childcare. If we live in an area where educational standards are low, let's provide homework clubs. It's OK to meet the social need.

The effect of Raikes' "little experiment" was unprecedented. Eight years later (in 1788) the Sunday School Society reported that 300,000 children were now attending Sunday schools in various parts of England. To give some idea of the magnitude of this figure, if all the New Churches'[4] attendance in the UK were added to all the Pentecostal Churches'[5] attendance in the UK, the number would be just over 300,000. The effect of just eight years of outreach to children was extraordinary.

The Raikes paradigm was rarely used in its entirety after the first 25 years. The Sunday-school movement was to peak in attendance in 1900, but the seeds of decline had been sown many years earlier when essential elements of the Raikes paradigm had been ignored. Today, however, there are many outstanding examples of children's ministry in operation through the UK, the majority of them (probably unknowingly) operating within the Raikes paradigm. Let's understand what outreach children's clubs looked like 200 years ago and ensure we don't miss out those essential elements in our 21st-century models.

We mustn't forget:

CHILD EVANGELISM IS A SIGNIFICANT KEY TO CHURCH GROWTH

Without children's outreach and good children's provision, churches are very unlikely to see any significant numerical growth.

4. This includes Pioneer, Ichthus, New Frontiers, etc.
5. This includes the Assemblies of God, Apostolic Church, Elim, Church of God of Prophecy, etc.

WE COVERED WHY; NOW HOW DO WE DO IT?

The aim of this section is to show you how to start a children's club from scratch. It will give you a timescale for activities and in some cases expected outcomes. The difficulty with presenting practice is that it doesn't always translate into every situation. Hopefully the preceding chapters will have built in enough principles to allow the discussion of practice. But again the warning: this section is meant to help, not to hinder. It is here as your slave, not your master. Use it, but don't be confined by it.

Before you start

There are many issues that need to be weighed before you start an outreach children's club, since once something is up and running it is very hard to change its form or shape. It has always been my preference to start from scratch, as taking over from someone else is always going to be difficult. But I am aware that this is not always a possibility and some diplomacy skills may be needed to reform an existing club.

In children's ministry, there is the temptation to wait until all the conditions are right before you start. You might feel you should wait until you have the right staff, wait until you are all experts at the programme, wait until you have all the equipment you need. Forget It! Start. It'll never be the perfect time, but God blesses people on the journey, not while they're waiting for the perfect conditions.

This section contains two parts:

1. The timetable for the first two years
2. The timetable for a normal year

Timetable for the first two years

The WHY section below is simply a reminder of what has been mentioned in the previous chapters. For a full explanation of WHY, refer to the appropriate chapter.

WHEN	WHAT	WHY
Pre-start	Take some time to pray and understand the area you are working in. If you are new to the area this is particularly important.	God may have a specific key that will enable you to establish the whole thing so much faster. Give God time to speak to you.
January to July (Year 1)	Make contact with one or more schools and schedule some assemblies.	Schools will be the place the children who attend your club will come from.
January	Begin to share your vision and form your team.	Your ability to reproduce leaders will be the single most important factor that determines the extent of your vision.

February	Begin to think finance. Are there local grant organisations that can help with start-up funding? Are there opportunities for child-based businesses? Can you start an after-schools project in your building? How about a holiday play scheme in the summer?	Vision will always need provision.
April	Send the schools letters advertising assemblies for June and July.	
August	If you have children already linked in, take them to summer camp.	Summer camp is an excellent opportunity to have significant input into your children's lives. It gives you six days away with them.
	Run your holiday play schemes.	A chance to bring in some extra income, but also an opportunity for spiritual input over a week.
September	Start your business opportunity or activate your other sources of income.	
	Begin to advertise your children's club in schools, in shop windows, by word of mouth.	People will not come if they don't know it exists.
	Staff training night, to complement all the informal training nights up until now.	Invest in your team. Give regular training and input.
October	Launch your children's club.	The rubber hits the road! Time to put it all together.
November	Hold a community event, e.g. a parents' party.	This never was and never will be just about reaching children. This is about winning families.
December	The Christmas special for all the children you now have contact with. Make it a big one with selection boxes for all those who attend.	The big end-of-year bash will close your first year in style. Make sure *all* your child contacts are invited: schools, holiday play schemes, children's club.
	Send schools letters out for January, February and March assemblies.	Get all your school assembly administration out of the way quickly.
	Send Christmas cards to all your contacts.	It's *always* about relationship.
	Staff/leaders' party.	Work hard but also play hard. Reward your leaders. If at all possible have a great night together and don't allow them to pay!

January (Year 2)	Restart the children's club.	
	Start small groups.	Purposeful discipleship happens best in small groups.
April	The Easter special for all the children you know.	
	If you are starting a church for children using the children's work as your start point, then start a Sunday service now. Make Easter Sunday your first service.	
	If no church plant, then run a community event here, e.g. a swimming night or a family fun day.	
	Don't do any children's activities or schools work in April; evaluate here.	Don't move into headless-chicken mode. Keep sharp and focused. You achieve this by stopping and evaluating from time to time.
	Send the schools letters advertising assemblies for June and July.	
May	Restart the children's club.	
July	Community event, e.g. barbecue with entertainer.	
August	If you have children already linked in, take them to summer camp.	
	Run your holiday play schemes.	
September	Begin to advertise your children's club in schools, in shop windows, by word of mouth.	
	If you started from scratch then start your youth activities now. If you didn't, then ensure your children are making a smooth transition into the youth department.	Children don't stay children for long. They will need to move into a dynamic youth programme eventually.
	Staff training night, to complement all the informal training nights up until now.	
	Send schools letters to advertise assemblies for October to December.	

October	Launch your children's club.	
November	Hold a community event, e.g. a parents' party.	
December	The Christmas special for all the children you now have contact with. Make it a big one with selection boxes for all those who attend.	
	Send Christmas cards to all your contacts.	
	Advertise your Christmas services to all your contacts, especially Christingle and Carols by Candlelight.	
	Send schools letters for January, February and March assemblies.	
	Staff/leaders' party.	

TIMETABLE FOR A NORMAL YEAR

January	Start your children's club.
	Start small groups for purposeful discipleship.
April	The Easter special for all the children you have contact with.
	Community event here, e.g. a swimming night.
	Send the schools letters advertising assemblies for June and July.
May	Restart the children's club.
July	Community event, e.g. barbecue with entertainer.
August	If you have children already linked in, take them to summer camp.
	Run your holiday play schemes.
September	Begin to advertise your children's club in schools, in shop windows, etc.
	Ensure all your children who are eligible are incorporated into youth group.
	Staff training night.
	Send schools letters to advertise assemblies for September to December.
October	Launch your children's club.
November	Hold a community event, e.g. a parents' party.
December	The Christmas special for all the children you now have contact with.
	Send Christmas cards to all your contacts.
	Advertise your Christmas services to all your contacts.
	Send schools letters out for January, February and March assemblies.
	Staff/leaders' party.

SECTION 2

Resources

THE PROGRAMME FROM BEGINNING TO END

The items of the teaching programme are listed on subsequent pages, but follow the following format:

	Programme	Timing *(this is maximum time for each item)*
Section 1	**Welcome**	3 minutes
	Rules	2 minutes
	Prayer	5 minutes
	Introductory Praise	7 minutes
	Game 1	5 minutes
	Praise	10 minutes
	Fun Item 1	5 minutes
	Game 2	5 minutes
	Fun Item 2	5 minutes
	Bible Text	3 minutes
	Announcements	2 minutes
	Interview	5 minutes
Section 2	**Worship Time**	10 minutes
Preaching	**Bible Lesson**	5 minutes
Time	**Illustration 1**	5 minutes
	Illustration 2	5 minutes
	Illustration 3	5 minutes
	Story	15 minutes
	Prayer	5 minutes

THE STEP-BY-STEP GUIDE TO RUNNING A CHILDREN'S CLUB

ARRIVAL

Arrival and departure is important. Have a good register that keeps track of names, addresses and any ailments that you should be aware of. Have a contact number for parents. Talk to parents; allow them to see your face. It's hard for a parent to trust an unknown name on the bottom of a sheet of paper. It's much easier to trust someone they've seen and met. For this reason, even though teenagers may man various activities and hold positions of responsibility it is better to place an adult at the reception area.

Charge a small admission fee. The more self-sufficient the club can be, the better. Remember: I am suggesting that these clubs can be the seeds for new churches. Some will need to be completely self-sufficient.

HALL SET-UP AND STRUCTURE

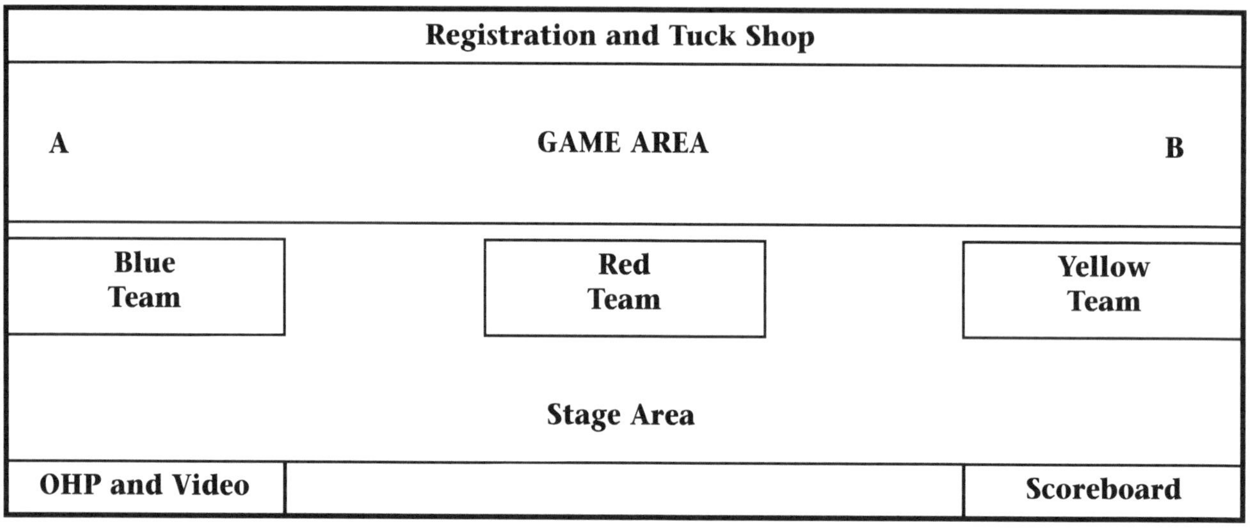

<table>
<tr><td colspan="3" align="center">Registration and Tuck Shop</td></tr>
<tr><td>A</td><td align="center">GAME AREA</td><td align="right">B</td></tr>
<tr><td align="center">Blue
Team</td><td align="center">Red
Team</td><td align="center">Yellow
Team</td></tr>
<tr><td colspan="3" align="center">Stage Area</td></tr>
<tr><td align="center">OHP and Video</td><td></td><td align="center">Scoreboard</td></tr>
</table>

Make the hall as colourful and as child-friendly as possible. You may not be allowed to decorate the building from top to bottom with the latest cartoon characters, but you can still use colourful banners and exciting background music. The hall should be at the appropriate temperature so children don't need to keep their coats on all night. The room should be brightly lit.

Why three teams?

If two teams are used, then usually there is a winning team and a losing team. Having three teams allows one team to win and the others to come joint second. It allows an element of healthy competitiveness without there needing to be a loser. Other children's groups (some very large groups) work on two teams, one of boys and the other of girls. There are two main disadvantages to this system: there is very rarely an equal mix of boys and girls; it leads to unnecessary tension between the teams and also with social services, who will frown on the practice. (Wherever possible it will pay you to keep government organisations positively inclined towards your work – Jesus had favour with God *and men.*)

STAFFING

Registration

Three team members should be responsible for registration. This is where you meet the parents. This is the initial contact point. First impressions do last, so put some of your best people here. The registration people will also need to be armed with information regarding trips, etc. This is the place to base your administrators.

Welcome person

An adult or several adults should greet the children on arrival and give a quick guided tour and breakdown of the format to those who are new. This is the place to base your pastors.

Activity supervisor

Each activity, such as bouncy castle, computers, etc., needs to be supervised by an activity supervisor. This can be one of your teenagers as long as they are prepared to be responsible.

Scorekeeper

A competent and upbeat member of the team is needed who will periodically announce the scores. We presently have a person called Gorgeous Nick to do the scores – the children's idea, not mine.

Tuck shop / Café area

This is fairly self-explanatory, but bear in mind that the café area does generate finance for the project and gives us an opportunity to talk to the children.

Technical support

A person who can operate PA systems, videos, OHPs, etc. is invaluable. If done well, this will help you greatly; if done badly, this can destroy your programme.

Front people

Two front people will be responsible for illustrations. If you work with two front people who know what they are doing and have obvious communication gifts, then introduce a third who can develop and learn. As they come to maturity in this gift, release more responsibility to them. This is a continuous process which allows you to move or sow out into other children's works. The choice of the third person is very important. He or she may not be particularly gifted, but they must be humble and teachable and have the heart of a servant. Don't choose anyone without these qualifications. The front is the place for your evangelists and teachers and maybe your apostles.

Floaters

The job description is in the title. These people float around, checking everyone is OK, talking to children, sitting in the café area with them, chilling with them, getting to know them, caring for them. People with pastoral gifts and a heart for children thrive in this position.

Others

If you run crafts as part of your programme then you will need artistic people. A qualified first-aider should not be overlooked. Members of the team will also need to be involved in the weekly visitation programme. You may also have a person to be the team leader of each team. Our Green Team leader is presently Gregory the Green!

Team Leaders

During the programme part of the evening there will need to be a sprinkling of leaders in each team. Problems should not be dealt with from the front but sorted quickly from within the team. For the staff as well as for the children it will be a process of education.

ACTIVITIES ON ARRIVAL

Because we believe that in order for the children to listen to us we must listen to them, and in order for them to listen to us we must have fun with them, and in order for them to listen to us we must be liked by them, we run the first 45 minutes of our programme with the children allowed to choose between a range of activities.

Give a quick guided tour to the children who are there for the first time. All the children need to be instructed that on arrival they need to place their coats on the back of the seats that they will later sit on and for the first 45 minutes they are free to join whatever activity they like. They may choose from:

- Crafts
- Bouncy castle

- Computer games
- Café area
- Outside play (weather and availability of a secure garden allowing)
- Snooker/Pool
- Video

The children also need to know that they don't have to stay at any of these areas; they may freely move from one to another. Some of the activities are simply there for the children to have fun; some of the activities are there to allow the children time to speak to leaders – the café area is an example of this.

Crafts

It is always useful to have a good craft activity that relates to the overall theme for the week. Assign a creative person to come up with an idea each week, based on the theme. When the children take things home it helps reinforce the message and at the same time allows a Christian activity into a possibly non-Christian home. Use paints, use glitter, use glass-painting, use textiles. Be creative.

Outside sports and bouncy castle

Joyfully, the more boisterous children always opt to go to these activities. The activities must therefore be well supervised. I say "joyfully" because it means they are expending energy that might otherwise be used in the disruption of the teaching programme. Bouncy castles, football, basketball, short tennis, etc. can all be incorporated according to the space available.

Computer games

I always have reservations about this area because children seem to spend so much time at home on computers, so it would be nice to give them a change. But in our experience some children initially attended because we had computers that they could use to show off to their friends how good they were on certain games. The club gave them an audience. Because they attract people to our teaching programme the computers have stayed.

Timing

After 45 minutes we play a specific piece of music that the children quickly learn to recognise. It is currently "Mission Impossible"! The children, on hearing the music, leave their activity and rush to their seats. It may not happen in Week 1 or 2, but by Week 3 they'll come running. As in all these things, it's a process of education.

The programme from beginning to end lasts for one hour and fifteen minutes (the numbers in brackets after each heading are maximum running times).

WARNING: **The 1989 Children's Act states that if an activity runs for more than two hours a week and for more than five days a year it must be registered – formerly with social services, now with OFSTED. OFSTED will not register you if you meet for less than two hours a week but it is vital that our clubs are safe places and it is important that our workers are police-checked – your denominational office should be able to give you further information on this process.**

TIP: **If your hall is small and you need the same space for initial activities as you do for the programme, then send the children to the back of the hall for a game of statues or a five-minute cartoon or whatever it takes to give you time to clear the floor. Clearly you are not going to use seats, but you can divide three areas using masking tape quite easily. However, be realistic. If it is not going to work in the church hall, and the main church has pews, then seriously consider booking the sports-centre hall for a couple of hours every Friday evening, or maybe a nearby local community centre. If you do take this route you will have to work harder to ensure your children's club has the correct associations with the church.**

If each item runs to the maximum time allowed, then you have a 107-minute programme. We are aiming for 75 minutes. Obviously each item must not go to the maximum, but it is better to be tight at the end than finish fifteen minutes early!

THE PROGRAMME

⇨ Welcome (3 minutes)

This is a chance to welcome the children, but also an opportunity to have fun with them. Remember, if you will not have fun with them, they will not listen to you. I prefer to lead the programme with others at the front, e.g. the scorekeeper, team leaders, a trainee leader. This allows comical banter between them. Think differently! Have leaders walk on dressed as Barney Rubble and Fred Flintstone and welcome the children. Be creative.

⇨ Rules (2 minutes)

If there are no clear rules, then the children have no discipline guidelines – they cannot be reprimanded for not obeying rules that they have never heard. Only two simple rules are necessary:

- Nobody leaves their seat. If a child needs to go to the toilet, he or she must put a hand up and ask permission from a leader.
- When the whistle blows, everyone stops speaking, sits down, focuses on the front and makes no sound. If you are uncomfortable with the use of a whistle, you can use a horn, or a special word.

These two simple rules will keep everything controlled. Children feel safer and more secure in a disciplined atmosphere.

There must be a method of enforcing the rules. We use the following twofold system:

Positive enforcement: If a team is particularly good, e.g. they sit well, listen well, cheer the loudest, or win a game, they get to roll dice. The score from the dice is added to their overall score. The team with the most points at the end of the term gets the biggest prizes; the other teams receive smaller prizes (e.g. at the end of the Easter term the members of the winning team receive Easter eggs; the other teams receive cream eggs).

Negative enforcement: If a child talks after the whistle has gone or is not sitting and facing the front, their team instantly loses six points off their score.

> **_TIP:_ You don't have to bring prizes every week. If you keep a running score for each team, inform them that they are working towards the best score for the end of term when the team that comes first will receive the largest selection box/Easter egg, and the other two teams will receive small selection boxes/cream eggs. Also, the age-old tactic of rewarding those who attend the most with attendance prizes at the end of term will ensure that you don't suffer from the spasmodic attendance common to many children's clubs up and down the country.**

⇨ Prayer (5 minutes)

This can be divided into two sections:

1. Giving thanks: Children who have prayed for something the week before (or several weeks before) and whose prayers have been answered should be asked to come and tell the others how God answered their prayer.
2. Bringing needs: Some of the children will want to pray for certain things. Allow them to come and mention what they are praying for, and ask God together to answer prayer.

	Programme
Section 1	**Welcome**
	Rules
	Prayer
	Introductory Praise
	Game 1
	Praise
	Fun Item 1
	Game 2
	Fun Item 2
	Bible Text
	Announcements
	Interview
Section 2 **Preaching Time**	Worship Time
	Bible Lesson
	Illustration 1
	Illustration 2
	Illustration 3
	Story
	Prayer

Remember, when children have prayers answered they need to be invited to the front to give God thanks.

➯ Longer prayer sessions (15 minutes)

Sometimes you may wish to hold an extra-long prayer section. You can do this in several ways:

P.R.A.Y.

The four corners of the building are given the letters P, R, A and Y respectively. If there are more than 40 children, then the centre point on each side will also need to be used, as follows:

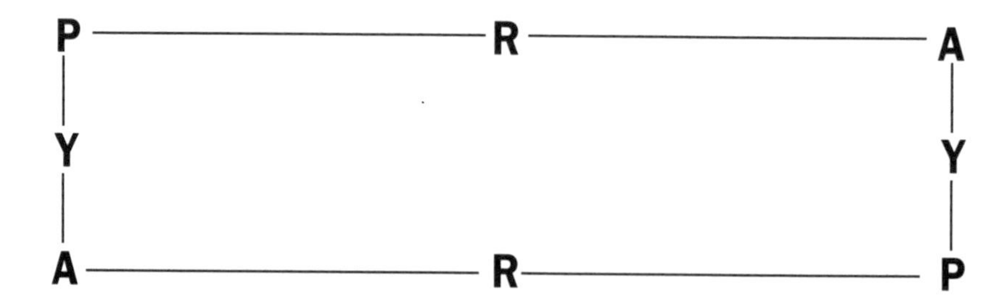

A leader is placed at each base and the children are split into four groups (eight for above). The children start at one of the bases, but only remain there for two minutes. After two minutes they move clockwise to the next base. The bases represent the following:

P is for Praise
At this base the children stand in a circle and give thanks for one thing that is good in their lives, e.g. "God, thank you for my family", "God, thank you for the children's club", "God, thank you that I'm healthy." If they visit another P base, then the leader may simply talk them through all the things we have to be thankful for, such as salvation, creation, life, eternal life.

R is for Repent
At this base the children are reminded by the base leader that we have all done things wrong, things that hurt God: "This would be a good time to think quietly about things we have done wrong that hurt God and maybe ask God to forgive us."

A is for Ask
At this base one or two children might lead in prayer and ask God for a good session, or maybe a safe journey home at the end. There may also be specific requests, for example, for parents who are sick.

Y is for Yourself
At this base the children are encouraged to ask God for something for themselves. Give them quick guidance on what sort of things, but allow the children to ask God to bless them, or to give them a good time at children's club.

From time to time children will spend their Ask and their Yourself time asking God to let their team win. Don't be worried by this; I'm not sure if God has ever got involved in the scoring system at children's club.

WALK

Send the children to walk around the building on the outside. Send a leader first and then, after he has travelled five metres, send the first child. His (or her) instructions are simple:

	Programme
Section 1	Welcome
	Rules
	Prayer
	Introductory Praise
	Game 1
	Praise
	Fun Item 1
	Game 2
	Fun Item 2
	Bible Text
	Announcements
	Interview
Section 2 **Preaching Time**	Worship Time
	Bible Lesson
	Illustration 1
	Illustration 2
	Illustration 3
	Story
	Prayer

1. He is going to walk and talk to God in the same way that he might walk and talk to a friend; he is going to tell God how he feels and what is bothering him, etc.
2. He is never going to lose sight of the person in front.
3. He is never going to catch up with the person in front; there will always be a five-metre gap.

When the child has gone five metres, send the next, until all the children have gone. This calls for close supervision and we need to send adults in between every five or six children.

CIRCLES

- Ask the children to find a space. Ask them to talk to God about themselves in that space for one minute.
- After one minute each child joins up with another child and together they pray for each other. They put their hands on each others' shoulders and in turn pray something like: "God, help my friend learn more about you."
- After one minute the two join with another two and pray in their foursome that God will give them a good session.
- After one minute the four join with another four and pray that God will look after their families – or something similar.
- After one minute the eight join with another eight and pray that God will...
- And so it continues, until you have one very large group. You then pray for the whole group.

THE HAND
The Church of England website suggests using the following:

Your **fingers** can be used to bring to your mind different things to pray for.

- **Thumb.** This is the **strongest** digit on your hand. Give thanks for all the strong things in your life, like home and family, relationships that support and sustain you.
- **Index finger.** This is the **pointing** finger. Pray for all those people and things in your life that guide and help you, e.g. friends, teachers, doctors, nurses, emergency services.
- **Middle finger.** This is the **tallest** finger. Pray for all the important people who have power in the world, like world leaders and their governments, members of parliament and local councillors, the royal family, other world leaders and their governments.
- **Ring finger.** This is the **weakest** finger on your hand. It cannot do much by itself. Remember the poor, the weak, the helpless, the hungry, the sick, the ill and the bereaved.
- **Little finger.** This is the **smallest** and the **last** finger on your hand. Pray for yourself.

⇨ Introductory Praise (7 minutes)

This involves singing some lively songs. There are two slots for praise. Make sure you use the first slot for songs the children know which contain lots of actions. New songs can be introduced in the second section. Some of the children may not enjoy singing – award six points for best team singing, and suddenly you'll find they enjoy it a lot more!

> *TIP:* **For the first section until Preaching Time, music is present almost all the time: quiet, ambient music for explaining rules; loud music for games. The contrast of total silence in Preaching Time seems to help the children listen and focus on the discussion.**

	Programme
Section 1	Welcome
	Rules
	Prayer
	Introductory Praise
	Game 1
	Praise
	Fun Item 1
	Game 2
	Fun Item 2
	Bible Text
	Announcements
	Interview
***Section 2* Preaching Time**	Worship Time
	Bible Lesson
	Illustration 1
	Illustration 2
	Illustration 3
	Story
	Prayer

➪ Game 1 (5 minutes)

Games differ from week to week. But the following points are important:

- In order to play a game the children must answer a question on the previous week's lesson.
- Choose one person from each team and then allow that person to choose the rest of the team.
- Give points for the teams that cheer people the loudest.
- Play music while the game runs – live music, if possible.
- The first team to complete the game must sit down.

➪ Praise (10 minutes)

The second praise slot is longer, with several songs being used together. Encourage banners, streamers, dancing, etc. Allow some of the children to form a praise group that stands with a microphone to lead the others. I have included a list of good CDs for children in Appendix 6.

➪ Fun Item 1 (5 minutes)

We use several fun items to enhance the programme. You can be creative with your ideas, but we recommend the following:

Guess The Leader: We reveal an interesting fact regarding one of the leaders, e.g. "This leader used to live in Spain." Then four leaders are chosen who all try to convince the children that they used to live in Spain. The children then have to guess the leader who was telling the truth. A variation on this theme is to show a picture of the leader as a baby; the leaders all have to try to convince the children that they are the person in the picture.

> ***COMMENT:*** **My favourite "Guess The Leader" involves a leader who was at the theatre. In the interval she went to the ladies' room and on her return she sat in her seat and leaned over to kiss her fiancé's neck (the children never fail to go "Ughhh!" at this point). Her "boyfriend" then turned around and his wife also leaned over and gave this particular leader a very annoyed look – the leader had sat in the wrong seat and kissed the wrong person. You'd be amazed at what your leaders have done, and also how keen their friends are to tell the stories!**

Strip Search: Here is an idea from Saturday-morning television that helps with getting to know the children or leaders. Play some background music. Invite a leader (or a child) to sit at the front. Then for one minute ask the leader questions such as: "Awake or asleep?" The leader then answers by telling you whether they prefer to be awake or asleep. These are some sample questions:

- "Awake or asleep?"
- "Music or reading?"
- "Chocolate or fruit?"
- "Kylie or Robbie?"
- "Sweets or chocolate?"
- "Shoes or trainers?"
- "Bath or shower?"
- "McDonald's or Burger King?"
- "Cap or hat?"
- "Dogs or cats?"
- "Spring or autumn?"
- "Pepsi or Coke?"
- "Cinema or video?"
- "Morning or evening?"

Buy It or Bin It: This is a chance for music and video reviews. Ask the children to bring in the videos they watch and the music they listen to. This may not seem overtly Christian, but it is incredibly educational!

	Programme
Section 1	Welcome
	Rules
	Prayer
	Introductory Praise
	Game 1
	Praise
	Fun Item 1
	Game 2
	Fun Item 2
	Bible Text
	Announcements
	Interview
Section 2 **Preaching Time**	Worship Time
	Bible Lesson
	Illustration 1
	Illustration 2
	Illustration 3
	Story
	Prayer

Form a panel of three (one leader and two children) and allow them to view three videos/CDs for 30 seconds each. Then ask them whether they would buy them or bin them, and why. Periodically introduce Christian music.

This game teaches the children critical thought, which is very important for their development. Don't allow the children to get away with reasons such as: "Because it's good" or Because I like it". They must at least try and explain why. They need their attention drawn to the lyrics: ask if they know what the song is about.

Who Wants To Be A Chocoholic?: This is based on the television game show *Who Wants To Be A Millionaire?* A child is chosen from the audience. They are asked questions in increasing degrees of difficulty. They are given four answers to the questions and have to choose the right one. For a right answer they gain more chocolate; for a wrong answer they lose it all. The trick is to know when to quit and take the chocolate. The children have two lifelines: they can ask the audience or ask a leader the answer to a question.

Aerobics Workout: A piece of music is played and the children copy the leader at the front performing their aerobic workout.

Double Dare: A child is chosen. He or she then chooses a leader. The child will then choose between several different envelopes. In each envelope there is a question; some questions are easy, some very hard. The child has to make a decision before the envelope is opened: Will he or she answer the question, or will the leader? The envelope is then opened and the question is put to whomever the child chose. If the child chose to answer the question but gets it wrong, then he or she gets a shaving-foam pie in the face. If he or she gets it right, then he or she gets to place the pie in the leader's face. If the leader answers the question the same rules apply in reverse.

This slot can also be used for all sorts of fun items such as puppet skits, etc. Use the time to have fun with the children.

> ***WARNING:*** **There exists a group of people called the "What's the point of that?" people. They watch with cynical faces. They shake their heads and ask, "What's the point of that?" It's perfectly legitimate to have fun. But I find it best never to defend the fun items. It's best to smile and simply say, "There's no point at all!" Watch the response.**

⇨ Game 2 (5 minutes)

Make sure that the people who take part in Game 2 are different from those who were involved in Game 1.

⇨ Fun Item 2 (5 minutes)

Other items may be added here, such as video clips of an outing. Use your imagination.

> ***SPECIAL NOTE:*** **All the items within the programme need to be joined together quite rapidly. The usual length of a session is just under two hours. Younger children may not cope with the full length of the programme. Condense the programme and introduce a simple craft time if you are working with children under seven years old.**

⇨ Bible Text (3 minutes)

We display the memory verse on the OHP from the start of Preaching Time and refer to it frequently, but you may prefer to encourage the children to memorise the text. There are many ways to teach a Bible Text. A few ideas are given below, but there are literally hundreds of possibilities. Be creative.

	Programme
Section 1	Welcome
	Rules
	Prayer
	Introductory Praise
	Game 1
	Praise
	Fun Item 1
	Game 2
	Fun Item 2
	Bible Text
	Announcements
	Interview
Section 2	Worship Time
Preaching	Bible Lesson
Time	Illustration 1
	Illustration 2
	Illustration 3
	Story
	Prayer

- Write the Bible Text on balloons and burst a balloon as each word of the verse is read.
- Make the verse into a jigsaw puzzle.
- Write the verse on an object which communicates its message, e.g. "You are a light to my path" can be written on a lamp or a drawing of a bulb.
- "The Lord is my shepherd" can be written on five cut-out sheep.
- Laminate the verse onto lots of tiny sheets of paper and give each child one to take home.

Remember that memorisation of the verse is not as important as understanding. Children may win a prize if they can quote "The Lord is my shepherd", but their lives will be changed if they understand it.

⇨ Announcements (2 minutes)

Summer camps, play schemes, colouring competitions, birthdays, special events, etc. all need mentioning here. If you are going to do birthdays you must be consistent – don't mention birthdays one week and then give them a miss for two weeks, as some children will miss out and feel hurt.

⇨ Interview (5 minutes)

Invite one of the leaders (or one of the children) to come and tell the group what Jesus has done for them; how he helped them in work or school; how he cares for them; how they first made their decision to become a Christian. If the person is very nervous, interview them. If they are more confident, allow them to speak freely, taking notice of the timing allowed for this section.

⇨ Preaching Time

The rest of the programme falls under the heading "Preaching Time". This will include all Worship, Bible Lessons, Illustrations and the Story. Take three minutes to explain the rules.

Time for a very special announcement. Inform the children that they are now moving into Preaching Time, which is the most important thing that happens. Inform them that this section can change their lives. There are special rules. When the whistle blows next, Preaching Time has begun. In Preaching Time:

- Nobody leaves to go to the toilet. In fact nobody moves.
- Anyone talking loses six points straight away, without discussion.

However, a leader will be walking around with tuck-shop tokens or sweets and will place them in the hands of anyone who really deserves one:

- You must be excellent to receive one. Being good is not enough; anyone can be good.
- You must keep facing the front. If you look at the leader (whom we refer to as a "quiet seat" watcher) he or she will not give you a token/sweet.
- If you get a token/sweet and play with it (or try and open it), it will be taken from you.

Sweets and tokens are given sparingly, perhaps one sweet or token every three to four minutes. Giving more than this means the sweets and tokens are no longer an incentive to listen; they become a distraction.

⇨ Worship Time (10 minutes)

This is a quieter time of worship, when songs such as Ishmael's "Father God" can be introduced. Encourage the children who know the words to close their eyes and begin to think about King Jesus. Take your time here; it is important to introduce them to worship.

Instruct the children that praise is generally loud and lively, a time when we have fun singing to God. Worship is when we come closer to God, and think about God more. Worship comes from our hearts and our minds. It involves all our emotions. The definitions of praise and

	Programme
Section 1	Welcome
	Rules
	Prayer
	Introductory Praise
	Game 1
	Praise
	Fun Item 1
	Game 2
	Fun Item 2
	Bible Text
	Announcements
	Interview
Section 2 **Preaching Time**	**Worship Time**
	Bible Lesson
	Illustration 1
	Illustration 2
	Illustration 3
	Story
	Prayer

worship may be much broader and more theological than this, but a bite-sized theological portion is more easily swallowed by an eight-year-old.

Blow the whistle at the end of Worship Time and inform the children again that this is Preaching Time (the whistle can be put away now; it will no longer be needed).

⇨ Bible Lesson (5 minutes)

There are various ideas to help with the presentation of the Bible Lesson:

- Dress some of the children up as characters in the story.
- Use videos. The list of recommended resources in Appendix 6 will give you some ideas.
- If you are presenting the story in narrative form, then tell the story as Hollywood would – don't just read the account.

⇨ Illustrations 1–3 (5 minutes each)

Illustrations can take many forms, as below:

Object lessons:
An object can be used to communicate a truth. For example:

Object needed: *A light bulb and a sheet of paper.*

People are always complaining that we are wasting things. They say: "Turn off the light; you're wasting electricity." "Use the back of that piece of paper; don't waste paper." "Don't leave the tap running; you're wasting water... "

All these things are important and we mustn't waste things. But I heard a story once of someone who wasted something even more important. It was an old woman and she said one of the saddest things I have ever heard. She said that God had told her when she was young that she should be a missionary for him and go to a faraway country. The old woman said that she hadn't gone because she had found something else to do and now she feels that she has wasted her life.

It's bad to waste money or electricity or paper or water. But it is the saddest thing in the world to waste a life. Being a Christian may be tough sometimes, but at least we will not waste our lives.

Short drama sketches
Short drama sketches are an excellent way to communicate themes. Here's an example:

Cheese: Hi everyone! It's me, the amazing Cheese. Has anyone seen the Chalk dude? He's not been around for a while. He's doing his exams.
Chalk: Hi, old chap! Did I hear you talking about me?
Cheese: Yes, I was just wondering when you're going to be back around playing and things. I've missed you over the last couple of months. All that work you've been doing for those exams!
Chalk: Yes, it's been quite difficult. I've had to work really hard. I've got to pass three different exams and then I get this really cool certificate that says that I am really clever.
Cheese: So, you've done two and you've got the last one really soon.
Chalk: No! I've had enough now. I've been working really hard and those two exams were really long and I don't want to do any more.
Cheese: But, dude, if you don't do the last exam then you won't get the certificate!
Chalk: That's true.
Cheese: Well, go and do the final exam!
Chalk: I don't want to; it's too much effort.
Cheese: But you've done two already; you're nearly there...

	Programme
Section 1	Welcome
	Rules
	Prayer
	Introductory Praise
	Game 1
	Praise
	Fun Item 1
	Game 2
	Fun Item 2
	Bible Text
	Announcements
	Interview
Section 2	**Worship Time**
Preaching	**Bible Lesson**
Time	**Illustration 1**
	Illustration 2
	Illustration 3
	Story
	Prayer

Chalk: No, old bean, I'm not going.
Cheese: But, Chalk, this is foolish!
Chalk: Yes, it is, but it's not as foolish as promising to do something for Jesus and then giving up halfway through.
Cheese: Well, I know it's not *that* foolish, but it certainly is foolish.
Chalk: Well, I guess you're right. I'll do the final test. I guess I'll see you soon.
Cheese: Go for it! We can always play next week.

What about you? Are you a good finisher or did you just start well? How many of you will finish the work God has given you to do?

Video clips
With a video camera, go to the streets and get a teenager to interview passers-by. People can be asked if they believe in God, if they own a Bible, what they understand by the word "trust", etc.

Commercial movie clips
Video clips can also be used to communicate. Here is an example:

Here's a clip from the movie *Hook*.

This is one of my all-time favourite movies. It's the story of when Peter Pan grows up and goes back to Neverland and finally defeats Captain Hook and saves his children. There's a great bit towards the end. Hook has been defeated and Peter stands opposite Tinker Bell and Tinker Bell says to him: "So, Peter, I guess your adventures are over now."

Peter looks at Tink and says these words: "Tink, to live is an adventure."

Those people who will give their lives to Jesus and allow God to do whatever he wants with them will discover that living for Jesus really is an adventure.

Testimonies: personal testimony
Things that happen to us often illustrate important truths. Here's an example:

I had to go on a journey once to a place in the north of the country. I got on a train very early in the morning and was on my way. We hadn't travelled very far when it started to snow. It kept on snowing and didn't look as if it was ever going to stop. When I was halfway there I had to change trains. When I got off my train the whole world had gone white. The snow kept on falling and most of the trains were cancelled. There were just a few trains left running; one was going back towards my home and another was going in the direction I was heading but not exactly the right way.

I had to make a decision. It would have been the easiest thing in the world to get back on the other train and go home. But I didn't. I got on the other train. You see, I had friends waiting for me, and I didn't want to let them down. So I got on the other train.

God is desperate for us to finish the journey we started with him. He doesn't want us to turn back; he wants us to keep going.

The train took me to somewhere near where I wanted to go and then I had to get in a taxi and travel the last 40 miles. The taxi couldn't get me all the way. So, in the freezing cold and well after midnight, I had to walk the last bit. And then to my horror I discovered the person I was going to stay with wasn't there. He hadn't been able to get home because of the snow. I had to phone someone else and finally managed to find someone to stay with. But I had got there. I didn't turn back. I finished the journey. I reached the destination.

God didn't tell us it would be easy serving him – in fact he promised that it would be hard at times. But we must keep going.

When we start something we need to see it through until the end.

	Programme
Section 1	Welcome
	Rules
	Prayer
	Introductory Praise
	Game 1
	Praise
	Fun Item 1
	Game 2
	Fun Item 2
	Bible Text
	Announcements
	Interview
Section 2	Worship Time
Preaching	Bible Lesson
Time	**Illustration 1**
	Illustration 2
	Illustration 3
	Story
	Prayer

Testimonies: stories of others

Not only are stories about our own lives useful, but things that happen to others can also be an excellent communication tool:

> Once during the American War of Independence an accident happened as several of the American troops were travelling along a muddy path. A wagon they were using had overturned and was blocking the road. The captain of the troops had lined up several of the men and was shouting at them to push and push and push to try and turn the wagon back over.
>
> When the wagon wouldn't budge the captain got even more annoyed and shouted louder at his men to push. After some time a man on horseback arrived at the place where the wagon had turned over and asked: "Captain, why don't you help these men rather than just shout at them?"
>
> The Captain was amazed at the request. "I am their captain," he replied. "I should not dirty my uniform in such a manner."
>
> With that, the rider got off his horse. His uniform was already dirty. He walked over to the men and said: "I will help! Let's push again." And now, with the help of this stranger, the wagon was pushed upright.
>
> The captain was glad that the wagon was restored but annoyed that this stranger should interfere. As the stranger got back onto his horse the captain demanded: "Who are you, sir? What gives you the right to interfere in my affairs?"
>
> The man, now on horseback, smiled. "I am General George Washington and I interfere because you are in my army. And from now on, Captain, you will lead by example."
>
> The captain didn't know how to answer. So he simply said: "Yes, sir!"
>
> That day the captain learned the importance of leading by example. Do we give a good example for others to follow, or not?

Basically, anything that will help to present the overall lesson can be placed here.

⇨ Story (15 minutes)

The story is a modern parable which rolls all the themes presented so far into one neat narrative package. Again, various methods can be used to enhance the presentation:

- Use some of the children as characters in the story.
- Draw some of the characters on flash cards or acetates.
- Keep it dramatic. Use your body and voice to maximise the presentation.
- Some of the stories that you plan to use often can be given to an artist to illustrate. From there it is fairly simple to photocopy onto acetate for display on your overhead projector. For the more computer-literate (and those who own a video projector) you can scan the pictures into your computer and use a package such as Microsoft PowerPoint to display them.
- Use crowd actions or a mimed response to certain words.

⇨ Prayer/Response (5 minutes)

Always ask for a response. Make an appeal. Ask the children who felt the lesson had applied to them to stand. If the lesson required forgiveness, pray a prayer of forgiveness together. Let the children respond by repeating the prayer after you. There should be a response.

⇨ Next Week (3 minutes)

Highlight next week's programme. Keep it exciting: "Next week everyone who comes will get a cream egg", "Next week we'll hear the concluding part of this exciting story", etc.

⇨ The Finishing Touch (2 minutes)

Ask a leader to dismiss the children a row at a time. Head for the door and say goodbye to the children, then talk to some parents. Mix!

	Programme
Section 1	Welcome
	Rules
	Prayer
	Introductory Praise
	Game 1
	Praise
	Fun Item 1
	Game 2
	Fun Item 2
	Bible Text
	Announcements
	Interview
Section 2	Worship Time
Preaching	Bible Lesson
Time	**Illustration 1**
	Illustration 2
	Illustration 3
	Story
	Prayer

PROGRAMME ENHANCEMENTS

It's always the little things that help make the programme just a little more special. Here are a few suggestions:

- The games each week can be run by the "Games Master". This is a person in costume, perhaps with their own theme music, who comes on to run the games sections. He or she could be dressed as a court jester or something similar.
- If you have the staff, one of the fun items could become a regular drama-group slot.
- Keep a diary of the club's activities and appoint a diary committee.
- Video cameras and projectors are becoming more and more common. If you have one available, use it. Do interviews in your local high street on the theme of the session. You could appoint a person from the team to do ridiculous things each week. Members of a church I know make a visit to a child's bedroom (in consultation with the parents) and film it for all to see. In another church the club leaders visit a child's home and cook the child their favourite meal. The clips are filmed and shown.
- These are just a splattering of ideas – add to these.

COMMENT: **Don't underestimate the importance of standing at the door and saying goodbye to the children and parents. Parents need to see a person they can relate to. Once again, the emphasis is on the establishment of long-term relationships. Say goodbye; allow the parents to ask questions; let them clarify with you when the Christmas or Easter special begins. Provide them with the opportunity to ask about how their child can get involved in a small group – all this by simply standing at the door.**

IMPORTANT* IMPORTANT * IMPORTANT

It is essential that our clubs are safe places and it is therefore imperative that our workers are police-checked (your denominational office should be able to give you information on this process).

However, do not fall into the trap of assuming that police checks stop child abuse. It is good practice that stops child abuse and not police checks. Have a clear policy in place as to what your workers should and shouldn't do. For example, they should never be alone in a room with a child for any reason. If private conversations are needed, they should take place in the same room as the rest of the crowd but in a different area. Rules like this will keep children safe from harm and leaders safe from allegation.

MACTAVISH

A Series in Five Parts

Introduction

Title	Themes covered
1 Elisha And Naaman	God wants us to come to him
2 Elisha And The Syrians	God is with us in every situation
3 Elisha Is Chosen	God chose us for something special
4 Elisha Keeps Going	God wants us to show perseverance
5 Elisha Brings Life	God wants us to bring light and love wherever we go

Elisha, the successor to Elijah, is an amazing individual with much to teach us. The series looks at some of the amazing adventures in Elisha's life – dealt with in non-chronological order. Issues such as: God choosing us even though we didn't deserve it; our responsibility to keep following Jesus; our need to trust him in every situation; and the glorious privilege of every Christian: to be able to bring the life and love of God to every situation.

1 Elisha And Naaman

	Programme	Item
Section 1	Welcome	
	Rules	
	Prayer	
	Introductory Praise	
	Game 1	Draw The Leader
	Praise	
	Fun Item 1	
	Game 2	Cut Up The Leader
	Fun Item 2	
	Bible Text	John 6:44
	Announcements	
	Interview	
Section 2	Worship Time	
Preaching Time	Bible Lesson 1	Naaman – You Can't Always Come When You Want
	Bible Lesson 2	You Can't Always Come As You Want
	Bible Lesson 3	There Comes A Time When You Have To Come
	Story	MacTavish
	Prayer	

Overview Naaman lived in a faraway land called Syria. He had a terrible disease called leprosy; he needed God to heal him or he would die. We have a terrible disease as well; it is called sin. But much worse than causing us to die, sin causes us to experience what the Bible calls "second death".

games

Game 1

Draw The Leader

PREPARATION A few crayons and a piece of paper per person placed at point B.

PLAYERS Four players per team.

SET-UP Players line up in relay formation at point A.

OBJECT The first person runs from A to B. At B the player attempts to draw any of the leaders. He must then run back to A and, without words being spoken, the team must identify the leader. Only then can the next player go. The team must not choose leaders already drawn by members of their own team.

WINNING The first team to complete the relay and sit down wins.

Game 2

Cut Up The Leader

PREPARATION A leader's name is chosen. The name is written out and cut into its component letters (the longer the name, the better).

PLAYERS A player for each letter per team.

SET-UP Players stand in standard relay pattern at point A with a letter each.

OBJECT The first person runs from A to B and places their letter on the floor. They then do a star jump to indicate to the next player to come. This continues until all the letters are on the floor. The team then sorts the letters to discover the name. The whole team then runs from A to B to inform the leader of the name.

WINNING The first team back with the correct name wins.

PreachingTime

BIBLE LESSON 1 **YOU CAN'T ALWAYS COME WHEN YOU WANT**

"No one can come to me, unless the Father who sent me makes them want to come." (John 6:44)

Object needed: *A sign with the above heading written on it.*

Display the sign at the front and leave it there (you will add the next two signs as you continue). Invite some of the children to come and act out the following:

Actors: Narrator
Syrian king
Israeli king
Servant girl
Naaman's wife
Elisha
Naaman
Naaman's servant

They will need to read out the parts that are associated with their character, so they will need a copy each.

Naaman was the commander of the Syrian army. The Lord had helped him and his troops defeat their enemies, so the king of Syria respected Naaman very much. Naaman was a brave soldier. But he had leprosy.

One day, while the Syrian troops were raiding Israel, they captured a girl, and she became the servant of Naaman's wife. Some time later the girl said to the wife: "If your husband Naaman would go to the prophet in Samaria, he would be cured of his leprosy."

When Naaman told the king what had been said, the king replied: "Go ahead! I will give you a letter to take to the king of Israel."

Namaan was a soldier; he lived many miles away from Elisha, in Syria. I'm sure he would have loved to come to Elisha many years earlier when he first got leprosy, but there probably wasn't time. He was too busy fighting. But remember, you can't always come to God when you want.

You can't always come when you want.

BIBLE LESSON 2 YOU CAN'T ALWAYS COME AS YOU WANT

Object needed: *A sign with the above written on it.*

Naaman left for Israel and took along 30,000 pieces of silver, 6,000 pieces of gold, and ten new outfits. He also carried the letter to the king of Israel. It said: "I am sending my servant Naaman to you. Would you cure him of his leprosy?"

When the king of Israel read the letter, he tore his clothes in fear and shouted, "That Syrian king believes I can cure this man of leprosy! Does he think I am God, with power over life and death? He must be trying to pick a fight with me."

As soon as Elisha the prophet heard what had happened, he sent the Israelite king this message: "Why are you so afraid? Send the man to me, so that he will know there is a prophet in Israel."

So Naaman set off on his chariot and came to Elisha's house. Elisha sent someone outside to say to him: "Go and wash seven times in the river Jordan. Then you will be completely cured." But Namaan stormed off, grumbling.

"Why couldn't Elisha come out and talk to me?" he complained. "I thought he would be sure to stand in front of me and pray to the Lord God, then wave his hand over my skin and cure me. What about the river Abana or the river Pharpar? Those rivers in Damascus are just as good as any river in Israel. I could have washed in them and been cured."

His servant went over to him and said: "Sir, if the prophet had told you to do something difficult, you would have done it. So why don't you do what he has said? Go and wash, and be cured."

The King of the universe had spoken to Elisha and told him what Naaman should do. Naaman would be foolish not to listen to the King of the whole universe. But some people *are* foolish.

BIBLE LESSON 3 THERE COMES A TIME WHEN YOU HAVE TO COME

Object needed: *A final sign with the above written on it.*

Namaan walked down to the river Jordan. He waded into the water and stooped down in it seven times just as Elisha had told him: 1, 2, 3, 4, 5, 6 (if he'd stopped here nothing would have happened)... 7... He was cured! His skin became like a child's skin. Naaman came the way that God wanted him to come, and everything went well for him.

There comes a time when, if you don't come, the whole thing gets serious.

• STORY – MacTavish (1)

MacTavish was a bear, but not a bear like Winnie the Pooh or Paddington. MacTavish was a proper bear: big, mean, tough. His fur was matted, and underneath the fur there were scars, long scars from the many battles he had fought. He had huge claws and, as he stood right now on the edge of the mountain wearing his battle armour, he did indeed look very formidable. This was real battle armour. It wasn't polished and shiny, it was tarnished and dented. It had been used – many times. MacTavish was a Leader of Bears.

He lived in the mountains with those who followed him. And this evening he was sitting in front of the camp fire, his back leaning against a tree that had only recently been upright. It had been upright until MacTavish needed something to lean against and then he had pulled it out of the ground and carefully positioned it near the fire, not so near as to singe his fur, but close enough to feel the warmth. He sat drinking the only suitable drink for a bear like MacTavish, Irn-Bru, and stared into the flames.

He began to think back to the day it had all begun. MacTavish's father had also been a Leader of Bears, but it looked certain that MacTavish wouldn't be the next leader. MacTavish had two elder brothers and they were certainly bigger and stronger than he, and there was a time when they were better fighters also. But not any more. MacTavish had been in too many fights not to be the best by now. You didn't get to stay Leader of Bears if you lost a challenge and in the early days there were plenty who wanted to challenge him.

That's how MacTavish had become Leader of Bears in the first place.

His dad had called all the bears to a gathering one evening and when they had formed themselves into a circle he made his big announcement: "I am MacTavish." (Because of course MacTavish's father was also called MacTavish, as was his grandfather and his great-grandfather and... well, it went back a long way.) "I have led you for many years and now I must step down. I am too old to live in the wild and to fight all the time. Soon I must return to the village where I will settle down and enjoy my old age. But one of you must succeed me. And the rules are the rules. I can only step down if one of you beats me in combat. So who will it be? Who fancies being Leader of Bears?"

There was absolute silence. Several bears nudged other bears, who shrugged and looked at the ground. MacTavish's elder sons exchanged looks but they would not enter into combat with their father – not out of of respect, but simply because he would surely win.

The silence continued for what seemed like an eternity. It was understandable. Many bears had taken on MacTavish Senior in combat. The last one to do so was still recovering – he had been recovering for nearly two years. MacTavish was a fierce fighter, although to say he was fierce didn't even begin to explain what he was like when fighting. He looked completely out of control, paws moving too fast to see. He was truly wild.

"Come on! Who will fight me?" he yelled once again. Still nobody moved. It would indeed be a brave bear who stepped forward, or a very stupid one. "Who will fight me?"

Then there was movement and MacTavish Junior got to his feet. There were sniggers and even some quite loud laughter from his elder brothers, but MacTavish Junior was going to enter the arena. He wasn't sure what would happen but he was going to be brave enough to enter the fight.

This is what we are talking about in this lesson, not about how well you know Jesus or how much Bible you've read. We want to know if you'll take a chance and come. Will you be brave enough to say, "God, I'm not even sure you are there, but if you are I want to come to you, and be close to you"? You can't always come *when* you want, or *how* you want, but sometimes you've just got to get brave enough to come anyway.

The laughter stopped. Nobody felt it right to laugh when somebody was about to get killed. All the bears stared into the centre of the circle.

"So, my brave, foolhardy cub. You dare to take on your dad in combat? I will tear you in half without even breaking sweat. Go and sit down." But MacTavish Junior would not sit. He stared into the eyes of his dad and said: "No! I will fight." There were some growls, some claws being stretched, some movement, and then... MacTavish knelt down and in front of the whole gathering announced: "I give in. My son shall be the new leader. He has dared to face me. I knew nobody could win, but I needed to know who would be brave enough to try. So, my son, you will be Leader of Bears." And with that MacTavish Senior took off his chainmail sash and hung it around his son. He hugged him as only a bear can do properly and said his goodbyes.

That was how it all began. Old MacTavish left and returned to the village, and MacTavish Junior was the new Leader of Bears. Many had challenged him, but he fought so hard and long that he had never been beaten. Now, the bears agreed, he was even more fierce and formidable than his father. Nobody dared challenge him any more. The last challenge had been two years ago!

MacTavish blinked as he watched the flames rising high. This was going to be a very interesting week. He might not live past the end of it, but he would be brave. He knew no other way. He closed his eyes and slept.

(To be continued...)

Elisha And The Syrians

	Programme	Item
Section 1	Welcome	
	Rules	
	Prayer	
	Introductory Praise	
	Game 1	Colours
	Praise	
	Fun Item 1	
	Game 2	Hop, Skip And Jump
	Fun Item 2	
	Bible Text	1 Peter 5:7
	Announcements	
	Interview	
Section 2	Worship Time	
Preaching	Bible Lesson	Elisha And The Syrian Army
Time	Illustration 1	Fan
	Illustration 2	"Whatifs"
	Illustration 3	Box Of Worries
	Story	MacTavish (2)
	Prayer	

We need to understand that God is with us in every situation. Even when we can't see him, God is still with us.

Game 1

Colours

PREPARATION	None needed as long as the hall contains sufficient objects of different colours. If necessary, place some red, yellow, blue and green items in the hall at various positions.
PLAYERS	Four players per team. Two blindfolded children players per team and two leaders per team.
SET-UP	Players line up at A.
OBJECT	The team must find an object which is yellow, an object which is red, an object which is green and an object which is blue. All the players may search at the same time. But none of them can see; they are each protected by a leader who guides them.
WINNING	The first team to collect all the coloured items and sit down wins.

Hop, Skip And Jump

PREPARATION	A skipping rope per team.
PLAYERS	Three players per team.
SET-UP	The players line up in standard relay pattern at point A.
OBJECT	The first person hops from A to B and back again. The next person skips and the last person jumps around (both feet together).
WINNING	The first team back and sitting down wins.

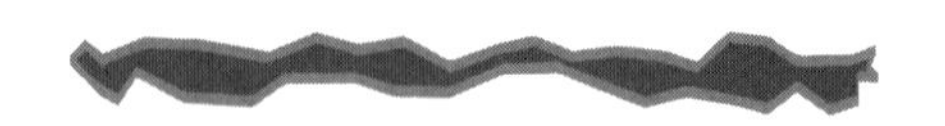

BIBLE LESSON

ELISHA AND THE SYRIAN ARMY

"God cares for you, so turn all your worries over to him." (1 Peter 5:7)

The Syrians were at war with Israel, but the Syrian king was becoming increasingly angry. Every time he sent his army to invade a certain part of Israel, the Israelite army was already there waiting to stop them. The Syrian king had called together all his generals and asked who was spying for the king of Israel, but they all said it wasn't them.

Then the king eventually learned the truth. Elisha was from Israel and he was a prophet. A prophet, as we know by now, is someone who hears from God and tells others what God has said. God was telling Elisha where the Syrians would attack, because God knows everything. Then Elisha was telling the king of Israel where to send his army.

The king of Syria was furious when he found this out and gave orders to his army: "Go and find this Elisha and kill him."

The Syrian army set off and early in the morning when Elisha's servant opened the front door he couldn't believe his eyes. The town was full of Syrian soldiers waiting to kill Elisha as soon as he came out. Elisha's servant was very worried and rushed back into the house to tell Elisha what he had seen.

You would think that Elisha would be very worried indeed. But Elisha knew God very well and he had learnt to see God in every situation, no matter how good or bad. Elisha prayed that his servant would also be able to see God in this situation. The servant had to blink twice and pinch himself before he could believe his eyes, for when he looked out again he could see that surrounding the Syrian army was God's army. He saw thousand of horses and chariots, all holding God's warrior angels. Elisha's servant didn't feel so afraid now. He had learnt to see God in the problem.

God wants to help us in every situation and with every problem. Elisha's servant could now see God helping, and we need to ask God to help us in every situation and then look for God helping us.

Elisha prayed another prayer and all the Syrians became blind. Elisha captured them all and led them away to the king of Israel. The king of Syria was now angrier than he'd ever been.

Fan

Object needed: *A fan and some confetti.*

We can't see God, so how do we know he's there? It's a fair question and I hear it lots and lots.

Let me put this fan on... Now here is an interesting thing: we can't see what is happening, but the air around this fan is now moving very quickly. We can't see it, but we know it's happening. Let me prove it to you.

Sprinkle the confetti in front of the fan.

You can't see the wind blowing but you can see what it does. In this case, it makes a mess with the confetti and I'll have to clean it all up later!

You can't see what God is doing, but you can see the effects. You can't always see God helping us and we can't always see him protecting us. But it doesn't change the fact that God really does help us and he really does protect us. We can't see God but sometimes we get to see the effect – God deals with the things that worry us. But very often he protects us even when we don't know about it.

"Whatifs"

Here's a poem about things that cause us worry.

Whatifs

Last night while I lay thinking here,
Some Whatifs crawled inside my ear
And pranced and partied all night long
And sang their same old Whatif song:
Whatif I'm dumb in school?
Whatif they've closed the swimming pool?
Whatif I get beat up?
Whatif there's poison in my cup?
Whatif I flunk the test?
Whatif green hair grows on my chest?
Whatif nobody likes me?
Whatif a bolt of lightning strikes me?
Whatif I don't grow taller?
Whatif my head starts getting smaller?
Whatif the wind tears up my kite?
Whatif they start a war?
Whatif my parents get divorced?
Whatif the bus is late?
Whatif my teeth don't grow in straight?
Whatif I tear my pants?
Whatif I never learn to dance?
Everything seems swell and then,
The night time whatifs strike again!

(Quoted from *Helping Children Handle Stress* by Norman Wright, published by Here's Life Publishers)

Box Of Worries

Object needed: *A box, with the word "worry" written on it, containing the list below and a helium balloon.*

Do any of you have worries? Most people have worries. This is a box of worries. Some people have massive boxes for their worries because they have so many. Some people have very, very small boxes for their worries because they have so few! This is a typical box, sort of average size really! You can't actually see people's boxes of worries, because they keep them inside. But most people have worries.

I need a volunteer. *(Choose someone to help you – you'll need them to hold the box of worries in their hand and you'll need to stick the helium balloon string on their back.)*

Now, what has he got in his box? *(Pretend to read.)*

"Whatif I fall out of a tree?"
"Whatif my teacher doesn't like me?"
"Whatif my girlfriend doesn't like me?"
"Whatif my house gets burgled?"

Lots of people worry about lots of different things: My mum and dad keep arguing – how will I cope? My granddad has died – what will I do without him? My sister's had an accident. My little brother isn't well. Lots of us have lots of different worries. Now here is the big question for the day: How can this person get rid of their worries?

Be prepared to field the following responses to the replies:

- "Throw the box away!" No, he can't. The worries are not really outside, they're inside.
- "Give them to someone else!" Well, we can give our worries away. If I took his box of worries I'd be able to handle some of these problems. I could handle the one about the girlfriend, I could handle the one about teachers not liking me, but ultimately I'd end up with more worries as well. No, I think I'll give the box back!
- "Run away from them!" You can't run away from your worries. But neither do we have to carry our box of worries by ourselves. We must learn to become like Elisha and see God in every problem. God loves us so much that he will be with us in every problem that causes us worry. If we learn to see God in every situation it will get us through.

● STORY – MacTavish (2)

MacTavish was the 17th MacTavish to be Leader of Bears. Before that, there had been a whole line of MacDougals. Being the Leader of Bears was not a very complicated job. He would live on the mountain with his army of bears and keep all harm away from the village.

Many brave bears would volunteer to serve in the bear army for ten years. The Leader of Bears would stay for 20 years. The bears would leave behind their mothers, their wives and often their children and they would protect the community. They would fight if need be, but they would always keep the village safe from harm.

Life in the village was wonderful. The cutting winds that blew across the mountains rarely made it into the valley, the snows were never as deep in the valley as they were in the mountains, and the warmth of the sun often shone there.

The cubs played in complete safety, while the grown-ups went about their daily tasks without worry of attack. Tens of thousands of bears lived in the village. They lived and worked and enjoyed themselves.

Far away on the mountain the Leader of Bears protected them all. There was no use denying it, MacTavish liked to fight and he was incredibly good at it. But he felt the responsibility of his position. Many enemies had attacked the village, many strange and wild enemies that would have done untold harm to those who lived their lives in safety and tranquillity. But the bears that lived in the valley would never learn about it. The enemies had attacked and the Leader of Bears had given the commands and the enemy had been dealt with, usually in such a way as to guarantee that they would never come back. There were casualties and many good bears had died. But this was what they did. They would fight and they would be protectors and far below in the valley the rest of the bears would be safe.

God protects us in much the same way. He sends his guardian angels to watch over us and keep us protected. We rarely see them but they are there protecting us and keeping us safe.

It wasn't always so tough. MacTavish had some wonderful friends who would stand with him in every situation. There was Campbell, who had a terrible habit of always getting injured in every battle they fought – they'd had to pull countless arrows out of his back and carry him away with broken bones on countless occasions and his head had received so many stitches his hair didn't grow there any more. He was the only bear to have a bald head.

Then there was Wee Jock and his brother, Big Jock. They were always playing tricks on people. One day they had managed to get some strange berries and had mixed them in with the food, so all the bears ended up with multicoloured fur. Sometimes they would put huge tree trunks outside the cabins of others bears so that when they opened the door the tree would fall on them. They'd even nailed MacTavish's door closed so that he couldn't get out in the morning – MacTavish had punched the door, which flew off its hinges, ripped half the wall down and landed ten metres from his cabin. He then made the two Jocks fix it. But they wouldn't be stopped. That night they'd mixed something in with MacTavish's Irn-Bru and he went to the toilet 47 times the next day!

Then there was Kenny. Kenny was a fighting machine. If Kenny heard the word "fight" he was off. MacTavish just had to point him in the right direction and let him go. Anyone in his way would be in trouble. They had eventually learnt to put Kenny at the very front of any battle. If Kenny was at the back he often started fighting with his own friends, he was so desperate to get stuck in. But he was a good friend and MacTavish knew that Kenny would always be there for him.

So the bears, with their leader, lived on the mountain. New bears would join them, and old bears would leave to return to the village. They would be protectors and at night sit by the fire and drink Irn-Bru. And below in the village the rest of the bears would live in safety.

(To be continued...)

3 Elisha Is Chosen

	Programme	Item
Section 1	**Welcome**	
	Rules	
	Prayer	
	Introductory Praise	
	Game 1	Speed Relay
	Praise	
	Fun Item 1	
	Game 2	Collect
	Fun Item 2	
	Bible Text	John 15:16
	Announcements	
	Interview	
Section 2	**Worship Time**	
Preaching	**Bible Lesson**	Elisha Is Chosen
Time	**Illustration 1**	Classroom Helper
	Illustration 2	Apple Trees
	Illustration 3	You Don't Have To Join
	Story	MacTavish (3)
	Prayer	

Overview Elisha was placed in a very privileged position. The great prophet Elijah wanted him to become his assistant and later his successor. Elisha had to think hard; he didn't have to follow Elijah. But he made the right decision.

Speed Relay

PREPARATION	One bouncy castle at point B. You can purchase cheap bouncy castles from many toy shops, priced approximately £30.
PLAYERS	Four players per team.
SET-UP	Players line up in relay formation at A.
OBJECT	The players in turn run from A, touch the back wall of the bouncy castle and return to B. The next player then begins.
WINNING	The first team to complete the relay and to sit down wins.

Collect

PREPARATION	Place various coloured boxes on the bouncy castle. Number them with a points value from one to twelve.
PLAYERS	Four players per team.
SET-UP	Players stand in standard relay pattern at point A.
OBJECT	The first person runs from A to B, collects the highest-point package they can find and returns to A. The next player then runs.
WINNING	The team with the most accumulated points from the boxes wins.

BIBLE LESSON

ELISHA IS CHOSEN

"You did not choose me (God), but I (God) chose you and sent you out to produce fruit, the kind of fruit that will last." (John 15:16)

Elisha hadn't always been a prophet of God. He used to be a farmer. He would spend his time ploughing fields, planting crops and bringing in the harvest. But God had very different ideas for his life.

Elijah was a prophet. He did some amazing things, which we talked about in another series *(see "To Boldly Go..." from* Fusion*)*. On one occasion he had even called fire to come down from heaven. But God had told Elijah that he wouldn't be on the earth for much longer and that he should choose Elisha to be his successor.

Elijah had listened to God and did what God wanted. He walked into the field where Elisha was ploughing and threw his coat over the young man's shoulders as a sign that he wanted Elisha to follow him. The amazing thing is that the Bible says: "Elisha stopped ploughing and ran after him." Elisha didn't need to be asked twice. He wanted to serve God so much that he just followed.

A similar thing happened many thousands of years later, when Jesus said to some fishermen, "Follow me", and instantly they laid down their nets and followed Jesus.

Jesus is still doing that now. He is inviting people to follow him. The Bible says that we didn't choose God, but he chose us. I think he's chosen some of you today to be his followers too.

Classroom Helper

It's nice to be chosen to do things. When I was in school I wasn't always as good as I should have been and so the teachers didn't choose me to do things very often. But when I did get chosen, I was very pleased. I used to enjoy being chosen to do special jobs for the teacher, even if it was just to go and take a message to another teacher in another room.

Sometimes I would be given very special jobs, like reading in assembly. When that happened I used to get very excited. I would tell everyone that I had been chosen to be the reader. I was very pleased.

But every one of you has been chosen as well, not by a teacher, but by the Creator of the universe. He chose you before the world itself was created. Before you were born, he had already chosen you to be his. Now that should make you feel really special. Because you are.

Apple Trees

Object needed: *An apple.*

What do these grow on? (Yes, of course, apple trees.) But not all apple trees. Some apple trees just don't produce apples. They produce flowers sometimes, they produce lots of green leaves, they produce long branches, but no apples.

When a person buys an apple tree, they do their best to help the tree produce fruit. They feed it with special chemicals. They put compost around its roots. They water it lots. But if after many years it still doesn't produce apples, it doesn't surprise me that the tree gets chopped down. It hasn't done what it was chosen to do.

Now God chose me because I'm me and for no other reason. Not for what I'm good at, or not good at, not for my skills or gifts, but just because I'm me. But once he's chosen me, he then wants me to produce fruit – not apples and oranges. I'd look very silly with a banana growing out of my nose. But "fruit of the Spirit", things like patience and kindness and gentleness. These are the things God looks for in us.

He chose us to bear fruit, fruit that lasts.

You Don't Have To Join

Object needed: *An invite to the children's club/group/congregation.*

Here's an invite to our children's congregation. I gave a lot of these out before we started back after the holidays. Lots of you came. But some children didn't. You see, you don't have to join. It's up to you.

And God has chosen you to be one of his followers. In the same way he chose Elisha and in the same way he chose the disciples, he also chose you. But you don't have to accept. God has chosen you today. Do you want to be one of his followers or not?

● STORY – MacTavish (3)

A rider had arrived in the early morning. It was very unusual for a bear to ride on a horse but when it was an emergency a cub would be placed on horseback and sent with a message. And this was an emergency – the elders had summoned MacTavish.

Each bear community was made up of the Leader of Bears who was in charge of an army of bears who in turn protected a village, usually of tens of thousands. There were twelve bear communities. All the communities were under the authority of the elders. These were very, very old bears who lived in a cave on Ben Pinion mountain. The elders were wise and knew many things. They had spies everywhere and they particularly kept an eye on the humans. To be summoned by the elders could only mean trouble.

MacTavish set off at once, leaving Kenny in charge. He made him promise not to attack any other villages or countries or anything until he got back. Solemnly Kenny agreed, though he really did like to fight. MacTavish began to run. He was too large a bear for a horse and, anyway, he was fairly sure he could get to places that a horse never could.

He ran with his long, striding pace throughout the day. He rested only briefly at nightfall. He waited for the full moon to rise high in the sky and then he continued his journey. By noon the next day he had arrived at the caves. These were enormous caves with ceilings that stretched up further than MacTavish could see. Other Leaders of Bears were also arriving. They hugged one another because they all knew each other; they had met before, but only when there was trouble. There was one new bear, named MacAndrew, but the other bears all knew his father and many of them knew his grandfather also, so they felt as if they had known him all his life.

The Leaders of Bears took their seats at a huge table. The elders with their grey and white fur joined them. In all, 25 enormous bears sat around the massive stone table. The head bear began to speak: "I will not waste time with small talk; there is no time for that. The humans are gathering an army. They will attack within a fortnight. One of you must lead his bears to war."

Now this wasn't like most gatherings of this kind, where everyone would probably look shocked. The humans often tried to invade. Several times they had succeeded and many bears had died and many villages had been destroyed. But all the bears who were gathered here were great fighters. They were Leaders of Bears because they were great fighters; they could not have taken the title otherwise. So with one voice they all shouted: "We'll go!"

The elders smiled. The elders had been chosen because of their wisdom and because they knew when to avoid fighting, but nonetheless they couldn't help admiring these bears – they were heroes, every last one of them, the stuff of legends. The chief elder spoke: "We have designed a competition. It has three exercises. The first will be to test your speed, the second will test your strength and the third will be the final test: it will be the most important test – it will test *you*. The winner will lead his bears to fight."

MacTavish hated tests but he would do what he had to do. The first test was a straight test of speed. The fastest bear around the mountain would win. The race began, but MacTavish was not built for speed. He ran as quickly as he could but MacAndrew was by far the youngest and by far the fastest. He sprinted so quickly around the mountain that he finished in half the time it took MacTavish. In fact, MacTavish finished last.

The next event was to test strength. MacTavish felt better about this, but he could plainly see that he was not the strongest bear. MacLeod was clearly the strongest. The event involved pushing enormous rocks up the mountain. The bear to push the most rocks would be the winner. So they began pushing. MacTavish did very well indeed, but in the end he could only finish third.

And then it was the final event: a race through a swamp with heavy backpacks on. Points were given for the previous events and those who had come first were allowed to start first and those who had come second would go next. Because of MacTavish's terrible performance in the first event he was in tenth place to start, but he wasn't unduly concerned. This event he liked. This was the event that tested the bears themselves, and MacTavish was confident. The swamp was enormous, fifteen kilometres in all. His bones were still aching from the other events but MacTavish set off. He soon moved into his long, striding run that covered so much ground and took very little energy.

MacAndrew had sprinted into the swamp and was sure he could run as he'd run around the mountain, but the swamp was deep and he lacked experience in that environment. After ten kilometres he could not go on and had to be helped out. MacLeod tore through the swamp, smashing anything that got in his way, but he was using so much strength and it was beginning to hurt. MacLeod was not fond of pain and soon gave up. The others at various points were dropping out and MacTavish overtook them as he went. His muscles were screaming in agony, but he was determined to keep going. He would look straight ahead, he would focus and he would keep going. And then at the thirteen-kilometre point he saw MacAdam leaning against a tree catching his breath – MacTavish was now in the lead. But he didn't slow down and he didn't speed up; he just kept going. Fighting for breath, his heart threatening to pound through his chest, he kept on going. He would look straight ahead, he would focus and he would keep going.

And then it was over and everyone was congratulating him! MacTavish had won, as the elders knew he would. The others were fast and strong, but MacTavish had the greatest gift of all: he kept going. The elders knew that if it was within his ability MacTavish would stop this human army, and if it wasn't, then he would try anyway.

And now his legs were striding again across the mountains. MacTavish must get home and prepare his bears. They had three days before they would fight. MacTavish, Leader of Bears, was going to war, a war he didn't know if he could win.

(To be continued...)

Elisha Keeps Going

	Programme	Item
Section 1	**Welcome**	
	Rules	
	Prayer	
	Introductory Praise	
	Game 1	Pole To Pole
	Praise	
	Fun Item 1	
	Game 2	Pole Rolls
	Fun Item 2	
	Bible Text	Galatians 6:9
	Announcements	
	Interview	
Section 2	**Worship Time**	
Preaching	**Bible Lesson**	Elisha Will Not Leave
Time	**Illustration 1**	Medal
	Illustration 2	Candle
	Illustration 3	Blindfolded
	Story	MacTavish (4)
	Prayer	

Elisha knew that Elijah was about to be taken back to God. He knew that if he was to receive God's blessing he must stay close to Elijah. Even when Elijah tested Elisha by asking him to go away, Elisha stayed very close.

Game 1

Pole To Pole

PREPARATION	Two sticks per team and one jar per team that both poles can fit into at the same time.
PLAYERS	Five players per team.
SET-UP	Players line up in relay formation at A. The first player holds the pole with the open jar placed on top. The second waits with his pole.
OBJECT	The players in turn run from A to B, balancing the jar the whole time. At B the next player puts his stick into the jar, takes the jar and sets off. The stick from the first player is passed to person three.
WINNING	The first team to complete the relay and sit down wins.

Pole Rolls

PREPARATION	One pole per team. Several toilet rolls placed at B.
PLAYERS	Five players per team.
SET-UP	The players stand in standard relay pattern at point A.
OBJECT	The first person runs from A to B, places a toilet roll on the end of the pole and then, with pole, returns to A. The next player then runs and repeats the process.
WINNING	The first team to collect five toilet rolls wins.

Preaching Time

BIBLE LESSON ELISHA WILL NOT LEAVE

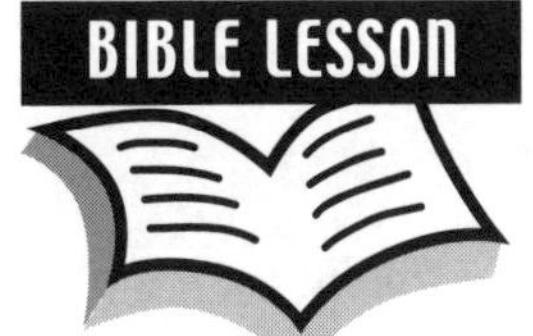

"You will be rewarded when the time is right, if you don't give up." (Galatians 6:9)

When the Lord was about to take Elijah up to heaven, Elijah and Elisha were on their way from Gilgal. Elijah said to Elisha, "Stay here", but Elisha refused and said, "I will stay with you."

At Bethel Elijah again said to Elisha, "Stay here, Elisha; the Lord has sent me to Jericho." But Elisha would not listen.

At Jericho Elijah again said to Elisha, "Stay here, Elisha; the Lord has sent me to Jordan." But Elisha would not listen. He knew that something amazing was going to happen and he knew that if he was to get God's blessing he should stay close to Elijah. We too will receive great things if we can learn to stay close to God and not stray away.

At the river Jordan Elijah took his cloak, rolled it up and struck the water. The water opened up in front of them and the two of them crossed over on dry ground. When they had crossed, Elijah said to Elisha, "Tell me, what I can do for you before I am taken from you?"

"Let me have your power, plus more," Elisha replied.

Then an amazing thing happened: Elijah was taken up to heaven in a fiery chariot, leaving his coat behind. Elisha picked up the coat – probably the same coat Elijah had thrown over his shoulders when he had chosen him – and went back and stood on the bank of the Jordan. He took the coat and struck the water with it. When he struck the water, it divided to the right and to the left, and he crossed over.

Elisha had refused to leave Elijah's side. He had stayed close. He now had the reward.

Medal

Object needed: *A medal or a trophy.*

Marathon runners are amazing people. Who knows how far they have to run before they finish the race? *(Field some answers.)*

Yes, 26 miles. But did you know that it's not just the winner who gets a medal in the marathon? The person coming second gets a medal, the person coming third gets a medal, as does the person who comes 400th.

You see, to get a medal in a marathon, you don't have to win. You have to finish. If you stop halfway around, no medal. If you fall over because you're too tired, no medal. You get a medal only if you finish.

God doesn't reward people because they are the fastest. He rewards people because they keep going. They don't give up when things are hard; they just stick in there.

Candle

Object needed: *A candle (lit).*

There are many advantages in staying close to God. One of them is that he shows me which way to go.

Several weeks ago I was trying to fix a problem I had in my house with one of the light sockets. I cut the wrong wire and all the lights in my house went out, leaving me in the dark. My wife, being a smart person, found a candle and lit it. But we only had one candle.

I could have tried to find my way around all by myself, falling over chairs, kicking the dog, smashing the ornaments. But I didn't. Wherever my wife went with the candle, I went too. She had the light. As long as I stayed close to her I wouldn't get lost in the dark. She could show me where to go.

The Bible says: "Jesus is the light of the world. Whoever believes in him doesn't need to walk in darkness." So, if you want to know which way to go, stay close to Jesus.

Sometimes we find it hard to stay close to King Jesus. But, if we do, one of the rewards is that he shows us which way to go.

Blindfolded

Object needed: *A blindfold and a large rope with a weight at the bottom to act as a pendulum.*

There are many advantages in staying close to God. Another advantage is that he keeps me safe.

Ask someone to stand on a chair swinging the pendulum backwards and forwards. Blindfold a person and ask them to walk past the swinging pendulum – they are guaranteed to be hit by the pendulum.

Sometimes our lives are like this. There are dangers ahead of us, but we can't see them. But God, who sees everything, can keep us safe if we stay close to him. You can't walk past this dangerous pendulum alone. But, if I help you, you can!

Take the person by the hand and lead them past the pendulum when it has swung backwards.

God is exactly the same! He leads us through all sorts of dangers, some of which we never even know about. But if we can learn to stay close to God, God will keep us safe.

Sometimes it's hard to stay close to King Jesus, but, if we do, one of the rewards is that he protects us.

● STORY – MacTavish

Just for effect, play "Brothers in Arms" by Dire Straits in the background as you tell this part of the story. Tell the story to the pace of the music – fade it out as you come to the end. It really does work very well.

The day had arrived. MacTavish walked up and down the lines looking into the eyes of his gathered bears. There were times when MacTavish would have preferred not to be Leader of Bears, but he was. He looked into the eyes of those gathered. They were brave, of that there was no doubt. They would fight until they no longer could. MacTavish stood in front of them all; some were only cubs several summer ago. MacTavish's mind was racing. He could not deny that part of him loved to fight, but he had been in too many battles not to know there was a cost. Many of the faces he stared into today he would not see again. He looked at Kenny and Campbell and Wee Jock and Big Jock. They would lead their respective units well. They would do their duty. But would MacTavish see them again? Would he himself return? He did not know. But what he did know was that he would lead these bears and he would fight. While there was still blood in his body he would fight.

He raised his gigantic arms in the air. There was instant silence. Every eye focused on MacTavish, Leader of Bears.

"So we must fight. It has come to this again. We will do what we were born to do. We will fight and our valley will be kept safe. We will fight and our mothers will sleep well at night. We will fight and our children will play safely in the streets. We will fight. For it is our duty and our right. We will fight. Some of us will not return, but we will fight. Some of us will shed bear blood today, but we will fight. And when the sun sets we will rest and when the sun rises on the battlefield we will stand together and know that we have fought bravely. Some of our friends will not return, but we will stand IN VICTORY!!!"

There was a deafening roar from the bears. Kenny was giving orders to his unit. The others followed and then they marched. What an impressive sight they were: nearly a thousand bears, marching to fight.

They marched for an hour and then they saw it in the distance: a huge moving cloud of dust coming closer. As they continued to march the cloud of dust took shape. This army of men had been working hard; they had gathered a large army this time, maybe twice the size of MacTavish's. But the bears did not comment. They would fight and they would win. Because they must.

The two armies stood on the flattest part of the mountain and looked at each other. They were very impressive. They stood and stared for some time. Then MacTavish looked across the battlefield into the face of King Kevin. The king had positioned himself at the very back of his army, as he always did. From there he would be kept safe and from there he would direct his troops. He was a very different leader from MacTavish. MacTavish would lead from the front and, if he was killed, then there were others who would give the commands. Kenny and then Wee Jock – they could lead if they needed to.

And then it occurred to MacTavish. He knew how to win. He smiled. He turned to his bears and they could see the change in him. His eyes sparkled, he looked enormous, he was ready. The Leader of Bears was ready, and they were ready too. MacTavish raised his arms and shouted: "AND NOW, *WE FIGHT!*"

There was a huge noise and a thousand bears ran forward. The men ran too. They would meet and they would fight. Swords hit shields and swords hit flesh. Men began to fall, as did bears. This battle would be intense; it would last all day.

MacTavish had only one thing in mind as he fought his way through these men: he would kill the king. Men ran at him but he knocked them aside as if they were made of paper. His sword was drawn. He was focused. He would not turn to the left or right; he would kill the king. And this is why he was chosen above all others. He was not the fastest or even the strongest, but he would keep going. No matter what, MacTavish would keep going.

Now there were men all over him but he threw them off and they landed with a crunch. He saw Wee Jock in the middle of the battle. There was a man about to drop down on him with his sword. MacTavish grabbed the nearest man, tore his sword out of his arms and threw it at the man. It was not the blade that hit first but the handle. But it didn't matter, the effect was the same: the man was knocked so hard he landed many metres away from Wee Jock. Wee Jock was safe. He shouted over the battle: "Thanks!"

And the fight continued. MacTavish was now only metres away from the king. He'd had to help Kenny out on the way. Kenny had got himself outnumbered 20 to 1 and so MacTavish had grabbed ten men and thrown them away from the battlefield. Kenny could deal with 10 men quite easily.

And now MacTavish was there. There was the king, screaming his orders, surrounded by the royal guard. The royal guard were the strongest of all the men. They had huge muscles and were very well trained. But because of the way they looked nobody had ever attacked them, so they had never been in the battle. MacTavish was surprised how easy it was. The guards attacked with their swords drawn. MacTavish took his sword and knocked them all out with one swoop. They lay on the ground moaning. They would not be getting up for some time.

And there was the king. He was incredibly agile. He moved very quickly, but he fought by the rules. These rules involved a lot of showy moves but very little else. MacTavish also fought by the rules. His rules said: We will fight and we will win. The two of them fought, but it was a very poor fight and the king turned and ran for it. MacTavish grabbed a rock and threw it at the king. It was a very good throw. The king would not get up.

With no more orders from the king the men were lost. They ran at MacTavish; it was all they could think of to do.

MacTavish fought hard. He thrashed with his sword and many men fell victim to his great blade. Then he was surrounded, and as he plunged his sword into the first attacker the man grabbed his sword as he fell. MacTavish was left with no weapon. The men charged with their swords, but MacTavish was not finished – he would fight with his paws. A man lunged with his sword, but MacTavish moved and then hit out with a ferocity that knocked the man back many metres. The man would not get back up for many days.

Now the men rushed all at once. There were many and there was much confusion. MacTavish fought with all his might, but there were so many of them. MacTavish fell backwards. The men dived, but MacTavish moved and rolled. He found himself next to the body of the king, grabbed the king's sword, and the fight continued...

And then night-time came and the battle was over. It would be morning before they would know if they had been victorious. It would be morning before they would know what had become of their leader. The moon rose high in the night sky. A mist fell on the battlefield. The bears were too tired to move. They tumbled to the ground and slept. In the morning they would know what had become of MacTavish, Leader of Bears.

(To be continued...)

5 Elisha Brings Life

	Programme	Item
Section 1	Welcome	
	Rules	
	Prayer	
	Introductory Praise	
	Game 1	Jelly Find
	Praise	
	Fun Item 1	
	Game 2	Jelly Eater
	Fun Item 2	
	Bible Text	1 John 5:1–12
	Announcements	
	Interview	
Section 2	Worship Time	
Preaching	Bible Lesson	Elisha And The Widow's Son
Time	Illustration 1	Paramedic
	Illustration 2	Watering Can
	Illustration 3	Smells
	Story	MacTavish (5)
	Prayer	

Overview Elisha had stayed with this family many times. He'd even prayed to God for the woman and God had blessed her with a son. But death invades the household. The son dies. What will Elisha do? Is life really stronger than death?

games

Jelly Find

PREPARATION	A bowl of jelly per team (five Maltesers placed in each jelly before the jelly sets). The jellies are placed at B.
PLAYERS	Five players per team.
SET-UP	The teams line up in relay position at point A.
OBJECT	The players in turn run from A to B and take the Maltesers out of the jelly, using only their mouths. Hands must be behind their backs. The first player returns to A, then the next player goes.
WINNING	The first team to complete the relay and sit down wins. Any team taking more than one Malteser at a time will be disqualified.

Jelly Eater

PREPARATION	A bowl of jelly per team. Five spoons given to each team.
PLAYERS	Five players per team.
SET-UP	The teams line up in relay position at point A with a spoon each.
OBJECT	The players in turn run from A to B. At B they eat as much jelly as they can in ten seconds and then return to A. Then the next player runs. This repeats for two minutes.
WINNING	The team with the emptiest bowl after two minutes wins.

ELISHA AND THE WIDOW'S SON

"And so, if we have God's Son, we have this life. But if we don't have the Son, we don't have this life." (1 John 5:12)

Once when Elisha was in the town of Shunem, he met a rich woman who invited him home for dinner with her husband and herself. After that, every time Elisha was in Shunem he would visit this family.

The family were convinced that Elisha was a prophet of God so they decided to build him a small room on top of their house so that he could come and stay whenever he wanted. Elisha was very appreciative of the couple's kindness and asked if there was anything he could do in return. They both said no. But Elisha's servant Gehazi knew that the couple didn't have any children and wanted a child. So Elisha prayed and, sure enough, the woman had a baby boy.

One day while the boy was playing in the fields he became very hot and fell over. By the time he was taken back to his mother he was dead. The woman set off at once to find Elisha. She knew that only God could give life and that he brought life through his servants. When she reached Elisha she pleaded with him to come.

Elisha sent his servant Gehazi to run ahead. He was given Elisha's walking stick to place on the child. But when Gehazi arrived and placed his walking stick on the little boy and prayed, nothing happened.

Eventually Elisha arrived. He walked into the little boy's room, closed the door and began to pray for the boy. And the boy came back to life! Elisha had brought God's life to the house. He picked up the boy and carried him to his mother.

Life had come. Life was stronger than death.

Paramedic

The cars smashed into each other. The driver should have been wearing his seatbelt, but he wasn't. He went flying through the windscreen and rolled down the nearby bank.

He was bleeding and almost certainly close to death. He was fighting for breath, he could barely keep his eyes open, many of his bones were broken. But that wasn't the worst. There was blood pumping out. Surely he would die. He began to close his eyes, fearing that he would never open them again.

Then he saw her. Through his half-closed eyes he saw her. Dressed in green, she was walking towards him. He closed his eyes. Later he awoke in the hospital. He was alive and he would heal. The woman in green had saved his life. She was a paramedic.

When he was well enough he thanked her. She smiled and responded: "I was just doing my job." And there it is. Her job was to bring life. Pretty much the same job as us!

Watering Can

Object needed: *A watering can.*

I absolutely hate gardening. I know absolutely nothing about it. I can't even get grass to grow properly in my garden. I really am very bad at gardening.

But I do know something. I know that if it's a very warm, sunny day and it's been warm and sunny for several weeks, then all my flowers will die unless I do something. What do you think my plants need?

This thing back here *(pick up the watering can)*, this is what I use to bring life to those little flowers. The watering can doesn't keep the flowers alive, but it carries the water which keeps them alive. The watering can is a carrier of life.

You may not know this, but if you are a Christian, you are a carrier of life. Every place you go, if you talk about Jesus, you bring life. The Bible says that people who know Jesus have life and those who don't know Jesus don't have life. It also says that Jesus is "the way, the truth and the life". We are carriers of life. Isn't that exciting?

Smells

Object needed: *Deodorant or perfume.*

Walk on and spray some of the deodorant or perfume in the air.

Can you smell that? This is my favourite deodorant/perfume. Some of my friends wear different types. I can always tell when they've been in a room for some time. The room smells of their deodorant/perfume. I can't always see them, but I know they've been there.

I wonder if you leave any smells when you visit places. Some of you may leave some very nasty smells if you've been eating the wrong foods. But even if you leave no smell at all, there will usually be a way of knowing you were there.

Whenever Jesus went somewhere, he also left life there. He would leave happiness, joy and kindness, he would leave good news, he would show people how to get to heaven. He would always leave life. But how about you? I told you earlier that it was your job to bring life, to be a carrier of life, bringing joy and happiness wherever you go, helping people, being kind, talking about King Jesus.

Are you a bringer of joy, happiness and life? Or do people feel upset when you have visited them? Do you bring life or do you bring death?

If you are a Christian, that is, someone who has asked God to forgive all the wrong things you've done and someone who lives for Jesus, then you should be bringing life. A person who knows Jesus should bring life.

● STORY – MacTavish

The mist began to rise. The field was covered with the bodies of the injured and the dead. But the bears had won. It would be a long time before the humans could re-form their army and attack again. It would certainly not be for many generations to come.

MacTavish and the bears had done what was needed. They had put their lives on the line so that the village could be kept safe. Thousands of bears and their cubs would now spend their time in safety and security. They would continue to play their games and enjoy their lives because MacTavish and his bears had kept them safe. But at what cost?

The battlefield was clear now; the mist had risen. The sun pierced through the clouds. Kenny dragged himself to his feet. He had been too exhausted to move at the end of the battle and had simply slumped to the ground and slept. Now he would have to look at the damage and face the thought that worried him the most: Who had died in this fiercest of battles?

He walked up and down the field, tears beginning to form in his eyes as he realised how horrific this battle had really been. Then he saw Wee Jock. He walked over to him. Rolling him onto his back, he leaned close to see if he was breathing. Close enough to hear Wee Jock mutter the gentle words: "Kenny, if you try and give me mouth-to-mouth resuscitation I will kill you even if the enemy didn't manage it!" A big smile spread over Wee Jock's face. Kenny laughed and, reaching out his hand, helped Kenny to his feet. Many of the bears were beginning to get up now. They had done well – judging from the numbers gathering around them, very well.

But where was MacTavish? They all began to look for him. But no matter how much they searched, there was no sign of him anywhere. They called his name, but there was no response. There were piles of bodies, but nobody else emerged from the battlefield. Campbell came hobbling towards them. He appeared to have a spear sticking out of his leg, but he insisted it wasn't serious and he would sort it out later.

The bears gathered together and a hush fell over them all. Wee Jock announced: "Let us be quiet for a minute for our departed MacTavish, Leader of Bears." There was a silence, heads were bowed, tears were being wiped away. They all began to think about the bravest bear of them all. They would miss him...

And then they heard it. It started as a slow moan, and then the moan became louder. The moan became a growl, louder and louder, and then, "Ahhhhhhhhhhh!" All the bears focused on the pile of bodies lying only ten metres away, where enemy was piled on top of enemy. And then the pile exploded. Enemy soldiers were flying everywhere, and there he stood. The humans groaned as they landed around him – they would not get up until the bears had left, even if they could. There he stood: MacTavish, Leader of Bears.

"Did you miss me, lads?"

The bears began to cheer. Then with much laughter they marched back to their camp. No one would even have imagined that they had been in a battle – unless they had seen the spear sticking out of Campbell's leg, of course. The celebration began. Irn-Bru flowed like water. This celebration would last for the whole week.

On the last night of the celebration MacTavish walked to the centre of the camp and asked in a loud voice: "Come on! Who will fight me?"

Nobody moved. It would indeed be a brave bear who stepped forward, or a very stupid one.

"Who will fight me?"

Then there was movement and MacTavish Junior got to his feet. There were sniggers and even some quite loud laughter from Wee Jock. Kenny was laughing so much there were tears in his eyes. But MacTavish Junior was going to enter the arena. He wasn't sure what would happen but he was going to be brave enough to enter the fight.

"So, my brave, foolhardy cub. You dare to take on your dad in combat? I will tear you in half without even breaking sweat. Go and sit down." But MacTavish Junior would not sit. Kenny and Campbell exchanged looks; they had seen this scene before. Young MacTavish stared into the eyes of his dad and said: "No! I will fight."

There were some growls, some claws being stretched, some movement and then... MacTavish knelt down and in front of the whole gathering announced: "I give in. My son shall be the new leader. He has dared to face me. I knew nobody could win, but I needed to know who would be brave enough to try. So my son, you will be Leader of Bears." And with that, MacTavish Senior took off his chainmail sash and hung it around his son. He hugged him as only a bear can do properly and said his goodbyes.

Then MacTavish left, and MacTavish Junior was the new Leader of Bears. Many would challenge him, but he would fight so long and hard that he would never be beaten.

MacTavish Senior made his way down the valley to the village. There children played and people relaxed. MacTavish Senior hugged his father. He had played his part. He had brought life to the village – or certainly kept death out. He had earned his rest. And now he *would* rest. He would enjoy himself. He would have a haircut and maybe even take a bath – maybe. For him the fight was over; for his son it had just begun. That was the way it had always been, and that was the way it always would be.

As the sun set on the village below, MacTavish Junior gazed into the fire. He too would bring life. He was MacTavish now. MacTavish, Leader of Bears.

A DOG CALLED SAM

A Series in Five Parts

Introduction

Title	Area of prayer
1 Pain	**Jabez was a man who got his name because of the pain he caused his mother.**
2 Personality	**But he was still the most respected son in his family.**
3 Prayer	**One day he prayed to God, "Please bless me and give me a lot of land."**
4 Protection	**"Be with me so I will be safe from harm."**
5 Patience	**And God did just what Jabez had asked.**

This short account of a man called Jabez forms the basis for the Bible Texts throughout this series. His interesting prayer, hidden away in the heart of the book of Chronicles, has been the subject of many books, most recently the writings of Bruce Wilkinson.

The Bible Lesson looks at the life of Job. This is not the most common choice for talks to children, but Job has much to teach us and within the many chapters that comprise the book of Job there are jewels of truth. The Story concerns a very special foxhound called Sam. The two run parallel through five lessons that deal with subjects from good character to tenacity. The overriding message from beginning to end is simply: "We may have had a rough start; but it's not about how we start, it's about how we live and how we finish."

Display each line of the prayer week after week until the whole prayer is displayed. Then offer a huge prize for any child who can come in the following week and recite the whole prayer. You could send a copy of the prayer to each of the children's homes to encourage their parents to help with the memorisation process.

SAM

1 Pain

	Programme	Item
Section 1	**Welcome**	
	Rules	
	Prayer	
	Introductory Praise	
	Game 1	Names
	Praise	
	Fun Item 1	
	Game 2	Names (x2)
	Fun Item 2	
	Bible Text	1 Chronicles 4:9
	Announcements	
	Interview	
Section 2	**Worship Time**	
Preaching	**Bible Lesson**	Job
Time	**Illustration 1**	Cheese!
	Illustration 2	Names
	Illustration 3	It's Not About How We Start...
	Story	A Dog Called Sam (1)
	Prayer	

Overview Names are very significant in the Bible. Names can show something good or something bad. But the important thing is this – the name we are given at the start doesn't need to be the one we finish with. Jabez may have come into this world causing pain, but he was going to leave having been a great blessing.

Game 1

Names

PREPARATION	The letters of the alphabet stuck to a nearby wall. Provide enough copies of the alphabet per team.
PLAYERS	Three per team.
SET-UP	The players are lined up at A. A leader's name is chosen (it must have enough letters to make the game interesting, but without duplication of the letters).
OBJECT	The players run from A to B, collect one letter associated with the name and return to A. The next player goes until all the necessary letters are there to construct the name.
WINNING	The first team to construct the name wins.

Game 2

Names (x2)

Play the above game as many times as you want within the programme time. If the leader's name has a meaning, then let the children know.

Preaching Time

BIBLE LESSON JOB

"Jabez was a man who got his name because of the pain he caused his mother... "
(1 Chronicles 4:9)

Job's sons and daughters were having a feast in the home of his eldest son, when someone rushed up to Job and said, "While your servants were ploughing with your oxen, and your donkeys were nearby eating grass, a gang of Sabeans attacked and stole the oxen and donkeys! Your other servants were killed, and I was the only one who escaped to tell you."

That servant was still speaking, when a second one came running up and saying, "God sent down a fire that killed your sheep and your servants. I am the only one who escaped to tell you."

Before that servant finished speaking, a third one raced up and said, "Three gangs of Chaldeans attacked and stole your camels! All of your other servants were killed, and I am the only one who escaped to tell you."

That servant was still speaking, when a fourth one dashed up and said, "Your children were having a feast and drinking wine at the home of your eldest son, when suddenly a storm from the desert blew the house down, crushing all your children. I am the only one who escaped to tell you."

When Job heard this, he tore his clothes and shaved his head because of his great sorrow. He knelt on the ground, then worshipped God... In spite of everything, Job did not sin or accuse God of doing wrong. (Job 1:13–22)

Job's friends told him to blame God and get cross, but he wouldn't do it. Job replied, "Don't talk like a fool! If we accept blessings from God, we must accept trouble as well." In all that happened, Job never once said anything against God.

Job has some extremely bad things happen to him, but never once does Job turn against God. Everything may look bad for Job right now but it is all going to change soon. You see, things at the moment may seem bad, things in the past may have been terrible, but that doesn't mean that things in the future will be bad. God promises us a glorious future.

Cheese!

Object needed: *A puppet stage, or use actors.*

Chalk: Hello, chaps!
Cheese: Hi, Chalky baby. How's it going?
Chalk: Hey, Cheese, has it ever occurred to you that you have a strange name?
Cheese: Well, no! There are lots of people called Cheese. I'll show you. Please can all the people called Cheese put their hands up? See? Lots!
Chalk: There were none! Well, none that were serious.
Cheese: Well, it's good to have an unusual name, isn't it? There are millions of people called Mark, but not many Cheeses. And not many Chalks, for that matter.
Chalk: I guess you're right! Did you know names can mean things?
Cheese: No, I didn't.
Chalk: Yes, Mark means "warrior". Nia means "brightness", Zoë means "life", Sophie means "wisdom".
Cheese: They are cool meanings. Does everyone have a nice meaning to their name?
Chalk: Well, this bloke today doesn't, does he? This Jabez person.
Cheese: What do you mean?
Chalk: Well, his name actually means "pain". Can you imagine that? I know some of these children here are pains – *joke* – but none of them are named "pain".
Cheese: That's a rough name. It sure is.

Illustration 2

Names

Object needed: *A book containing the meaning of names.*

OK. Are there any people who want to find out what their name means? *(Allow the children to tell you their names, and read out their meanings from the book.)*

There are some really good names there. Sometimes we give each other some extra names as well. We call these nicknames. Some of these names can be fun.

When I was in school we used to have a boy in our gang called Spew. It wasn't because he was sick a lot; it was just that his name was Hugh and it rhymed. We had another bloke called Spanner because he was good at fixing things. And they used to call me Arms, for the simple reason that I have long arms. Now that can be fun, but some names can be not so good.

I've heard of children called Dumbo, Thicko and Dafthead. Now these are not such good names. And of course you remember the person from the Bible we talked about, called Jabez.

So what do we do when we are called bad names? The thing we mustn't do is begin to believe them. If you get called Dumbo it doesn't mean that you have to walk around being dumb. We must learn to say: "I am *not* dumb. I'm smart!" Don't believe the bad things.

Jabez's name meant "pain". Can you imagine having a name that meant "pain"? If you walked down the street and tripped over, you'd say: "Oh! The Jabez!"

But, again, Jabez made a decision. He wouldn't become what his name was. He was not going to be a pain. In fact, quite the opposite.

It's Not About How We Start...

Object needed: *A picture of the cross.*

In long-distance races there are usually lots of very good starters. You see them all lined up at the start of the marathon. They all look keen and fresh. They are jumping up and down doing their warm-ups. Then the race begins.

The runners set off, going at quite a pace. Several hours later at the finish line the sight is very different. The first thing we notice is that there are not so many people. The next thing we notice is that they don't look so fresh any more. Then, as we cast our eyes back across the track, we see a whole range of people who just didn't make it to the finish line.

You don't get a medal for starting well; you get a medal for finishing well.

It's not so important how you started off. Things may have not been so good in our lives; our parents may have left us; people may have been unkind to us. But it is not about how we start. It really is about how we finish. Lots of people have come from some very difficult backgrounds but have done amazing things. It's all about how we finish.

Let's make a decision that we are going to finish well.

You see, if you had seen Jesus hanging on the cross with blood coming from his wounds you might have thought that everything had gone wrong, that Jesus himself had failed. But you would be very wrong indeed. It really is not about how you start. It's about how you finish. And Jesus was far from finished: he would rise from the dead and he would be alive for evermore. He went to the cross – suffered the bad things – but he knew that wasn't the end. Sometimes we have to get through the bad stuff and keep going.

• STORY – A Dog Called Sam (1)

The wind blew hard and cold as Sam crawled through the backyard. Until recently, the little dog had been huddled together with her mum and the rest of the puppies in the barn, curled up behind a comfortable haystack, happy and contented.

Then for no real reason the other puppies had become mean and had driven her out of the barn. She had tried to get back to her mother but they just snarled and tried to bite her. So in the end she had just left. She could feel the wind biting into her tiny body.

She kept walking. The journey from the barn to the main house seemed to take an eternity. She wasn't even sure why she was going there. She had seen people coming from the house and bringing food to her mum and she thought they seemed kind. So she kept walking.

Sam was less than two weeks old and already she felt what it was to be alone and afraid. She was less than two weeks old and felt rejected. She began to scratch at the door or the house, and whimpered. She thought that the whole thing wasn't going to get any better. She wasn't sure why she was here. She scratched some more and then she fell over and lay there. It couldn't have looked worse. The wind kept blowing and Sam was sure she was going to die.

It may not look very good for Sam right now – poor, freezing, hurt, rejected Sam. But this is just the start.

Do you get what I'm trying to say? Lots of us might have had rough starts. We could be in the middle of quite a mess right now. But God does not want us to end up there. If we can just trust God, then he will make the end glorious.

(I'll tell you a little more about Sam next week.)

2 Personality

	Programme	Item
Section 1	**Welcome**	
	Rules	
	Prayer	
	Introductory Praise	
	Game 1	Pedigree Chum
	Praise	
	Fun Item 1	
	Game 2	Puppy Pass
	Fun Item 2	
	Bible Text	1 Chronicles 4:9
	Announcements	
	Interview	
Section 2	**Worship Time**	
Preaching	**Bible Lesson**	Job
Time	**Illustration 1**	Honour
	Illustration 2	Knight
	Illustration 3	Whoops!
	Story	A Dog Called Sam (2)
	Prayer	

Honour is not a fashionable word right now. However, honour is essential to ensuring that no matter how we start, we end gloriously and triumphantly.

Pedigree Chum

PREPARATION A tin of Pedigree Chum at A and three plates of melted Mars Bars at B. A fork per player.

PLAYERS Three per team.

SET-UP The players are lined up at A.

OBJECT The first player runs from A to B, eats some Mars Bar (tell the children that it's dog food; this makes it a whole lot more fun) and comes back. The second player repeats this and they keep going until all the "dog food" is gone.

WINNING The first team to eat all the food wins.

Puppy Pass

PREPARATION A stuffed puppy dog per team.

PLAYERS The whole team.

SET-UP The person at the back of the team holds the toy puppy.

OBJECT The puppy is passed from hand to hand until it reaches the front. However, everyone in the team must take and then pass the puppy. Nobody is to be missed out. When the puppy reaches the front, the person at the front runs to the back with the puppy and the pass continues until all the players have run to the back once.

WINNING The first team to complete the rotation wins.

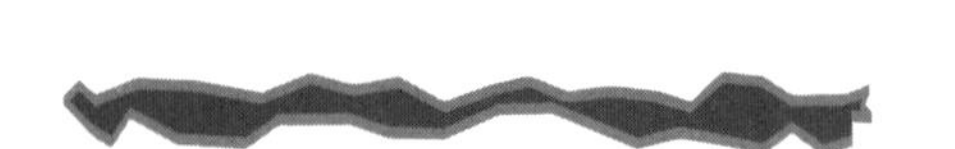

BIBLE LESSON **JOB**

"But he was still the most respected son in his family." (1 Chronicles 4:9)

Do you remember what we talked about last week, to do with this man Job? Let me briefly go over what happened to him. *(Retell some of last week's Bible Lesson.)*

Now, to me, the amazing part of that story is this. Again and again the phrase comes up: "In all that happened, Job never once said anything against God."

All his things were taken away from him. But he never said anything against God.

All his animals died. But he never said anything against God.

His children were taken away. Again he doesn't say anything against God.

I don't know about you, but with so many things going wrong I might well have been a little bit upset with God and might well have shouted some fairly crazy things up to heaven.

But not Job. He kept trusting God and loving God and obeying God. And I think here lies part of the reason that everything would end up brilliantly for Job. He always did the right thing and kept himself right even when things were not going so well.

Honour

Object needed: *A board with the word "honour" written on it.*

Now, I have put this word up on our board. It is the word *"honour"*. I've put it up there because in some people's Bibles it actually says that Jabez was more *"honourable"* than his brothers, and I was just wondering if you could help me work out what this word actually means.

Simply allow the children to answer. Put lots of their answers on the board. Words such as "respect" should go up there, maybe "integrity", maybe "being good", "doing what is right always", but at some point introduce also the word "dignity".

OK, there are our words. That's what Jabez was like, so maybe we shouldn't be too surprised that even though things started out a little rough, they ended very well indeed.

Knight

Object needed: *Two characters playing the parts of king (or queen) and a brave person. You'll also need a plastic sword.*

What's going on here?

Allow one of the leaders to walk on with a sword and a crown, and another leader to walk up and kneel before him or her. The king (or queen) will now honour the brave person by knighting him – by touching the sword on each of his shoulders in turn and then announcing the words: "Arise, Sir [his name]. You are now a knight." Then continue…

This person is being honoured for what they have done. Honour is like respect, only stronger. In real life some people (not all) are honoured because they have worked tirelessly doing things that are right and good. An honourable person is one who lives right even though they may never be honoured by a king or queen.

Whoops!

Object needed: *A puppet stage, or use actors.*

Chalk: Hey, Cheese old chap!
Cheese: Yer!
Chalk: What did you do in school today?
Cheese: Oh, just the usual stuff.
Chalk: Nothing interesting?
Cheese: Well, we didn't have our normal teacher. She was off sick.
Chalk: Who did you have instead?
Cheese: Oh, just some old woman. It was quite fun really; we all started being naughty and John down the front threw some bits of paper at her and she got really upset and then someone else threw something and then everyone was throwing things!
Chalk: Except you, of course!
Cheese: Are you kidding? Everyone else was throwing things, so there was no way I was going to miss out.
Chalk: But, Chalk, what happened to doing the right thing even when nobody else does? What happened to being honourable and respectful?
Cheese: Well… I forgot. It was easier just to do what everyone else was doing.
Chalk: Well, yes, it always is, but it's not always easy doing the right thing. That doesn't mean we *shouldn't* do the right thing.
Cheese: I guess. I wish I had done the right thing now.
Chalk: Why? Do you feel that you let God down by not being honourable?
Cheese: Well, yes. And also because we've all got detention every lunch time for a week!

• STORY – A Dog Called Sam (2)

Sam began to scratch at the door of the house, and whimpered. She thought that the whole thing wasn't going to get any better. She wasn't sure why she was here. She scratched some more and then she fell over and lay there.

Sam woke up looking into the eyes of a very friendly-looking girl. Her name was Emily and her dad was the owner of the huge house. Over the next couple of weeks Emily looked after Sam, taking care of her, giving her bowls of milk to drink. She was going to be just fine. She might have had a rough start but she was going to be fine.

The time came for Sam to rejoin the rest of the dogs. Although they looked at her a little strangely at first, they seemed to have forgotten who she was. They seemed to have forgotten what they had done to her. Sam was a foxhound, as were all the other dogs on the farm. Their job was to hunt foxes. The person in charge of them was called Giles.

One day, Giles sat all the dogs down and announced: "Right! Today is your first time hunting. But there's nothing to worry about. All you have to do is follow the other dogs. They know what they are doing; just follow them."

The horn blew and the hunt was on. The other dogs straightened their legs. Sam straightened her legs. The other dogs stuck their tails in the air. Sam stuck her tail in the air. The other dogs started running up the track after the horses. Sam started running... straight through the hedge and into the field.

Sam knew that she was supposed to follow the other dogs, but she didn't much feel like following today and, anyway, she had smelt something interesting through the hedge. She sniffed her way through the long grass and eventually found her nose pushing against someone else's nose. She lifted up her head and there facing her was a small fox.

"Who are you?" asked Sam.

"My name is Georgina. I'm a fox," the fox replied politely. "And who are you?"

"My name is Sam. I'm a foxhound!"

The two animals looked at each other curiously for some time. Sam began to think. She was sure she was supposed to know something about foxes. Fox... foxhound... "I know!" she said at last. "We must be related – cousins or something. That's it. Cousins."

Georgina agreed and they began jumping and frolicking around on the grass. Just then Mrs Fox returned, and when she saw the foxhound she got very worried. She knew that foxhounds sometimes killed foxes. She shouted to Georgina: "Georgina! Come away at once!" Georgina didn't understand. She was having a wonderful time, but who was she to argue with her mother?

Georgina wandered away. It was then that Sam realised she was alone. She didn't know her way back and began to cry. Mrs Fox looked back. She knew that Sam was only very young and couldn't hurt her. She felt sorry for her. "Follow me!" she shouted. Sam followed Mrs Fox, who led her all the way back to the farmhouse where she lived.

Sam had begun to run down the hill to the farmhouse when she realised that she hadn't said thank you to Mrs Fox. She turned around but both the foxes had gone. Sam rushed down the hill, very happy about meeting her new friend. She ran all the way to the bottom. She was going so fast she couldn't stop, and BASH! She ran right into Giles. He was very angry and would surely have shouted at her a lot more if Emily hadn't stopped him.

"Be kind to her," she said. "She's only young."

"Young she may be," replied Giles, "but she had better learn fast. She will be the leader of the pack one day." Sam was confused. She didn't know what a leader was. How could she be one if she didn't know what it was?

The spring came to an end, the summer came, then the autumn and then the winter returned. It was time to go fox-hunting again.

"Now, listen to me, Sam. When that horn blows you must follow those other dogs." Giles gave his usual speech.

The horn blew and the hunt was on. The other dogs straightened their legs. Sam straightened her legs. The other dogs stuck their tails in the air. Sam stuck her tail in the air. The other dogs started running up the track after the horses. Sam started running up the track after the horses. The other dogs started to sniff the ground, looking for the right smell. Sam started sniffing the ground.

Then, she realised what scent she could smell. It was Georgina. These dogs were hunting Georgina. Well, they might be hunting Georgina but there was no way she was going to hunt her friend. She turned around and ran back to the farm.

Giles was furious: "Sam, what are you doing? You are a foxhound. Foxhounds hunt foxes!" Sam just lay down on the ground as if to say: "Other foxhounds may hunt foxes, but not this foxhound."

Giles took her by the collar and tied her to the gate. "There you will stay until you learn to hunt foxes," he said. Sam sat down. If she had to stay there until she hunted her friend Georgina, then she was going to stay there for a long, long time.

There she sat for many weeks. Giles brought her food and water and asked her every day if she was ready to hunt foxes yet, and every day Sam just looked at the ground.

Sam could easily have joined everyone else. She could easily have hunted the foxes. But Sam was determined to do what was right. Doing what is right is not always easy. Living with dignity and respect and honour is not always easy. But if we want the end to be great, then we need to learn to live as Jabez did – with honour and respect and dignity.

(To be continued...)

3 Prayer

	Programme	Item
Section 1	Welcome	
	Rules	
	Prayer	
	Introductory Praise	
	Game 1	Ask (for boys)
	Praise	
	Fun Item 1	
	Game 2	Ask (for girls)
	Fun Item 2	
	Bible Text	1 Chronicles 4:9
	Announcements	
	Interview	
Section 2 Preaching Time	Worship Time	
	Bible Lesson	Job
	Illustration 1	P.R.A.Y.
	Illustration 2	Important People
	Illustration 3	Tuck
	Story	A Dog Called Sam (3)
	Prayer	

As we move on, we discover more about this hero Jabez. First Jabez prayed. But not only did he pray, he prayed a seriously bold prayer.

Ask (for boys)

PREPARATION None.

PLAYERS One player per team.

SET-UP The player stands at A.

OBJECT The leader whispers an item to the player, who must then go into his team and find the item – he can only collect the item from a boy in the team. The item could be a coin, a watch, a sock or a shoe. Repeat the process a couple of times. The first player to collect the object from his team and return each time gains a point.

WINNING The team with the most points after a couple of goes wins.

Ask (for girls)

PREPARATION None.

PLAYERS One player per team.

SET-UP The player stands at A.

OBJECT The leader whispers an item to the player, who must then go into her team and find the item – she can only collect the item from a girl in the team. The item could be a coin, a watch, a sock or a shoe. Repeat the process a couple of times. The first player to collect the object from her team and return each time gains a point.

WINNING The team with the most points after a couple of goes wins.

JOB

"One day he prayed to God, 'Please bless me and give me a lot of land.'" (1 Chronicles 4:9)

Job listens to his friends giving all sorts of interesting advice. Some think it's his fault that bad things have happened to him. Others think he should just give up and die. In the Bible the conversations between Job and his so-called friends go on for pages and pages. It really is quite difficult to read. It lasts over 30 chapters.

Then, when you think you probably couldn't read any more, Job begins to get smart. He turns away from his friends and he begins to have a conversation with God. He realises that asking his friends is not going to help. He needs to start talking to God. Now Job is a little stupid when he starts to talk to God, as we will find out in a couple of weeks, but at least he starts to talk to someone who really can help.

Our friends don't always give us good advice, but when we learn to turn to God and pray to him, then anything is possible. Jabez knew how powerful prayer could be when you learned to ask for the right things.

I'll let you know in a couple of weeks what happens to Job when he begins to talk to God. Next week I want to tell you how Job got into all this trouble in the first place.

P.R.A.Y.

Object needed: *A puppet stage, or use actors. A white board to show the words on.*

Chalk: Hey, that's a great prayer that Jabez prayed.

Cheese: Sure is. I wish I could pray like that. But I find praying a bit tough.

Chalk: I know what you mean, I used to find praying hard too. But I learned something.

Cheese: What?

Chalk: I learned that if you take the letters of PRAY, you can use them to help you pray.

Cheese: Sometimes I'm not sure you're really speaking English. What *are* you talking about?

Chalk: I take the P from PRAY and I use it to remember PRAISE. So I start my prayer with PRAISE.

Cheese: With what?

Chalk: PRAISE. You know, saying thank you to God for the things he's done and getting excited about how great he is.

Cheese: Oh. OK. That's the P. Hey, bozo with the pen! Write up "P for PRAISE". OK, Chalky, what's next?

Chalk: R. PRAY is spelt P and then R. I use the R to remind me to REPENT.

Cheese: Chalky, baby! Once again, speak in English! What on earth does REPENT mean?

Chalk: OK! Well, you know we all do things wrong?

Cheese: Well, I know *I* do, but I didn't know that *you* did.

Chalk: We *all* do things wrong. Anyway, REPENT means we ask God to forgive the wrong things we've done and try not to do them again.

Cheese: OK! Got it. Bozo, write up "R for REPENT".

Chalk: Then "A for ASK". Now this is the bit most people don't believe. You can ask God for things.

Cheese: I'm on it, babe. God, I need a new car, a red one. And a new Xbox and a new pair of trainers. And some gum. And how about a gorgeous puppet girlfriend and...

Chalk: Stop!

Cheese: And some pizza and some...

Chalk: Stop!

Cheese: What do you mean, stop?! I'm just getting started.

Chalk: When I say ASK, we need to remember not to be selfish in our asking.

Cheese: Oh! I get it. God, I need half a bit of gum and an old rickety pushbike and a cardboard box to live in and...

Chalk: Cheese, get a grip! We mustn't be selfish, but at the same time God does still wants us to be blessed. He wants us to have good things. We just need to be asking him. He's happy for us to have good things and then we can use the good things to help others. But also when we ASK we should maybe use this bit to ask God for other people. You know, like: God, help my mum and dad to know you better, and prayers like that.

Cheese: OK. I got it. Bozo, it's your turn again! Write up "A for ASK".

Chalk: Then we come to the bit for ourselves. The Y is for YOU.

Cheese: For me.

Chalk: No, YOU.

Cheese: No, Me.

Chalk: Stop! OK, bozo person, write "Y for YOU" before Cheese drives me insane.

Cheese: Right, this is my bit... God, I need the car and the trainers and the gum and the pizza and... Oh God, no anchovies on the pizza...

Chalk: Some people may never learn!

Important People

Object needed: *Pictures of important people.*

Put your hand up if you can think of an important person or an important position.

Lead the children so that they don't just say "prime minister", etc. but also include things like "class monitor", "school council member".

When Jabez asked for land he was asking that God would make him an important person. In those days the more land you had, the more important you were. So Jabez was praying: "God, make me important."

You see, it isn't wrong to want to be important.

Tuck

Object needed: *A pile of confectionery and a sign saying "Ask for what you want".*

Ask for a volunteer who likes sweets. Then, when they arrive on the stage, just stand there. Shrug your shoulders, pull funny faces, but don't say anything (the sign should be on display).

After a while, and after several sniggers from the audience – who are in Preaching Time and therefore not allowed to talk! – ask the child why he or she is there.

One of two things will happen. By now the keen child will have asked for a Mars Bar or something. Other children may just shrug their shoulders and say "I don't know". If they don't know, send them back to their seat; if they ask for the Mars Bar, give them the Mars Bar.

If they ask for the whole lot, give them the whole lot! You may go through several volunteers until they eventually get it. After the principle has sunk in and the sweets are gone, say:

Anybody could have come up here and asked for all the sweets at any time. I was looking for someone who would be bold and who would be brave and would ask...

God is looking for some people who will ask him for risky things, who will say, "God, let me be the best at what I do." God, let me be the best doctor so I can save lives, or the best teacher or the best postman or the best friend, or the best footballer.

It's OK to ask God for things, as long as we are not simply trying to be greedy. But you know, you are always fairly safe; God won't give you anything that will harm you, but it's good to ask.

I asked God to make me one of the best children's workers in the country – I really did. I wanted to be able to tell as many boys and girls about Jesus as I could and I wanted to teach others how to do the same, so I asked God to help me be the best.

Replace the last paragraph with your own prayer request of God.

Ask!

• STORY – A Dog Called Sam (3)

Sam would have stayed there tied to the gate a lot longer except that on one very special day Emily decided she would sneak Sam out on her visit to London. She undid the rope and quietly smuggled Sam into the back of the car. They drove to London.

Sam found London very exciting, but she didn't like being tied up outside the shops when Emily went in. She was getting bored. So, when Emily went into the next shop, she decided to go exploring herself. She wriggled free of the rope and made her way down the street. It wasn't long before she came to a rather curious-looking road. She looked up at the sign. It said: "Downing Street".

"This is a strange street," thought Sam. "Why does it have these iron bars and why are all these policemen here?" Sam began to make her way up the street. She came to a big door with two policemen outside.

"I wonder what's in there?" she thought. "I'll go and look." And as quick as a flash she shot past the policemen and straight into the house.

"STOP!" shouted a policeman, and he started running after Sam. She ran into the house, over the chairs, up the stairs, under the bed, back down the stairs and out of the back gate – and straight into the strangest dog she had ever seen. It looked as if the dog had run into a wall and squashed his nose flat.

"Who are you?" asked Sam.

"I'm Barney. I'm a bulldog. But not just any bulldog. I'm the bulldog of the prime minister!"

"What's a prime minister?"

Barney couldn't believe that Sam had never heard of the prime minister. He tried to explain. "He leads the country."

"What's 'leading'?" asked Sam.

Barney thought she was joking but soon realised she wasn't. Again he tried to explain: "Well, he makes the decisions and decides where to go and people follow him." Sam understood. But she didn't have a chance to talk further because the policeman eventually caught up with her, took her by the collar, led her to the front door, down the street and through the gates and handed her back to Emily, who was waiting for her.

All the way back in the car, Sam just lay and thought. She thought about what a leader was: "A leader is someone who decides where to go and people follow them." She made a decision. She had an idea. She had a plan. When they arrived home, Emily tied Sam back up. Giles didn't even know she had gone.

The next day, when Giles brought Sam her food he asked the usual question: "Sam, are you ready to hunt foxes now?" This time, to Giles' surprise, Sam started barking frantically. He let her off the lead.

Over the next couple of weeks Sam practised her running until she could run faster than all the other dogs. She practised her jumping until she could jump further than all the other dogs and she practised her sniffing until she could sniff smells that none of the other dogs could sniff.

Then came the day of the next fox-hunt.

"So, Sam, when the horn blows all you have to do is follow the rest of the foxhounds and run up the path! Have you got that?" Giles asked. Sam nodded. Giles still wasn't convinced, but he stood back and watched.

The horn blew and the hunt was on. The other dogs straightened their legs. Sam straightened her legs. The other dogs stuck their tails in the air. Sam stuck her tail in the air. The other dogs started running up the track after the horses. Sam started running; she ran up the path and past the front dog. She took the lead. She started sniffing until she found the smell she wanted. Then off she went, running.

She led the dogs and the horses and the men down the mountain, through the stream, over the hedge, up the next mountain, through the field, over the river. In fact she led them all over the countryside. She led them everywhere, except of course where her friend Georgina was. Sam was the leader and so she could decide the direction and everyone would follow her.

That day everyone had a great time – the horses, the dogs, the riders – and, now that Sam was the leader, even the fox had a nice day.

Sam had learnt to be a leader.

She was in an important position. And because she was in an important position she could help others.

(To be continued...)

4 Protection

	Programme	Item
Section 1	Welcome	
	Rules	
	Prayer	
	Introductory Praise	
	Game 1	Hailstones
	Praise	
	Fun Item 1	
	Game 2	Hailstone Groups
	Fun Item 2	
	Bible Text	1 Chronicles 4:10
	Announcements	
	Interview	
Section 2 Preaching Time	Worship Time	
	Bible Lesson	Satan!
	Illustration 1	Big Cheese
	Illustration 2	Goal!!!!
	Story	A Dog Called Sam (4)
	Prayer	

Overview It is amazing to understand that the God who created the entire universe, the same God who fills all time and space, is the same God who has decreed that he will never leave or forsake us. The same God with unlimited resources has chosen to protect us.

Hailstones

PREPARATION	Table-tennis balls (or rolled-up pieces of paper) and an umbrella per team.
PLAYERS	Four per team.
SET-UP	The players are lined up at A.
OBJECT	All the players must run from A to B with the leaders dropping table-tennis balls on them, and then from B to A. They must *all* stay under the umbrella to avoid being hit.
WINNING	This first team to complete five runs wins.

Hailstone Groups

PREPARATION	Table-tennis balls (or rolled-up pieces of paper) and an umbrella per team.
PLAYERS	One player per team to begin with.
SET-UP	The player is lined up at A.
OBJECT	The first player must run from A to B with the leaders dropping table-tennis balls on them. When they return to A they must select someone from their team and set off again. They must *all* stay under the umbrella to avoid being hit. On their return they select another person and set off again. This continues until one of the players is hit by the "hailstone" ball.
WINNING	The team with the most players when they are eventually hit wins.

SATAN!

"Be with me so I will be safe from harm. And God did just what Jabez had asked."
(1 Chronicles 4:10)

This is this week's part of the Bible Text. Is there anyone who thinks they know it all up to this point?

> Jabez was a man who got his name because of the pain he caused his mother during birth. But he was still the most respected son in his family. One day he prayed to God, "Please bless me and give me a lot of land. Be with me so I will be safe from harm."

Now this may be a strange way round to look at it, but having told you about all the terrible things that happened to Job I'm now going to tell you how it all started:

> One day, when the angels had gathered around the LORD, and Satan was there with them, the LORD asked, "Satan, where have you been?"
>
> Satan replied, "I have been going all over the earth."
>
> Then the LORD asked, "What do you think of my servant Job? No one on earth is like him – he is a truly good person, who respects me and refuses to do evil."
>
> "Why shouldn't he respect you?" Satan remarked. "You are like a wall protecting not only him, but his entire family and all his property. You make him successful in whatever he does, and his flocks and herds are everywhere. Try taking away everything he owns, and he will curse you to your face."
>
> The LORD replied, "All right, Satan, do what you want with anything that belongs to him, but don't harm Job." Then Satan left. (Job 1:6–12)

There is only one main thing I want you to see. Even though God allowed all these terrible things to happen to Job – and I'll explain next week why he allowed it – God would not let Satan harm him. God insisted on protecting Job no matter what. God would ensure that Job was kept perfectly safe.

Big Cheese

Object needed: *A puppet stage, or use actors.*

Chalk: Hello, chaps! Hi, Cheese. What's wrong?
Cheese: No problems! Some big lads were picking on me.
Chalk: But that must be a huge problem, surely.
Cheese: Well, for some people it would be, but not for me. I have this brother, see.
Chalk: Really? I didn't know.
Cheese: You must have heard of him; he's called Big Cheese.
Chalk: Oh! Yes, I think I have. Is he the big cheese?
Cheese: No, that's my dad, but he's certainly *a* big cheese. Anyway, I told the lads and they have decided not to pick on me any more. Because if they did, my brother would knock their blocks off!
Chalk: I can see how that would work. I guess it's nice to have a big brother.
Cheese: Well, yes, but we all have someone who protects us, you know.
Chalk: What? We all have a big cheese?
Cheese: Something like that; he's called God. He has promised to take care of us if we ask him.
Chalk: Oh, I see.

Goal!!!!

Object needed: *Some goals, a goalkeeper and a ball.*

Shoot towards the goals with the ball.

He is the goalkeeper and I'm trying to get the ball in the net. Lots of sports have goalkeepers. You have them in football, you have them in hockey, you even have them in netball. Their job is to make sure the ball doesn't end up in the net. The opposition kicks the ball or throws the ball. Their job is to try and get the ball past the goalkeeper.

The Bible tells us that the devil also throws things at us – not footballs, but more like lies and bad words and things that can hurt us. But the Bible also tells us that we have been given a shield to stop the things the devil throws. It's called the shield of faith.

Now, I don't want to go into what the shield of faith is; we may save that for a different lesson. What I want to do is tell you this: there are some things that we have to keep out ourselves, and some things that God keeps away. The stuff we can't handle, God protects us against. But sometimes *we* have to deal with some things. When the lie comes we have to say: "Hey! I'm not listening to that lie and I'm certainly not going to believe it."

So God protects us from things, but there are times when we have to protect ourselves.

● STORY – A Dog Called Sam (4)

Eventually, after all that running, Sam was ready for a well-deserved rest. She walked over to the barn where all the dogs slept and she lay down. Her muscles ached and although she felt good that she had saved Georgina, she was also very, very tired.

Sam had become the leader and she had kept her friend safe. She thought that everything would be great now. She thought that all the other dogs would respect her, and that the dogs that had driven her out would now apologise and be kind to her. But it wasn't to be. Many of the dogs were jealous. They had thought that they would become the leader of the dogs, not this Sam. And another thing – she was a girl. Surely, girls couldn't be leaders!

The whispers became louder and once again the dogs turned and began to snarl at her. "We want Old Snarler back," they said. "He was a much better leader."

Old Snarler had been the leader of the dogs right up until the time when Sam had taken control in the last hunt. He had seen this girl dog drawing level with him and then pushing past him, and he had done nothing to stop her. In fact, if any of the dogs could have looked into Old Snarler's face just then, as Sam had run past him, they would have seen the little sparkle in his eyes. If dogs could smile he would have been smiling. But they couldn't see his face; they were behind him.

Sam stood up and looked at the other dogs.

Her mind raced back to the time when she was such a small puppy and they had driven her out of the barn. Her mind remembered their bites and the way they had driven her across the windswept yard, the way she had collapsed in the doorway of Emily's house. But she wasn't going to be driven out this time. She opened her jaws and showed her teeth. The dogs' snarls were answered by her own snarls. She would do whatever she could. But at the same time she knew it would be useless. There were at least five of them – five dogs who wanted to make trouble. There were another 20 dogs in the barn who just ignored them; they were happy to follow anyone who would lead them.

The angry dogs walked towards Sam. Their mouths were wide open now. They were determined to drive her out again, out into the cold once more. They were many and she was all alone. They were now ready to pounce. Sam would fight and Sam would undoubtedly lose. But she would fight.

Then Old Snarler himself walked into the middle of the five. He pushed his way in, making them almost fall over each other in an attempt to move aside. The dogs looked even more confident now; Old Snarler had come to join them. They knew without doubt that he was the best fighter in the barn; there was nobody who would dare to challenge Old Snarler. They became bolder and began to growl a low, menacing growl.

But Old Snarler didn't stop. He pushed on through the five and stood beside Sam. Then he turned and faced the dogs. The thought crossed their minds: "Shall we attack?" Then they remembered who it was who stood before them. One by one, the dogs bowed their heads and retreated. This was one fight they could never win.

Sam looked at Old Snarler with surprise and relief. Why had he done this? Why had he stepped in like this? Old Snarler bowed his head slightly and walked away. Nobody would dare challenge Sam now, not now and not ever.

What Sam didn't know, and what she would probably never know, was that Old Snarler was her father and he would protect her no matter what.

And for us the exciting thing is this: we may have a father who loves us and cares for us and protects us, or we may not, but we still have a heavenly Father who takes care of us all the time. He protects us no matter what.

(To be continued...)

5 Patience

	Programme	Item
Section 1	**Welcome**	
	Rules	
	Prayer	
	Introductory Praise	
	Game 1	Walk The Wire (for girls)
	Praise	
	Fun Item 1	
	Game 2	Walk The Wire (for boys)
	Fun Item 2	
	Bible Text	1 Chronicles 4:10
	Announcements	
	Interview	
Section 2 Preaching Time	**Worship Time**	
	Bible Lesson	Job
	Illustration 1	Cheese The Farmer
	Illustration 2	Seasons
	Story	A Dog Called Sam (5)
	Prayer	

Overview Instant soup, instant coffee... instant character! That's the one we can't get. God forms and shapes us over time. Character-building takes times. But God knows what he is doing. He has seen the end from the beginning.

Walk The Wire (for girls)

PREPARATION A long(ish) piece of wire, fairly thick, bent into a wiggly shape. A stick with a metal hoop at the top. Each team needs the wire and the stick.

PLAYERS Three girls per team.

SET-UP The players are lined up at A.

OBJECT The first player holds the stick and tries to steer the hoop through the wire without touching the wire. If they touch the wire they restart. When they complete the length of the wire the next person goes. And then the third.

WINNING The first team to get the three girls through the wire wins.

Walk The Wire (for boys)

PREPARATION As Game 1, but this time for boys.

PLAYERS –

SET-UP –

OBJECT –

WINNING –

BIBLE LESSON **JOB**

"And God did just what Jabez had asked." (1 Chronicles 4:10)

Can anyone now remember the whole prayer that Jabez prayed?

> Jabez was a man who got his name because of the pain he caused his mother. But he was still the most respected son in his family. One day he prayed to God, "Please bless me and give me a lot of land. Be with me so I will be safe from harm." And God did just what Jabez had asked. (1 Chronicles 4:9–10)

Most of the book of Job is made up of a long discussion between Job's friends in which they constantly blame Job for what has happened. Job himself doesn't really understand what is going on. He doesn't understand why God would allow these horrible things to happen to him. And towards the end of the book Job even thinks that maybe God has made a mistake.

Then suddenly God answers Job. The sky is illuminated with lightning, thunder rumbles on, and then, in the midst of this incredible storm, God speaks:

"Answer me, Job. Are you the one who laid the foundation of the world? Are you the one who spoke and creation happened? Are you the one who created the animals? Have you ever once commanded the morning to appear, and caused the dawn to rise in the east? Have you ever commanded the sun to shine?"

Job doesn't know how to answer. He cowers before God. He cries before God: "I am nothing, God. I don't know the answers. I was foolish to dare to stand up to you."

Then God concludes: "Job, I am God. I am not answerable to you and I owe you nothing." Job bows his head. How can he respond?

You see, God always knows better than us. He may be a God of love and compassion, but he is still all-powerful and all-knowing. He speaks and mountains themselves shake. And God knew what he was doing with Job's life. At the end of everything, God has made Job better. He has made him stronger, and now see what God does: having shown Job that he doesn't owe him anything, God does something out of his amazing kindness – he gives back all the things that Job has lost! His family, his possessions, everything. And just for good measure God gives him even more.

Now, why did all that happen to Job? I think it's all in one last verse at the end of Job. It says this (this is Job speaking): "God, before all this I knew *about* you, but now I have *seen* you."

Job has seen God. Sometimes God allows us to have difficult starts so that he can show his greatness through our lives. He is a great God. He is not a tame God. But he does love you.

Cheese The Farmer

Object needed: *A puppet stage, or use actors. Cheese wears a farmer's hat.*

Cheese: Oooh aaah. Oooh aaah.
Chalk: Hey, Cheese, are you in pain?
Cheese: No, I'm being a farmer. Oooh aaah, stone the crows.
Chalk: What *are* you talking about?
Cheese: Isn't this how farmers talk?
Chalk: Not unless they've been standing in the sun too long.
Cheese: Oh!
Chalk: Why are you trying to sound like a farmer anyway?
Cheese: Because I've been doing some farming. Well, I threw a couple of seeds in the ground in my garden. So I'm a farmer.
Chalk: I think you have to do more than that to become a farmer. Anyway, what are you planting?
Cheese: Flowers!
Chalk: What type?
Cheese: Um! Purple ones, I think. I'll show you – they should be ready by now.
Chalk: Don't be silly! If you've only just planted them, they won't be ready yet.
Cheese: Well, I'll go and check. I'm sure they're there already.

Cheese disappears, and after a series of crashes and bangs – and maybe a toilet flush – Cheese returns, clutching a plastic flower.

Cheese: See, here it is! What a gorgeous flower!
Chalk: Old chap, that isn't real, is it?
Cheese: Oh, yes! This is a real flower that I grew in my garden this morning.
Chalk: I don't think so!
Cheese: How could you doubt me, Chalk? I am a farmer, oooh aaaah...
Chalk: Cheese, the flower is plastic.
Cheese: Yes. I planted plastic seeds!
Chalk: Cheese, they don't believe you! I don't believe you! Flowers take a long time to grow and quite a few things have to take place before they look gorgeous. These things need time. Sorry, Cheese. You can't get instant flowers.
Cheese: Oh. Well, I'm sure my girlfriend will like it anyway.
Chalk: I'm sure she will.

Cheese disappears.

Chalk: You see, some things just take time. God wants to do amazing things in our lives, but not everything happens as quickly as we want.

Seasons

Object needed: *Pictures that evoke thoughts of summer, winter, spring and autumn.*

When a farmer plants his crops he knows that the crops will be in the field through a lot of different seasons before they are ready to be gathered in. Before we are the way God wants us to be, we to have to go through a lot of seasons.

Summer: The summertime is a lovely time. It's nice to feel the warmth of the sun. It's nice to see the bright blue sky. But if plants only had sun, the land would become a desert and they would die.

We have summertimes too. Summertime is that time

when everything is going well and everyone likes us, and our friends are kind and our parents are taking us to nice places. Summertime is when we feel good inside.

Autumn: The autumn is when the trees lose all their old leaves.

And for us, autumn is that time when God is taking things away from us. He knows that some of the things in our lives are not good for us, so he takes those things away. If we are unkind, then God will try and take the unkindness away. But *we* have to let it go.

Winter: The wintertime is the time for frost. Some things die in the winter.

And for us, wintertime is the time when things maybe are not going so well. Wintertime for Job would have been the time when everything had been taken away from him and he felt all alone. Everyone has wintertimes when things go wrong and times are hard, and things at home are not as nice as you would want, and things at school are not as nice as you would want. But wintertime is important too, because it is in the winter that God tests us to see how strong we are.

Spring: The springtime is the time when things begin to grow.

And God wants us to grow too: he wants us to grow physically, that is, get bigger. He wants us to grow intellectually, that is, get smarter – learn things. He wants us to grow spiritually, that is, get to know him better.

We need all these times. God uses all these times to help us, to make us what he wants us to be, so that no matter how we started we are going to finish in an amazing way.

STORY – A Dog Called Sam (5)

And so it was over. Sam would never again be challenged as leader of the pack. Her place was secure. Her father had ensured she would stay there.

This was the dog who all those years earlier had crawled out of the barn, forced into the cold by those who had turned against her. She had stood in the bitter wind, with tears streaming down her face. The whole thing could have ended there and then, but it didn't.

It doesn't matter how you start; it's how you finish. And some of you tonight need to come and pray this prayer that Jabez once prayed. Some of you have had some pretty rough starts and some of you aren't doing great right now, but come and pray the prayer. Some of you have had great starts and maybe you're doing great right now, but you come and pray this prayer too. Let's ask God to bless us, let's ask God to make us great, let's ask God to make it all happen so that we can do amazing things in this world for Jesus.

You see, Sam led the dogs time and time again. They respected her, they followed her, they listened to what she said and she led them properly and rightly.

Some of you also are going to be great leaders. If you are praying this prayer with honesty and you are ready to promise God that if he makes you a leader you will lead properly, and you will be honest and always do the right thing, then we need to pray for some of you as well.

Many years would come and go, and Sam would later have her own pups. She cared for them and taught them to be kind to others and in time they too grew up to be great leaders. Again, it could all have ended so sadly, but it didn't. It's not about starts; it's about finishes.

This story has been about Sam the foxhound, but more importantly it is about what you can do and what you can be.

In some contexts and with some audiences this will be altogether too heavy. Tone it down if you need. However, this is the level of intensity that children's ministry must touch on, even if only occasionally, to produce boys and girls who can change things.

THE GENERAL

A Series in Six Parts

Introduction

Title	Themes covered
1 The Call	I saw a need
2 Making History	Doing worthwhile things
3 Sacrifice	It usually costs us something to do something worthwhile
4 Teamwork	We don't have to do it alone
5 Opposition	There's always some persecution
6 Dreamers	The dream becomes reality

By now most people are familiar with the Salvation Army. There are mixed responses to the work that they do. Some would say that they exist only to fulfil a social role and have no part in the preaching of the gospel. Others would maintain that their social action is only an excuse to tell others about Jesus. The Salvation Army itself can point to the writings of James and show clearly that faith without works is dead, and also to the writings of Paul that inform us that people do not come to God unless they hear the message and they never hear the message without a messenger.

Whatever people's views on the Salvation Army, and there will almost certainly continue to be many, there can be little doubt about the significance of its founder, General William Booth. His life shines out in the darkness, a life of sacrifice and commitment to reaching out to those whom God loves. In his own words: "Go for souls and go for the worst." His life shines into our time, when people do what they like without thinking of others. This man stands as an example of what God can do through a life that is given to God.

The series will give us a very brief insight into a man who shook nations and whose efforts have changed history.

1 The Call

	Programme	Item
Section 1	Welcome	
	Rules	
	Prayer	
	Introductory Praise	
	Game 1	I Need A...
	Praise	
	Fun Item 1	
	Game 2	Find Me What I Need...
	Fun Item 2	
	Bible Text	James 2:17
	Announcements	
	Interview	
Section 2 Preaching Time	Worship Time	
	Bible Lesson	Nehemiah
	Illustration 1	Meeting The Need
	Illustration 2	Doing Something
	Illustration 3	Project
	Story	The General (1)
	Prayer	

Overview A man once preached a message entitled "What to do while we're waiting for the burning bush". The implication is that we don't have to stand around waiting for God to tell us what to do when there are huge needs right in front of us. The need is the call.

games

Game 1

I Need A...

PREPARATION A box full of rubbish and a few useful items such as a brush, a shoe, a sock, a pair of sunglasses, etc.

PLAYERS Four per team.

SET-UP The players are lined up in relay formation at A. The box is at B.

OBJECT The Games Master calls out the name of an object, in this way: "I need a ... comb". The players run from A to B, collect the object and return. The first person back with the object gets a point for their team. The game continues until all objects have been called for and retrieved.

WINNING The team that finishes with the most points wins.

Find Me What I Need...

PREPARATION A box full of rubbish and a few useful items such as a brush, a shoe, a sock, a pair of sunglasses, etc.

PLAYERS Four per team.

SET-UP The players are lined up in relay formation at A. The box is at B.

OBJECT This time the objects are not specifically named, but just descriptions given, for example: "I need something that I can comb my hair with... I need something I can go swimming in... "

WINNING The team that finishes with the most points wins.

Preaching Time

BIBLE LESSON NEHEMIAH

"Faith that doesn't lead us to do good deeds is all alone and dead!" (James 2:17)

For the next six weeks we will be looking at the Bible character called Nehemiah. At the start of our story about Nehemiah he is working in the palace of King Artaxerxes. His job was very simple and he enjoyed doing it. All he had to do every day was to bring the king his cup of wine – not the most difficult job in the whole world, but Nehemiah was happy doing it.

Happy, that is, until his brother came to him with news about Jerusalem, the place where he used to live and the place that he loved very much. His brother told him that the city was in ruins and the walls of the city had all been pulled down.

Nehemiah began to pray, but he also did something else: he decided that he would go and do something about it. You see, praying is important but, as well as praying, sometimes we need to go and do something. Nehemiah was determined to do something about it; he was going to rebuild the walls and restore the city.

Meeting the Need

Object needed: *A narrator holding a can of fizzy pop, a man lying on the floor begging and a couple of actors, as listed.*

Man: Help me! I'm so thirsty!

(Narrator takes drink of water.)

Narrator: There are lots of people like this. I mean, lots of people who need something. When we see people like this, we do a couple of different things. Some people do this:

Man: Help me! I'm thirsty!
Lady 1: Oh, dear me, seeing people like this makes one quite upset. Oh dear.
Narrator: Other people do this:
Man: Help me! I'm thirsty!
Lady 2: Oh, splendid, a person in need! I'm writing a book and I was wondering if you would mind answering some questions? No? Oh well, please yourself.
Narrator: And there are even some crazy people who do this:
Man: Help me! I'm thirsty!
Lady 3: Oh, you need something? Here you go, have some crisps... What do you mean, you're thirsty, not hungry? Some people are *so* ungrateful.
Narrator: So we get lots of people doing lots of things but not many people doing this:
Man: Help me! I'm thirsty!
Narrator: Here you go, mate, have a drink. *(Hands him the drink.)* You'd be surprised how many people do anything but just meet the need. If someone is thirsty and you can give them a drink, then do it. If they are hungry and you can feed them, then do it. If they are cold and you have a spare coat, then clothe them. It's really very simple.

Doing Something

Object needed: *A video clip of Live Aid (or a photograph of Bob Geldof) and the Pudsey Bear symbol (BBC Children In Need logo).*

(If there is a more up-to-date character or event, please use it.)

In the mid-1980s a man called Bob Geldof saw pictures of children and adults starving in a country called Ethiopia. He was so touched that he went to see the country for himself. What he saw was to have a profound effect on Bob for the rest of his life. It made him feel sad; it made him feel very upset as he watched many people dying with no food. Their harvest had failed, the rains hadn't come and the people were dying.

He was very upset. Lots of us get very upset at some of the things we see on television, or hear on the news. Some of us get upset by the sad things that happen all around us every day. But Bob Geldof did more than just get upset; he decided to do something about it. He would hold a concert to raise money to help these people. He would organise the largest concert the world had ever seen, with some of the biggest names in music appearing in it. He would hold it in London and in New York. It was called Live Aid.

Live Aid raised millions of pounds for starving people around the world. Bob did more than get upset; he did something about it. *(Again, adapt this to your locality.)*

There are other charity events that take place every year. This symbol is Pudsey Bear, the logo for the BBC's Children In Need programme. It is a great night of fun which we will try to be involved in this year. Again it gives us a chance not just to feel sad about things or to feel sorry for people who are not as well off as us, but it gives us a chance to get involved.

Project

Whether it be Children In Need, or Tear Fund, or the NSPCC, this is the slot to promote a charity that you would like the children to get behind and support. It is the best possible form of object lesson if you can motivate the children to get involved in a project that makes a difference.

Sponsor a child in a developing country. Organise a bring-and-buy sale. Clean up a nearby river. Visit old people's houses and clean up their gardens. Do *something.*

● STORY – The General (1)

He came up Mile End Road, East London, as the saffron light of evening flooded the sky – a tall, black-bearded man in a dark coat and wide-brimmed hat. He was walking quickly.

He stopped outside a pub called "The Blind Beggar", drew out an old Bible from his pocket and began to read out loud. He was nearly two metres tall and the passers-by soon stopped to stare at this strange man with his unusual Midlands accent. People were drawn to listen. The man continued to speak in his "sing-song" accent, but there was something else that could clearly be detected through his words: this man sincerely cared for people.

He continued to speak to the gathering crowds about how much God loved them. Then suddenly from the nearby pub came men who began to make fun of him. One threw an egg which broke on the man's cheek. The man calmly wiped the yolk away, bowed his head and prayed. Then he turned and continued his journey. For a long time he had thought about where God wanted him to go, and what God wanted him to do. He had dreamt of a journey to a faraway jungle with strange inhabitants whom he could preach the gospel to. But God had a different idea: on this special night the man, William Booth, walked through a human jungle, a city of over 3 million people.

He walked on, passing children as young as five years old who staggered about blind drunk. He watched fight after fight as man turned against man in a desire to conquer the other, in a futile attempt to wound the other before they were wounded. He looked into the squalid houses where the sick, the dying and very often the dead lay side by side on the cold cement floors. He walked on past countless tramps and homeless men, women and children. He walked avoiding the countless drunks who had spent the precious pennies they had earned on drink, while their families sat hungry at home, their children desperate for food.

William had thought long and hard about what he should do for God. Today he knew where he should go. The need was his call. God wanted him to start where he was, to make a difference to these men and women, to these boys and girls, not to a world far away, but to a world under his very nose. God wanted him to change these people's lives, to make things better for them.

Eventually, around midnight, he placed a key in his front door. As he entered, he turned and there sat his wife; she was not ready to sleep until her beloved William had returned. He stared at her, his grey eyes piercing and preparing the way for his announcement: "Tonight, darling, I found my destiny."

William had seen a very clear and desperate need and he was going to do something about it. He was going to help others.

2 Making History

	Programme	Item
Section 1	**Welcome**	
	Rules	
	Prayer	
	Introductory Praise	
	Game 1	Dates And Events
	Praise	
	Fun Item 1	
	Game 2	Events And Dates
	Fun Item 2	
	Bible Text	Matthew 3:8
	Announcements	
	Interview	
Section 2	**Worship Time**	
Preaching	**Bible Lesson**	Nehemiah
Time	**Illustration 1**	Bad History-makers
	Illustration 2	Good History-makers
	Illustration 3	Eternal History-makers
	Story	The General (2)
	Prayer	

Williams Booth was about to make history, not bad history, not even good history; he was going to make eternal history. He was going to affect the world for ever.

Dates And Events

PREPARATION Several sheets of paper per team, each with the following dates and historical events:

1066	Battle of Hastings
356BC	Birth of Alexander the Great
1100	The Crusades
1595	William Shakespeare writes *Romeo and Juliet*
1605	Guy Fawkes arrested

PLAYERS Five per team.

SET-UP The players are lined up in relay formation at A. The dates are placed at B and the events are placed on a board at A.

OBJECT The players run from A to B in turn and collect a date from B. They then return and match the date to the event on the board.

WINNING The team that gets the most dates right wins.

Events And Dates*

PREPARATION Several sheets of paper per team, each with the following historical events and dates:

1066	Battle of Hastings
356BC	Birth of Alexander the Great
1100	The Crusades
1595	William Shakespeare writes *Romeo and Juliet*
1605	Guy Fawkes arrested

PLAYERS Five per team.

SET-UP The players are lined up in relay formation at A. The events are placed at B and the dates are placed on a board at A.

OBJECT The players run from A to B in turn and collect an event from B. They then return and match the event to the date on the board.

WINNING The team that gets the most events right wins.

NEHEMIAH

"Do something to show that you have really given up your sins." (Matthew 3:8)

Nehemiah returned to Jerusalem and began to look at the walls. But here is the important point: if we are to be history-makers, then we have to do more than just look around. It is important that we do look around, but then we have to decide to do something. Nehemiah decided that he was going to rebuild the walls. His city was in ruins. No one else seemed ready to do anything about it, but Nehemiah was going to do something about it. He would fix the walls of the city, he would rebuild the houses and he would rebuild the temple.

Nehemiah was sad to see the mess the city was in, but he was going to become a history-maker. He was going to do something that people would remember. He was going to change things.

* In theory the game should be very easy the second time around as the children should have remembered the matchings from the first game.

Illustration 1

Bad History-makers

Object needed: *A list of the following names: Adolf Hitler, Osama Bin Laden (if you also have pictures, that will help).*

Let me show you some names/pictures. Does anyone know what these people have in common? Well, they actually have several things in common. They are both famous and they both made history. But they both made history in a very bad way. Adolf Hitler was the man responsible for killing 6 million Jews in the Second World War.

Osama Bin Laden was the man responsible for sending the two aeroplanes that flew into the World Trade Center in New York – killing 3,000 people.

Illustration 2

Good History-makers

Object needed: *A list of the following names: Neil Armstrong, Winston Churchill, Nelson Mandela (if you also have pictures, that will help).*

How about this list/these photos? Does anyone know what they have in common? They are all also very famous, but for different reasons. These are all people who made history because of the good things that they did.

Neil Armstrong was the first man to walk on the moon. What an exciting thing to do. To be the very first man to walk on the moon, to stare back at the earth from such a faraway position.

Winston Churchill was the British prime minister who did much to win the Second World War.

Nelson Mandela was kept in prison for 25 years for what he believed in. He believed all people should be treated equally, no matter what the colour of their skin. He became the first black president of the Republic of South Africa.

Eternal History-makers

Object needed: *A list of the following names: Peter, Hudson Taylor, Amy Carmichael (if you also have pictures, that will help).*

Now how about these names/pictures? Maybe they are not so familiar to you, but nevertheless they are very famous indeed. These people changed history in a different way from the others. The others changed history for a short time, but these people changed history in a way that will last for ever. They changed history in a similar way to William Booth, whom we will talk about again shortly. They changed history because they told people about Jesus and they helped people for God. So, what they did will last for ever. People will be in heaven right now because of these people and they will stay there for ever.

Peter was the man who learned from Jesus himself and then spent the rest of his life telling others about the love of God.

Hudson Taylor travelled all the way to China to tell people there about Jesus. He was so determined to tell

them that he was nearly killed on several occasions.

Amy Carmichael is one of my personal heroes. She went to India to tell people about Jesus and to open many orphanages for children whose parents no longer wanted them.

● STORY – The General (2)

William's wife's name was Catherine. She wanted to go with her husband and tell people about Jesus, but she was afraid. She had seen what had happened to him sometimes as he stood on street corners telling people about Jesus. Sometimes people swore at him. Sometimes he was beaten up. Sometimes people spat at him. But all the time he kept on telling people about Jesus. Catherine didn't know what to do, so she did what she always did when she didn't know what to do – she prayed.

As Catherine knelt in prayer, Jesus himself appeared before her. Catherine looked up at Jesus and asked: "Jesus, is there no other way?"

Jesus showed Catherine the nail prints in his wrist where he had been nailed to the cross and said: "Catherine, sometimes people who follow me suffer."

Catherine, still looking at Jesus, asked one more question: "Then, Jesus, will you go with me?"

Jesus looked into Catherine's eyes and replied: "Catherine, I will be with you until the very end." Catherine stood up and joined her husband. She began to tell people about Jesus. She didn't care what happened because Jesus was with her.

And we also must never be afraid. Jesus is with us and will look after us.

There is certainly an opportunity here to ask if the children would like to be prayed for, for that assurance that God will also be with them, no matter what. The story has not been elaborated so that time is available to do this.

3 The Sacrifice

	Programme	Item
Section 1	Welcome	
	Rules	
	Prayer	
	Introductory Praise	
	Game 1	Time
	Praise	
	Fun Item 1	
	Game 2	Treasure
	Fun Item 2	
	Bible Text	Luke 14:28
	Announcements	
	Interview	
Section 2 Preaching Time	Worship Time	
	Bible Lesson	Nehemiah
	Illustration 1	Time
	Illustration 2	Talents
	Illustration 3	Treasure
	Story	The General (3)
	Prayer	

Overview Whenever we want to do something of great worth, then it usually means that we have to sacrifice something. We usually have to give something up. It will mean sacrificing our time, our talents or maybe our treasure – possibly, as in the case of William Booth, all three.

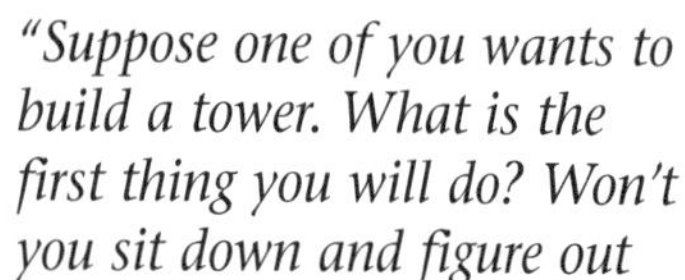

Game 1

Time

PREPARATION	Print out a picture of a clock per team and cut it into four pieces.
PLAYERS	Four per team.
SET-UP	The players line up at A. The pieces are placed B.
OBJECT	The players run in turn from A to B, collect a piece of the clock and return to A. When all the pieces are collected the team has to construct the clock.
WINNING	The first team to construct a clock wins.

Treasure

PREPARATION	Photocopy some Clipart money and place it at B.
PLAYERS	Five per team.
SET-UP	The players line up at A and on the word "Go" they run from A to B, collect one piece of money and return.
OBJECT	To collect as many pieces of money as possible within two minutes.
WINNING	The team with the most money after two minutes wins.

BIBLE LESSON NEHEMIAH

"Suppose one of you wants to build a tower. What is the first thing you will do? Won't you sit down and figure out how much it will cost and if you have enough money to pay for it?" (Luke 14:28)

While Nehemiah was still in Babylon he had an excellent job. He worked for the king and was almost certainly paid a lot of money. He had a job that he enjoyed and people looked up to him. But Nehemiah had heard about the country where he had grown up and what had happened to it. He cared more about Jerusalem than he did about his job.

There are lots of things that may seem very important to us. But sometimes we have to give up these things to get what's really important.

You see, sometimes, to do something that is really important we have to give something up. Nehemiah gave up his job and his important position in the king's palace. He gave up his comfortable bed and his nice food. He gave all this up so that he could go and live in a decrepit and broken-down city. He would live on food that was not as nice; he would sleep in places that did not compare with the king's palace. But he would give all this up to work at rebuilding Jerusalem.

Sometimes, to do something that is really important we have to give something up.

Time

Object needed: *A sheet of paper with the word "time" written on it.*

Some of us will have to give up our time. You see, to go and help others or to go and do something worthwhile takes time: time that you may want to use for hanging out with your friends; time you may have wanted for playing on your PlayStation; time you may have wanted for sitting down and watching television.

It will mean giving up your time. And the older you get, the less time you may have. When you get just a couple of years older you will have even more school work and even more things to do.

But if something is really important, then you must give up time. If you think that visiting old people is worthwhile, then it will take your time, but it is worth doing. If you think that helping people who are disabled is worthwhile, then it will take your time, but it is worth doing. If you think that helping people who have less than you is worthwhile, then it will take your time, but it is worth doing.

Talents

Object needed: *A sheet of paper with the word "talent" written on it.*

Can anybody think of a talent? *(Take some responses.)* Yes, these are all talents. We all have talents, but how we use those talents is important. Sometimes at Christmas we go with some friends to sing in an old people's home. Now we don't sing that well, but the old people like it very much – amazing, really. But when we use our talents to help others it's a good use of our talents.

We know some people who are excellent at painting and decorating and they can make a lot of money by painting and decorating people's homes. But from time to time these people use their talents to decorate the homes of people who could never afford it otherwise.

We know some people who are good with computers who could become very rich using their talents in this country, but instead they have gone to faraway countries to use their talents in helping others.

We know teachers who could easily use their talents in this country and have a nice job in a nice school and live in a nice home, but instead they have gone to countries where they get £10 a week for doing their work, where they live in homes that are too hot or too cold and usually full of mosquitoes. They do this so they can teach poor children how to read and write.

We can use our talents to be selfish or we can use our talents to help others. We all have talents; it really is how we use those talents that's important. Let's have a little think right now. Who has got a talent that they can use to help others? Any ideas?

Treasure

Object needed: *A sheet of paper with the word "treasure" written on it.*

It is usually possible to get people to give up their time. It's even possible to get people to use their talents, but most people are not very keen to give up their treasure.

Once, a long time ago, I needed to get home from college and back to my parents' house. It was a journey of about 200 miles. I was surrounded by lots of very talented people. They really could do some amazing things. There were people who could play all sorts of instruments. There were people who could draw anything I could think of, but these weren't the things I needed.

There were lots of people who wanted to spend time with me, and lots of people listened to my problem. But only one person decided to help me. He didn't give me his talents; he didn't give me his time; he simply gave me the money I needed to go home.

Sometimes we need to help people by giving them our treasure.

A couple of weeks back, we all gave some money to Children In Need, and the money we sent from here will help some people.

● STORY – The General (3)

Have three sheets of Flash Paper, marked "time", "talents" and "treasure" respectively.*

William Booth was a man who was so determined to do good that he gladly gave of his time, talents and treasure.

He never complained about the vast amount of time he gave to helping others. *(Set the first Flash Paper sheet, marked "time", on fire.)* Every night of the week William would arrive home well after midnight. He had no car or other transport and would make his way walking between the scores of people gathered on the street, arriving home with his clothes torn and, inevitably, blood on his face from a smashed egg, or worse, a bottle.

But William was determined. On Christmas Day, when other people were enjoying potatoes and turkey, William and his family, from Evangeline, the youngest, right up to Bramwell, the eldest, would be out preaching in the frost at Whitechapel or visiting thousands of poverty-stricken families and giving them what they could.

And what of Booth's talents? *(Set fire to paper marked "talents".)* William Booth was a professional man. He could have become a wealthy banker; he was a gifted speaker; he could have become a rich politician; but none of these things were important to William. He was committed to the job of winning people to Jesus.

His children were the same. They dreamed of being great speakers and of turning people away from the silly things they were doing, from violence, from getting drunk, from hurting each other. They dreamed of helping people come to Jesus, where they would find love and peace.

And he never had much money to give to others. *(Set fire to paper marked "treasure".)* He was living on less than £3 a week and with that he had to feed and clothe his family. It wasn't easy; his son Bramwell constantly complained that the other children in school laughed at the patches on his trousers. He was embarrassed but, just like his father, he was prepared to give up things to be able to help people.

William and his family gave up their time, talents and treasure to help others. How about you? Are you prepared to give things up to help others?

* Flash Paper is available from www.tricksfortruth.com

4 Teamwork

	Programme	Item
Section 1	Welcome	
	Rules	
	Prayer	
	Introductory Praise	
	Game 1	Building Up The Temple (for boys)
	Praise	
	Fun Item 1	
	Game 2	Building Up The Temple (for girls)
	Fun Item 2	
	Bible Text	Philippians 1:27
	Announcements	
	Interview	
Section 2 Preaching Time	Worship Time	
	Bible Lesson	Nehemiah
	Illustration 1	Armour-bearer
	Illustration 2	Building
	Illustration 3	The Body Of Christ
	Story	The General (4)
	Prayer	

William Booth was determined not to work with only middle-class "nice people". He was determined to go to the neediest. It came as a little surprise where his help would come from.

games

Building Up The Temple (for boys)

PREPARATION Four outfits (an electrician, a plumber, a carpenter, a bricklayer*). This can be done by purchasing a range of low-price dressing-up outfits, or the "bricklayer" can carry a brick, the "plumber" a pipe, etc.

PLAYERS Four per team.

SET-UP The players are lined up in relay formation at A. The props are placed at B.

OBJECT To build anything significant it needs lots of different types of people. Here we have some would-be tradespeople. When the game begins the first person will run to B, put on the outfit and return.

WINNING The first team that has all its members dressed in outfits wins.

Game 2

Building Up The Temple (for girls)

PREPARATION Four outfits (an electrician, a plumber, a carpenter, a bricklayer*). This can be done by purchasing a range of low-price dressing-up outfits, or the "bricklayer" can carry a brick, the "plumber" a pipe, etc.

PLAYERS Four per team.

SET-UP The players are lined up in relay formation at A. The props are placed at B.

OBJECT To build anything significant it needs lots of different types of people. Here we have some would-be tradespeople. When the game begins the first person will run to B, put on the outfit and return.

WINNING The first team that has all its members dressed in outfits wins.

BIBLE LESSON **NEHEMIAH**

"I will know that you are working together and that you are struggling side by side to get others to believe the good news." (Philippians 1:27)

Nehemiah returned to Jerusalem and looked at the walls. But he knew that he could not rebuild them alone. He had a plan, he had a dream, he had some amazing ideas, but he knew he couldn't do it himself. In a chapter of the Bible called Nehemiah 3 there is a list of the people who began to build the walls with Nehemiah. Let me read a few to you:

> The high priest Eliashib and the other priests rebuilt Sheep Gate and hung its doors. Then they dedicated Sheep Gate and the section of the wall as far as Hundred Tower and Hananel Tower.
>
> The people of Jericho rebuilt the next section of the wall, and Zaccur son of Imri rebuilt the section after that.
>
> The family of Hassenaah built Fish Gate. They put the beams in place and hung the doors, and then they added metal bolts and wooden beams as locks.
>
> Meremoth, son of Uriah and grandson of Hakkoz, completed the next section of the wall.
>
> Meshullam, son of Berechiah and grandson of Meshezabel, rebuilt the next

* Costumes are available from Early Learning Centre or similar toy shops, or online at www.toyshop.co.uk

section, and Zadok son of Baana rebuilt the section beside that.

The next section was to be repaired by the men of Tekoa, but their town leaders refused to do the hard work they were assigned.

The list goes on and on. Over 100 names are listed as people who built the wall. I don't want to read the whole list to you (there are too many names and they're too hard to pronounce), but I want you to see that in order to do the job there were lots of different people.

Armour-bearer

Object needed: *A picture of a man with a sword and armour.*

In the early part of the Bible, when the king or prince went into battle he would have with him an armour-bearer. The armour-bearer was something like a bodyguard. He would ensure that nothing happened to the man he guarded. But he did more than that.

Whenever the king or prince went into battle, he would march forward and he would slash at those ahead with his sword. They would fall to the ground and the armour-bearer would come behind and kill the men who had fallen. If this didn't happen, then the king's back would be exposed and the men who had been cut down could get up and stab him in the back. The armour-bearer would protect the king's or prince's back.

Let me ask you an important question: Are you the type of friend who watches your friend's back and if anyone tries to say anything bad about your friend you defend them? Or are you the kind of friend who stabs your friend in the back? Not with a knife, but when you hear something bad do you just agree and say bad things about your friend yourself? What sort of friend are you?

Building

Objects needed: *Using the four girls who are still wearing the outfits from Game 2, begin...*

Girl 1 is an electrician. Girl 2 is a plumber. Girl 3 is a carpenter and Girl 4 is a bricklayer. What could Girl 1 do if she was by herself? She could probably wire your house with electricity, wire a plug, replace fuses. Girl 2 could unblock your toilet, fix your leaking pipes. Girl 3 could build you some tables and chairs, and Girl 4 could put up a nice brick wall.

This is what they could do if they worked by themselves.

But if they worked together there is nothing they couldn't do. If they worked together, they could build houses – not only build them, they could wire them with electricity, put the sinks, toilets and central heating in, build your kitchen units, make your tables and chairs. When they work together they can build offices and schools and factories. While Girl 2 is by herself she can unblock toilets, but when she works with others she can do anything.

The Body Of Christ

Object needed: *Pictures of a body, a brain, a hand, a leg, etc.*

The Bible talks about the people who love Jesus being like one enormous body, with each person being like a different part of the body. Some people are like this *(show picture of a brain)*. Some of you are like the brain. You like to think. You have lots of ideas.

Some people are like this *(show picture of a hand)*. You like to be doing things. You like to be involved in things.

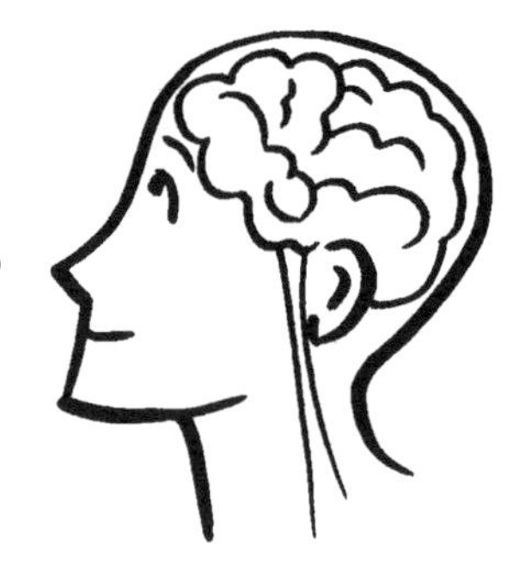

Some people are like this *(show picture of a leg)*. You like to go places.

Now if we were all like the brain, then we would have lots of great ideas but nothing would ever get done. If we were all like the hand, then we would do lots but it probably wouldn't be as good as it could be if we thought about it. If we were all like the leg, then we would be always going somewhere, but we wouldn't have thought about where we are going or what we are going to do there when we arrive.

• STORY – The General (4)

The route that William Booth had walked on that first night was not unusual. He would often go to the most needy. He would often go to those who were drunk and desperate. And he would often stand outside "The Blind Beggar" pub and tell the people about Jesus.

On one occasion he stood in his usual position, staring at a group of men who looked as if they had been drinking all day long. It was on this occasion that William first met Peter Monk. Peter approached William and asked him what he was doing. William responded: "I am looking for work." Peter thought that William needed money so he reached into his pocket to hand him some money, but William waved him away and said: "I don't need money, sir. Over there, those men are my work. Men forgotten by man and God."

Peter Monk was puzzled by these strange comments, but he agreed with one thing: "You are right, sir, these men are forgotten by God and man, and if you can do anything for them, it would be a great work."

"Well, I'm preaching tonight in the tent on the corner. You can come and bring a few of these people with you," replied William.

Peter Monk nodded. He didn't know why, but he had agreed to attend. William knew very little about Peter Monk. He probably didn't know that Peter was a prizefighter. Peter would fight other men for money. The boxing match usually took place behind "The Blind Beggar" pub. Peter had agreed to go to the tent to listen to William, but before he could go he had a fight.

Peter made his way to the usual place and stripped off his top. He watched as men bet money on who would win and he watched as his opponent took off his top and got ready to fight. The two boxers exchanged looks, walked towards each other and began to fight.

It was a ferocious battle, with both men fighting for all they were worth. There was much damage to both men's faces and it looked as if it could last for many hours. When Peter Monk brought it to a conclusion with a combination of dazzling blows to his opponent's body and a cracking finisher to his jaw, Peter's friends cheered and collected their money.

Peter was cut badly but remembered his promise to go and listen to William. He put on his shirt and jacket and went to find the tent. When he arrived he was surprised by the sight. William was standing at the front trying to speak while some local troublemakers were yelling insults and throwing things. There was no way William could be heard. Peter remembered that William wanted to help people like these and decided to help him.

Peter took off his jacket and went and stood beside William with his arms folded. Peter was a very tough man, but the cuts and fresh blood on his face just made him look even tougher. A hush fell over the crowd and the troublemakers sat down to listen.

William spoke to them about how much God loved them. Within a few days Peter Monk gave up boxing and decided that he too would give his life to helping people and telling them about the love of Jesus, just like William Booth. And with men like Peter Monk and with the help of his wife, Catherine, William began to gather together an army of people who would help others and tell them about the love of Jesus.

5 Opposition

	Programme	Item
Section 1	**Welcome**	
	Rules	
	Prayer	
	Introductory Praise	
	Game 1	Tug Of War
	Praise	
	Fun Item 1	
	Game 2	
	Fun Item 2	
	Bible Text	Romans 5:4
	Announcements	
	Interview	
Section 2	**Worship Time**	
Preaching	**Bible Lesson**	Nehemiah
Time	**Illustration 1**	Monopoly
	Illustration 2	Harry Potter
	Illustration 3	Stephen Hawking
	Story	The General (5)
	Prayer	

Overview William Booth had heard what God wanted him to do. He had given up much and his followers would also be asked to give up much. But his followers, like their leader before them, would never give up. They had a job to do, a world to win, and they would do it.

games

Tug Of War

PREPARATION	A rope with a middle marker.
PLAYERS	Four per team.
SET-UP	One team is lined up on one side of the rope, the other team on the other. *If there are more than two teams you will need to run a very quick tournament. You may want to use Game 2 for this purpose. If you have two teams, then Game 1 involves girls and Game 2 boys. If you have more than two teams, then happily mix the teams. In my experience, at this age the girls can more than hold their own.
OBJECT	Quite simply, to pull the other team more than one metre towards you.
WINNING	The team that completes the object wins.

* See note above

BIBLE LESSON NEHEMIAH

"And endurance builds character, which gives us a hope..." (Romans 5:4)

Even when Nehemiah and his team began to build the walls it wasn't easy. There were lots of people who didn't want to see the walls completed and did everything they could to try and stop the walls being rebuilt.

The main enemy was a man named Sanballat. When he saw what Nehemiah was doing he began to call Nehemiah's people all sorts of insulting names and became quite angry with them. But Nehemiah simply prayed to God for help and kept building.

It's important to see this. As soon as we start to do something good for God, then people will begin to insult us and call us all sorts of nasty names. But we, like Nehemiah, must learn to ignore it, ask God for help, and keep going.

Sanballat became even angrier when he saw that Nehemiah was ignoring him and continuing to build the walls, so he gathered some men together and was ready to attack the work that was being done and pull it down.

But Nehemiah and his team kept working. They were determined to build the walls. And to make sure that all went well, Nehemiah commanded that half the people should build the walls and the other half should keep guard. After several hours they would swap over. The wall was guarded day and night and even the men who were building had a sword strapped to their side in case danger came against them.

In this way, despite the threats and the anger, the walls began to be built higher and higher. And then the houses were restored and then the people moved on to rebuild the temple. These people would not give up until the job was done.

Monopoly

Object needed: *The board game Monopoly or at least a picture of it.*

Have any of you ever played Monopoly? Has anybody ever won? I like Monopoly; I win quite often. But we nearly didn't have the board game Monopoly. It was invented by a man called Charles Darrow. And when Charles first brought his invention to a company called Parker Brothers in 1934, with a view to them selling it for him, they laughed at him. They told him that his game was stupid and nobody would ever play it. They told him that there were 52 things wrong with the game.

Charles Darrow could have listened to them and given up. But people who give up so quickly have no way of doing anything worthwhile. To do anything worthwhile it takes determination and a decision to keep going and to make it happen. Charles Darrow decided he would sell his game himself and began to approach department stores himself. That year he sold 5,000 copies.

Parker Brothers found out what had happened and called Charles Darrow up. They said they were wrong and they asked if they could still be involved in selling the game. Charles reluctantly agreed. Parker Brothers have since sold 100 million copies of the game and Charles Darrow is a multimillionaire.

Harry Potter*

Object needed: *A picture of Harry Potter.*

Does anyone know who this is *(display photograph)*? That's a huge number of people who know! But, you know, we nearly didn't find out who he was. His creator, J.K. Rowling, sent the first book to over 20 publishers, who all said they weren't interested. They told her that nobody would be interested. They told her that it would never sell.

Can you imagine getting all the letters back saying that your work was no good and still you send it on to somebody else, who also sends it back saying it's no good? That must have been very difficult, to get turned down so many times.

But J.K. Rowling kept on going. She kept on sending the book to more and more publishers until one publisher eventually said yes. The publisher is now glad they did and all the ones who said no are probably very unhappy. The book made the publishers a lot of money and the book made J.K. Rowling very rich indeed.

Her first book, *Harry Potter and the Philosopher's Stone*, has sold millions of copies. Not bad for a book that they said was no good!

Sometimes you've got to keep going even when people say that your stuff is no good.

Stephen Hawking

Object needed: *A picture of Stephen Hawking.*

Does anyone know this man's name? His name is Stephen Hawking and, as you can see, he is very disabled. He developed a serious illness which left him seriously disabled and many people thought that he would never be able to do anything worthwhile. Many thought that he would simply wait to die.

But they hadn't counted on the determination of Stephen Hawking. He taught himself to talk and he continued to develop his amazing ability with numbers, which was far greater than that of those around him who were not disabled. He refused to be pitied, and instead he worked hard to continue learning. Although he could hardly move, he knew that his brain worked very well.

Right now he is Professor of Mathematics at Cambridge University. He has written many books and is regarded by many as one of the best thinkers in the world.

He could have spent his life doing nothing,

* Feel free to change this illustration for an alternative if you have theological problems with Mr Potter.

but he soon realised that if he worked hard he could be great. He worked hard and he *is* great.

• STORY – The General (5)

William Booth's work began to grow very quickly now and spread from the East End of London into all of the United Kingdom and then into Europe. Eventually Booth's people would be all over the world. Booth decided to call his team of people an "army", and since they were so concerned with seeing people won to Jesus they called themselves the Salvation Army.

They were committed and the work grew very quickly. But it was not without some major opposition. When the Salvation Army started their church in Switzerland, and tried to run a children's meeting like the one you're in right now, the effect was that the leader of the Salvation Army was locked up in jail for three months because they weren't allowed to tell children about Jesus.

A year later the Swiss government closed all Salvation Army churches and told all the people who had come to run the churches to get out of the country. But these people didn't run away, they never gave in, and they were ready to fight for what they believed in. They refused to go.

On the 2nd November in Geneva the police smashed down the door and ran into one of their services. They began to kick one young girl who was kneeling in prayer on the floor and threw three other people down a flight of stairs. They were determined to get rid of the Salvation Army. They didn't want these people here telling others about God. But the Salvation Army weren't going anywhere. Many of them spent more time in jail but still they refused to go.

And two years later the government gave in. They knew that they would never get rid of these people who were so determined to stand up for Jesus. They knew that even if they killed them, more of them would come. God was with them and they would never give in.

The opposition didn't stop; many people still threw stones at the Salvation Army. But they kept on growing, more and more Salvation Army halls were opened, and more and more people attended their meetings.

The almost comical conclusion came 50 years later, when the Salvation Army had eventually been accepted in Switzerland and had over 120 churches in the country, led by 400 people. The Swiss government were trying to think of pictures to put on their new stamps. They decided on the special hats the Salvation Army wear.

These people never gave up. They believed in something so strongly that they never stopped working for it.

6 Dreamers

	Programme	Item
Section 1	Welcome	
	Rules	
	Prayer	
	Introductory Praise	
	Game 1	Rollerball
	Praise	
	Fun Item 1	
	Game 2	Gunge Diver
	Fun Item 2	
	Bible Text	Hebrews 12:1
	Announcements	
	Interview	
Section 2 Preaching Time	Worship Time	
	Bible Lesson	Nehemiah
	Illustration 1	Martin Luther King's Dream
	Illustration 2	Nelson Mandela's Dream
	Illustration 3	Your Dream
	Story	The General (6)
	Prayer	

William Booth had heard what God wanted him to do. He had given up much, he was determined and he rallied many people around himself. Now the dream would become reality.

games

Game 1

Rollerball

PREPARATION Several balls (footballs, basketballs, tennis balls – it doesn't matter).

PLAYERS Three per team.

SET-UP The players line up at A. Several leaders are placed to form a runway through which the players have to run – there should be approximately five metres between the leaders for the players to run through.

OBJECT The first player runs from A to B and then returns. The leaders throw the balls from side to side. If the child is hit with the ball they score 0; if not, they score 1.

WINNING The team with the highest score wins.

Game 2

Gunge Diver

PREPARATION A bowl of beans with a Malteser at the bottom per team.

PLAYERS One per team.

SET-UP The players line up at A. The bowls are at B.

OBJECT The player runs from A to B and retrieves the Malteser with their mouth alone.

WINNING The first player to complete the object wins.

PreachingTime

BIBLE LESSON **NEHEMIAH**

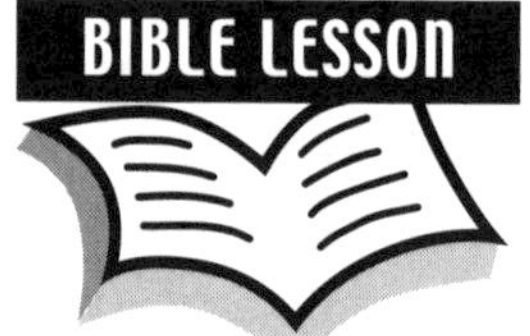

"So we must get rid of everything that slows us down, especially the sin that just won't let go. And we must be determined to run the race that is ahead of us." (Hebrews 12:1)

Let me read you some great news from the book of Nehemiah in the Bible:

> On the twenty-fifth day of the month Elul, the wall was completely rebuilt. It had taken fifty-two days. When our enemies in the surrounding nations learned that the work was finished, they felt helpless, because they knew that our God had helped us rebuild the wall.

Nehemiah had seen the need, he had prayed about it, he was prepared to give things up to see it happen, he gathered a team of people, he kept going even when it was hard and he got the job done.

Nehemiah saw his dream come true.

Martin Luther King's Dream

Object needed: *A picture of Martin Luther King.*

Martin Luther King was born in 1929. When he was 18 years of age he became a church minister. He would speak in churches and in city squares and in parks where thousands of people would come and listen to him. He preached about God, but he also spoke about fairness. He was determined that all people should be treated the same, no matter what the

colour of their skin, or how much money they had in their pockets.

Many people respected him and followed him, but many others hated him and tried to hurt him. Eventually he was shot while he was speaking in a large meeting. But his message had been heard by thousands of people.

Martin had seen the need, he had prayed about it, he was prepared to give things up to see it happen, he gathered a team of people, he kept going even when it was hard and he got the job done.

Martin Luther King's dream came true.

Nelson Mandela's Dream

Object needed: *A picture of Nelson Mandela.*

Like Martin Luther King, Nelson Mandela also fought for what was fair and right. You see, God is interested in justice as well. He's very interested in us doing the right thing. Nelson was born in 1918 in South Africa. South Africa was in the middle of something called "apartheid". This meant that white people and black people were not allowed to mix. White children and black children went to different schools, with the black children usually going to the poorer schools with no money. White people and black people were not allowed to ride on the same trains. And white and black teenagers were not allowed to play in the same sports teams.

Nelson felt this was wrong, and with others such as Bishop Desmond Tutu he began to speak out against apartheid. He began to gather others around him. He was determined to change things. Many of the people in the government hated what Nelson Mandela was saying and they locked him in prison. He spent 25 years in prison for standing up for what he knew to be right. Eventually things in South Africa changed and Nelson Mandela became South Africa's president.

Nelson had seen the need, he had prayed about it, he was prepared to give things up to see it happen, he gathered a team of people, he kept going even when it was hard and he got the job done.

Nelson Mandela saw his dream come true.

Your Dream

Object needed: *A mirror.*

Finally, I have a picture of another history-maker. You may know this one; let me show you.

Invite some of the children to come and look at the "picture" – allow them to look in the mirror.

Yes, you too can do amazing things for God. You can help others; you can change history. You can do anything you want with God's help. You could be the next William Booth and show the whole world how great God is, help the poor, make things fair for everyone. You can do that, if you allow God to take your life and make it into what he can.

You can see the need, you can pray about it, you can be prepared to give things up to see it happen, you can gather a team of people, you can keep going even when it's hard and you can get the job done.

You can see your dream come true.

• STORY – The General (6)

William Booth made history. To best explain how he made history, invite a member of the local Salvation Army to come and explain what the Salvation Army are doing around the world right now. Make sure you inform them that you have been talking about William Booth so they have a starting point. If you can't get someone to come, then tell the following:

And the last part of the William Booth story isn't a story at all. It's just some facts.

- The Salvation Army work in over 100 countries using more than 125 languages to preach the gospel

- There are over 3 million members of the Salvation Army today
- They serve 23 million cut-price meals every year
- They look after the sick, the homeless, alcoholics, young mums
- They run schools, maternity homes, children's homes and hostels

And all because one man trusted God and allowed God to do whatever he wanted with him. Today the world is a better place.

General William Booth had seen the need, he had prayed about it, he was prepared to give things up to see it happen, he gathered a team of people, he kept going even when it was hard and he got the job done.

General William Booth had seen his dream come true.

We have left lots of time this evening/ morning so that we can pray for some people, people who think that maybe God wants to use them to do some great things. So let's close our eyes...

Feel free to pray for some children who are willing to be prayed for. This is a great way to close a series on a remarkable man.

THE ADVENTURES OF ZOË AND OLIVER

A Series in Eight Parts

Introduction

Title	Themes covered
1 **We Believe In One God,** **the Father, the Almighty,**	**What is God like?**
2 **Maker Of Heaven And Earth,** **and of all that is,** **seen and unseen.**	**God is our maker, lover and keeper.**
3 **We Believe In One Lord, Jesus Christ,** **the only Son of God,** **eternally begotten of the Father,** **God from God, Light from Light,** **true God from True God,** **begotten, not made,** **of one Being with the Father.** **Through him all things were made.**	**Who was Jesus really?**
4 **For Us And For Our Salvation** **he came down from heaven;** **by the power of the Holy Spirit** **he became incarnate of the Virgin Mary,** **and was made man.** **For our sake he was crucified under Pontius Pilate;** **he suffered death and was buried.**	**Some people live interesting lives; some do amazing things; others make great sacrifices. Jesus did all three.**
5 **On The Third Day He Rose Again** **in accordance with the Scriptures;** **he ascended into heaven** **and is seated at the right hand of the Father.**	**The resurrection**

Title	Themes covered
6 He Will Come Again In Glory **to judge the living and the dead,** **and his kingdom will have no end.**	**The second coming**
7 We Believe In The Holy Spirit, **the Lord, the giver of life,** **who proceeds from the Father and the Son.** **With the Father and the Son he is worshipped and glorified.** **He has spoken through the Prophets.**	**The empowerer**
8 We Believe In One Holy Catholic And Apostolic Church. **We acknowledge one baptism for the forgiveness of sins.** **We look for the resurrection of the dead,** **and the life of the world to come. Amen.**	**The church**

The Nicene Creed was first written down in 381AD. It was written as a statement of belief in the Trinity and the deity of Christ. It became a backbone of stated belief for the church throughout the centuries. It forms a systematic theology of Christian belief and as such is very useful to build into the lives of children as soon possible. The creed in this form is almost certainly too difficult to teach the children; there are two options: either display the section of the creed on an OHP and allow the children who are able to to read it themselves, or teach a simplified version of the creed. Experience has taught me that the former works best.

The story of Zoë and Oliver, the troublesome siblings, accompanies each of the lessons. The Bible Lessons are built on the creed but form what shall be entitled the "Jesus Story".

We Believe In One God, the Father, the Almighty

	Programme	Item
Section 1	**Welcome**	
	Rules	
	Prayer	
	Introductory Praise	
	Game 1	Which One? (for boys)
	Praise	
	Fun Item 1	
	Game 2	Which One? (for girls)
	Fun Item 2	
	Bible Text	Isaiah 45:6
	Announcements	
	Interview	
Section 2	**Worship Time**	
Preaching	**Bible Lesson**	Genesis 1
Time	**Illustration 1**	One God
	Illustration 2	The Father
	Illustration 3	The Almighty
	Story	The Adventures Of Zoë And Oliver (1)
	Prayer	

Overview

Our aim is to show that God is one God, but he has within himself characteristics that are fatherly and characteristics that are almighty.

games

Which One? (for boys)

PREPARATION Fifteen table-tennis balls. One third are marked with a "1", one third marked with a "3" and the remainder marked with a "5".

PLAYERS Five boys per team.

SET-UP One female leader per team stands at position B. The teams stand at A in relay formation (i.e., one behind the other). The leaders will each have in their hand a table-tennis ball – one will have a "1", one a "3" and one a "5". Each time the balls are taken, the leaders will take another ball but ensure that each time one has a "1", one has a "3" and one has a "5".

OBJECT The players run from A to B in relay formation. At B they collect a ball from whichever leader they want. Clearly, the first there will get to choose from three leaders, the second from two and the third will have to take what is left.

WINNING The team with the most points when the table-tennis balls are added up wins.

Which One? (for girls)

PREPARATION Fifteen table-tennis balls. One third are marked with a "1", one third marked with a "3" and the remainder marked with a "5".

PLAYERS Five girls per team.

SET-UP One male leader per team stands at position B. The teams stand at A in relay formation (i.e., one behind the other). The leaders will each have in their hand a table-tennis ball – one will have a "1", one a "3" and one a "5". Each time the balls are taken, the leaders will take another ball but ensure that each time one has a "1", one has a "3" and one has a "5".

OBJECT The players run from A to B in relay formation. At B they collect a ball from whichever leader they want. Clearly, the first there will get to choose from three leaders, the second from two and the third will have to take what is left.

WINNING The team with the most points when the table tennis balls are added up wins.

Preaching Time

THE BEGINNING

"[You] will learn that I am the Lord. No other gods are real." (Isaiah 45:6)

In the year 381AD – that's nearly 1,700 years ago – some people held a meeting. They held the meeting to talk about what God was like and who Jesus was. After talking and reading their Bibles they wrote down what they believed. What they wrote down has a title; they called it the Nicene Creed, as it was written in a place called Nicaea. It helps us remember what we believe, so today lots of churches throughout the world say the creed to remind them what God is like.

Over the next eight weeks we will be looking at some of the words these people wrote down. This week we look at the very first part: "We believe in one God, the Father, the Almighty."

At the same time as looking at the creed we will be looking at the "Jesus Story". We will be looking for ourselves at who Jesus is. Our place for beginning the "Jesus Story" might surprise some of you.

There's nothing. No people, no mountains, no skies. In fact, no planet earth, no universe. There's nothing. Nothing at all. Oh... there is something. No, not a something! A some*one*.

This is the point before the beginning of time itself. There is nothing except God. God, waiting, ready, to start it all off. God is very complicated. God is one. Yet he is three. There is God the Father, God the Son and God the Holy Spirit. They are all God. Three separate persons, but only one God... I told you God was complicated. And there he is, right at the start of the universe, waiting to create everything. God. And this is where the Jesus Story begins for us. Jesus is the Son of God. Before the world began, Jesus was.

Very soon, the whole world is going to come into existence. But before any of that, before time itself, there was Jesus, the Son of God. The Jesus Story really has no beginning, because Jesus has always existed. But we'll start it right here, at the beginning of the universe.

One God

Object needed: *A map of the world and six volunteers.*

This is our world. It is quite a big place really. There are 6 billion people living on this world. That's a "6" with nine zeroes after it. It's a lot of people. Let me show you something interesting about these 6 billion people.

Let's pretend that each of these people at the front represents 1 billion people each. If that was the case, how many do you think believe that there is only one God? *(Take some answers.)* Well, the answer is four. That's most of them.

The other two mainly believe not in "no God", but rather strangely they believe in lots of gods. They believe in gods in trees and gods in mountains and gods of love and gods of anger; they believe in house gods and war gods, lots and lots of gods. It is a bit strange and I don't think it makes a lot of sense.

Now, how many do you think believe that there is no God at all? *(Take answers again.)* Well, there are no whole people left. Four believe in one God. Most of two believe in many gods. But if you want to know how many believe in no God at all, well, it's about the amount of this last person's left arm. That means, hardly anyone believes there is no God. Curiously, most of the people who do, live near to us. The Bible has a special name for the people who believe in no God. The Bible calls them "fools!"

The Father

Object needed: *A white board, or something to write on.*

Who can give me some words that you think would describe a perfect father?

As soon as you get words such as "loving", "giving", "caring", etc., begin to write them on the board.

The Almighty

Object needed: *The same items as above and the same sheet or board with the words that were given for father already on it.*

Who can give me some words that you think would describe someone who was almighty?

This time you're looking for words such as "powerful", "strong", "enormous", "tough", etc. Begin to write these on the board. When the board is full, stop.

And there we have it. This is what God is like. He is both the Father and the Almighty. He is loving and caring and giving, but he is also strong and powerful and certainly shouldn't be messed with. God is both of these things, but he is one God.

● STORY – The Adventures Of Zoë And Oliver (1)

Zoë and Oliver lived in a lovely house in the countryside. In the front garden there was an enormous tree and hanging from the tree was a swing that their dad had put up. Zoë was five; her older brother was seven.

Every evening Zoë and Oliver would come in from playing in the garden and they would be sent upstairs to take their bath. There would be the usual fight over who would go first. Oliver was the oldest and he would usually win most of the fights – but he was also the one who usually got into trouble with Mum when Zoë would burst into tears. Mum would wash their hair and after their bath they would come downstairs for their dinner and then it would be time for bed and their favourite time of all – storytime with Dad.

Dad was great at stories. And their favourite story was "Mandy and the Munchies Monster". Dad would do the voices and then he would do the growls of the monster as it walked through the city squashing all the tiny people below. Whenever he stepped on someone he would make the "squelch" sound that made Zoë and Oliver laugh uncontrollably. When they laughed too loud, Mum would shout up the stairs and call Dad back down. At this point Dad would give them a kiss goodnight, say prayers, turn off the light and go back downstairs.

Zoë and Oliver loved Dad's stories. They loved Dad. He was always so kind and caring and always made them laugh so much. They didn't think they had ever seen Dad angry, or even raise his voice. Not yet, anyway.

It's great to know that even if we don't have a dad, or if we have a dad who we don't live with, we still have a God in heaven who wants to be our Father and show us his love. Even if we have a dad who is here with us and loves us dearly, it's still good to know that God loves us also.

The next day it was raining and Mum drove Zoë and Oliver to school. They usually walked. It was less than half a mile from their house to the village school. Mum dropped them off and passed them their lunch boxes and book bags. Zoë and Oliver had begun to walk through the school gates when Mum shouted: "Zoë, Oliver! Dad will be picking you up after school. Wait here for him."

School was OK. Zoë enjoyed listening to stories about Victorians, and the whole class laughed when they saw what huge dresses they had to wear. Oliver did PE in the morning, which he really thought was his favourite lesson of all. After lunch there were sums, and he really thought that was his least favourite lesson.

School eventually came to an end and a very happy Zoë and Oliver ran out of school to the school gates. They both arrived at exactly the same time, although Oliver insisted he was first. They stood and waited, but there was no sign of Dad. This was 3pm. At 3:15pm they were beginning to worry. By 3:30pm everyone else had made their way home and Zoë and Oliver were the only ones left. They argued for a little while over what to do. Zoë said they should wait and Oliver said they shouldn't. In the end Oliver said he was going, and because Zoë wouldn't come he walked off by himself.

This was not a smart thing to do, but he was sure that he would be able to walk the half-mile to his house.

Oliver hadn't gone far when he began to wish that he had never set off. He had forgotten that he would have to walk past Gerald's house – and not just Gerald, but all his friends who were usually there with him. Gerald was fourteen and Gerald was a bully.

Sure enough, as Oliver got close, Gerald saw him. "Get him!" shouted Gerald. And Gerald and three of his friends ran towards Oliver. Oliver did what you might expect. He ran for it. He decided to run into the woods and to come out round the back of his house. He took off and ran as fast as he could. He could hear the bullies getting closer and closer. He didn't know how it happened but he ended up running right to the edge of the river. It was flowing very quickly and would surely sweep Oliver away if he stepped into it.

The bullies had arrived and were surrounding him. They were coming closer and closer and Oliver had to choose between being swept away by the river and being punched a lot by the bullies. He had braced himself ready for the first punch when suddenly...

"What do you think you're doing?"

The voice was like thunder and although Oliver thought he recognised the voice it was more frightening than he had ever heard. The bullies spun round and there stood Oliver's dad. Oliver had never seen him looking so angry. He looked as if he was going to turn into the "Munchie Monster" and make the bullies go "squelch"! The bullies took one look at Oliver's dad and began to run away very quickly. Oliver had never seen him like that before.

And God is the same: he is loving and kind and gentle like a great father, but he is also powerful and mighty like a dad who is protecting his children.

Oliver took Dad's hand and they walked to the car. Zoë was already safely in the back seat. Dad explained he had been stuck in traffic and that Oliver should have waited for him. Oliver got into the back. Zoë did feel sorry for him, but she couldn't resist it. She turned to Oliver and said: "I did tell you so, Oliver."

Maker Of Heaven And Earth and of all that is, seen and unseen.

	Programme	Item
Section 1	Welcome	
	Rules	
	Prayer	
	Introductory Praise	
	Game 1	Play Dough 1
	Praise	
	Fun Item 1	
	Game 2	Play Dough 2
	Fun Item 2	
	Bible Text	Genesis 1:1
	Announcements	
	Interview	
Section 2	Worship Time	
Preaching	Bible Lesson	Creation
Time	Illustration 1	Maker
	Illustration 2	Lover
	Illustration 3	Keeper
	Story	The Adventures Of Zoë And Oliver (2)
	Prayer	

God is our maker. But, more than this, he is our lover and our keeper.

games

Play Dough 1

PREPARATION	A ball of play dough per team.
PLAYERS	Two per team.
SET-UP	The players stand at A with a ball of play dough each.
OBJECT	When the game begins the players must construct their favourite animal that God created (even Tyrannosaurus rex).
WINNING	The best creation after two minutes wins.

Play Dough 2

PREPARATION	A ball of play dough per team.
PLAYERS	Two per team.
SET-UP	The players stand at A with a ball of play dough each.
OBJECT	When the game begins the players must construct any leader they want.
WINNING	The best creation wins. There is a bonus point if the team can recognise the leader.

Preaching Time

BIBLE LESSON **CREATION**

"In the beginning God created the heavens and the earth." (Genesis 1:1)

This week the part of the creed we look at is: "Maker of heaven and earth, and of all that is, seen and unseen."

The Jesus Story continues. Time has started. Everything has been created – well, nearly everything. There's one thing missing. The most exciting part is about to happen. God the Father and God the Holy Spirit and God the Son have a conversation. (Who can remember the name of God's Son? Yes: Jesus.)

They decide, "Let us make man in our image." Before Jesus is born in Bethlehem, he is involved in creating the universe, and, more than that, he is involved in creating you and me.

Maker

Object needed: *A hazelnut.*

Julian of Norwich was quite an unusual person. Firstly, Julian was a woman, and, secondly, she lived nearly 700 years ago. She lived within the walls of a church and spent a lot of time praying and listening to God.

On May 8th 1373 Julian was shown a lot of things by God, things we would call visions. She saw 16 visions, but probably the most famous is "The Hazelnut". God showed a hazelnut to Julian and told her three things about it:

1. God made it
2. God loves it
3. God keeps it

And through this vision he showed her the same thing was true of people. So let's look at this.

God made us. We are not an accident, we didn't come from monkeys and we certainly didn't start off as natural yoghurt, although lots of people might believe that. We were all made by God. God himself put us together. He formed us as Psalm 139 tells us, while we were in our mummy's tummy. God took the time to make us exactly the way we are. And we are made in an amazing and wonderful way.

Lover

Object needed: *A hazelnut.*

Julian also felt God saying that he didn't just make the hazelnut, but he also loved it.

God didn't just *make* us, he *loves* us. When I was in school I had to do woodwork. I was rubbish at it. Everything I made fell to pieces. I made a coat hanger that snapped when somebody hung a coat on it, I made a tape holder that was too small to hold tapes, and I made a sculpture that looked rather frightening. There wasn't a single thing that I made that I loved.

This is exactly the opposite of God. Everything God has made he loves, especially you. There is a wonderful verse in the Song of Solomon – a book in the old part of the Bible – that says: "With one glance of our eyes we captured his heart".

God loves us absolutely. He loves us more than words could explain. He loves us as much as he loves his own Son, Jesus.

Keeper

Object needed: *A hazelnut and a clock.*

And the final part of the vision that Julian saw. She felt God tell her that he didn't just make the hazelnut and love the hazelnut, but he kept the hazelnut.

Some people think that God is like a great big clockmaker, and the universe and all that is in it is his clock. He made it, he wound it up and now it runs by itself. The planets go around the sun, the moon goes around the earth, all because God set them to do that at the start of time and so they keep doing it.

I'm not completely sure where they think God is. They may think he's taking a tea break, or he's maybe popped off to the seaside for a couple of thousand years, I don't know.

In fact I do not believe this, and this is not what the Bible teaches. The Bible teaches that God is holding all things together and if for one moment God stepped away from the universe the whole thing would stop working.

You see, God didn't just make us and love us. God keeps us, he wants to look after us, he wants to be involved in our lives. He wants us to talk to him and to talk to us. That's what God is like. He didn't create and walk away. He is always there. Leading and guiding – if we'll let him.

• STORY – The Adventures Of Zoë And Oliver (2)

A travelling funfair had arrived in the village, and now that Gerald and his bully friends were too frightened to even look at Oliver and Zoë, they felt perfectly safe in wandering into the village to take a look – they told Mum where they were first, of course.

There was so much to see: waltzers and huge slides, a bungee jump that shot you upwards in a shiny cage, bumper cars that went so very fast. Oliver wanted to go on anything. He queued and got on the ride and then he queued for the next and the next.

Zoë wasn't as interested in the rides. She had been distracted by something else: a whole pile of goldfish bowls and a man inviting people to come and throw a table-tennis ball into them. "Come on, ladies and gentlemen, roll up, roll up, roll up. What could be easier? Throw the ball into the bowl and win yourself a goldfish. Come on, who'll be next? Come on, only £1 a go. Roll up, roll up."

Zoë couldn't resist. She desperately wanted a goldfish and this was her big chance. She ran over to the stall as fast as her little legs could carry her and handed the man her £1. He in return gave her three balls. She threw the first and it bounced on the edge of the bowl and then bounced away. The second was nowhere near and the third annoyingly rolled around the edge but eventually fell out. She handed the man another £1. But she had no better fortune. She handed him another and another and another, until the £5 that Mum had given her was all gone and she had only two balls left.

She threw the first. It hit the side and bounced off, nearly hitting the man in the eye. She was about to throw the second when she was distracted by Oliver running over to her. He was very excited. He'd been on everything. "What are you going on?" he asked Zoë, excitedly.

Zoë only shrugged. "I have no money left; I've spent it all here." Oliver couldn't believe it. How could his sister be so silly?

"Zoë, you can buy goldfish for £2 and you've spent £5 trying to win one!"

Zoë didn't know this and it made her very cross. She threw the ball onto the counter, yelling as she did so: *"Why didn't you tell me?"* But the ball bounced high into the air and then to Oliver and Zoë's amazement it landed straight in the middle of the bowl.

Zoë was overjoyed. She had won a goldfish! She would call him Goldie and she would look after him so well. She carried him home in a plastic bag and when she arrived she put him in his own special goldfish bowl – after taking out all the nails and screws that Dad had been keeping in it.

Zoë really did look after her fish. She may not have created it, but she certainly loved it. One afternoon she had seen Tiddles the cat desperately trying to get his paw into the bowl, but she had shouted so loudly and swung her brush at poor Tiddles so hard, it was fairly safe to assume that Tiddles would not be back again.

Then, the next morning, she caught Oliver stirring the goldfish bowl with a big wooden spoon, making Goldie go round and round. She had kicked him very hard and he was going to tell Mum on her, but then he thought that if he did, Zoë might tell Mum why she had kicked him, so he said nothing.

That evening, Zoë sat and chatted to Goldie about how the day had gone. She explained to Goldie where she sat in the classroom and who her friends were. She promised Goldie that he could come and see the school soon – she really did love this goldfish. Goldie had now been with Zoë for three whole days and the fair had left the village.

Then, the following morning, Zoë awoke to find a terrible thing had happened. There was Goldie floating on top of the water. She talked to him but he did nothing except float. He was dead.

Zoë burst into tears. "How could this have happened?" she sobbed. But it didn't take Dad to work out how. Zoë may have loved Goldie but she certainly didn't feed Goldie. Nobody had fed Goldie. Loving the fish wasn't enough; someone needed to feed it.

And God doesn't go halfway like this; God goes the whole way. He created us, he loves us and he keeps us. He is always involved in our lives, if we let him.

From then on Zoë didn't try to win any more goldfish; she simply played with Tiddles instead – after all, Mum fed Tiddles. That night at bedtime, Oliver called: "Hey, Zoë, maybe next year you'll come on the bumper cars and not waste your money on silly fish."

We Believe In One Lord, Jesus Christ

the only Son of God,
eternally begotten of the Father,
God from God, Light from Light,
true God from True God,
begotten, not made,
of one Being with the Father.
Through him all things were made.

	Programme	Item
Section 1	**Welcome**	
	Rules	
	Prayer	
	Introductory Praise	
	Game 1	L.O.R.D.J.E.S.U.S.C.H.R.I.S.T
	Praise	
	Fun Item 1	
	Game 2	T.H.E.S.O.N.O.F.G.O.D
	Fun Item 2	
	Bible Text	John 1:14
	Announcements	
	Interview	
Section 2	**Worship Time**	
Preaching	**Bible Lesson**	John 1
Time	**Illustration 1**	Legend
	Illustration 2	Liar
	Illustration 3	Lord
	Story	The Adventures Of Zoë And Oliver (3)
	Prayer	

Who was Jesus really? This is the big 21st-century discussion-starter and the subject of constant debate. The lesson looks at the alternatives: legend, liar and lunatic, or Lord.

games

L.O.R.D.J.E.S.U.S.C.H.R.I.S.T

PREPARATION	Cut out the individual letters L.O.R.D.J.E.S.U.S.C.H.R.I.S.T.
PLAYERS	Five per team.
SET-UP	The letters are placed at B in order. The players line up at A in relay formation (i.e., one behind the other).
OBJECT	The first person runs from A to B, collects the first letter and returns to A. At A they begin to construct the sentence while the second player starts running. They keep going until all the letters are collected.
WINNING	The first team to construct the sentence wins.

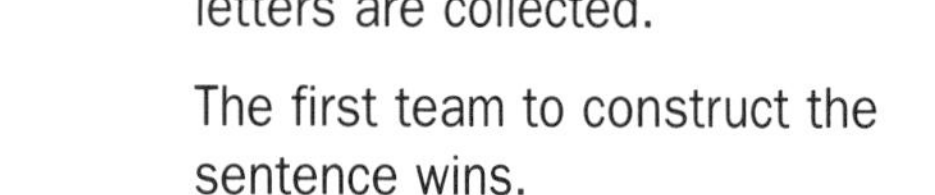

T.H.E.S.O.N.O.F.G.O.D

PREPARATION	Cut out the individual letters T.H.E.S.O.N.O.F.G.O.D.
PLAYERS	Five per team.
SET-UP	The letters are placed at B in order. The players line up at A in relay formation (i.e., one behind the other).
OBJECT	The first person runs from A to B, collects the first letter and returns to A. At A they begin to construct the sentence while the second player starts running. They keep going until all the letters are collected.
WINNING	The first team to construct the sentence wins.

BIBLE LESSON JOHN 1

"The Word became a human being and lived here with us. We saw his true glory, the glory of the only Son of the Father. From him all the kindness and all the truth of God have come down to us." (John 1:14)

This week's section of the creed is:

> We believe in one Lord, Jesus Christ, the only Son of God,
> eternally begotten of the Father, God from God, Light from Light,
> true God from True God, begotten, not made,
> of one Being with the Father. Through him all things were made.

And the Jesus Story continues:

Now imagine this. The same Son of God who was there at creation, the same Son of God who created the universe, the same Jesus who created Adam and Eve, and who is involved in creating every new life, is about to do something spectacular. He's about to do something that would amaze even the angels, if that were possible. He is about to come to our planet. He is going to spend time with human beings. He's going to come and visit us.

But he's coming in disguise, a disguise that nobody would ever have guessed. Jesus will be born as a baby in a stable in Bethlehem. The creator of the universe, who talked with God the Father and God the Holy Spirit and decided to make you and me, enters this world as a tiny little baby. He is wrapped in blankets and stares into this world with wide eyes. He cries, he sleeps, he feeds, he grows.

He never does anything wrong. He walks on our planet and he chooses disciples and performs miracles and raises the dead and calms storms. This is Jesus, the Son of God.

Nobody would have believed that a great God could make himself so tiny. But what happens at the end of his time on our planet is even more surprising.

Legend

Object needed: *A picture of Robin Hood.*

There are three main things people say when they are trying to explain who Jesus was. The first they say is: Jesus was a legend – a bit like our picture here. Who knows who this is? Yes, lots of us know Robin Hood. But it is fair to say that Robin Hood never really existed. Robin Hood has been put together from the lives of lots of other people, so that it comes up with one person.

It would be like me picking five of you, taking one story that happened to each of you and wrapping them all together with a pile of stories I'd make up. Then I'd also make up a new person (let's call him "Bouncing Bob") and then I'd say that Bouncing Bob did all those things. We would have created a legend, the "Legend of Bouncing Bob". And in years to come, people would discover that Bouncing Bob was not real, but some of the stories were.

Now, that's pretty much what happened to Robin Hood. Lots of different stories that have been made up or that happened to different people are said to have happened to Robin Hood. So we have the "Legend of Robin Hood".

Lots of people would have us believe that Jesus Christ is also a legend, the "Legend of Jesus Christ". They say that lots of good things happened to these other people and they were eventually said to have happened to this made-up person, Jesus Christ.

However, this is very difficult to believe. Lots and lots of people spoke about Jesus; lots of people said they met Jesus. People who were writing history books at the time – people like a man named Josephus – wrote about Jesus existing. People who dig in the ground to discover things about the past – people called archaeologists – are convinced that Jesus really did exist. People who have been able to look at the records that were kept at those times have become convinced that Jesus really was born.

In fact, someone once said that there is more evidence to support the fact that Jesus really did exist than there is to support the Battle of Hastings having taken place. Now we all know that the Battle of Hastings happened and I hope we are all clear that Jesus is no legend. He really did exist. He really did walk on our planet.

Liar

Object needed: *A big question mark.*

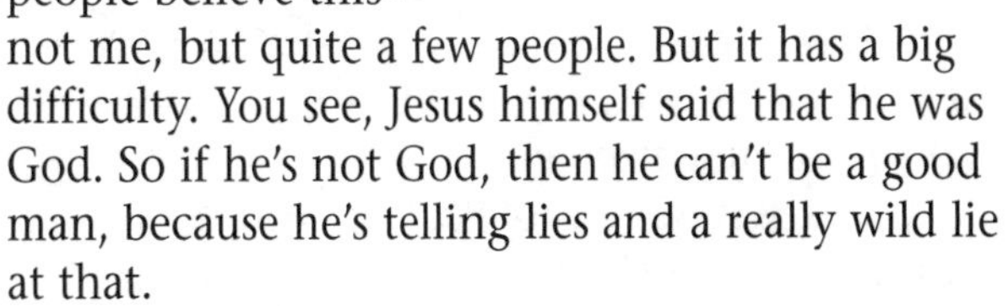

Some people say: "Well, yes, Jesus did exist, but he wasn't God. He was a just a good person, who went around doing good."

Quite a few people believe this – not me, but quite a few people. But it has a big difficulty. You see, Jesus himself said that he was God. So if he's not God, then he can't be a good man, because he's telling lies and a really wild lie at that.

So Jesus can't be a good man – either he's a liar or he really is God.

The old part of the Bible was written 450 years before Jesus was born in the stable in Bethlehem, but it is full of promises explaining what the Son of God would do when he arrived. It even tells us he would be born in Bethlehem. The odds of this happening by chance are quite high, but you could say it was just luck. 450 years before Jesus was born somebody made a lucky guess and guessed where Jesus would be born. It's possible. But there wasn't just one thing that was correct about Jesus – there were 298 things said about him that all happened. This is not by chance.

It would be like someone 500 years ago saying that you, John *(choose a person)*, would be sitting here at this time, wearing those clothes and having had egg and chips *(check what they had for tea first! This may not be a good time to practise your own personal prophecy gift!)* for dinner tonight. That would be just three things. They would also have to list where you were born, maybe what you would do when you grew up and a pile of other stuff too. And all this would have to be written down at least 450 years before you were born. I think it's a safe bet to say Jesus was not a liar – he is God. The Jesus who walked with us really is God.

Lord

Object needed: *None.*

There is a third option. This is what I believe. Jesus is not a legend; he is not a liar; he is Lord and God. I know this because I talk to Jesus, I feel his presence and I read about him in the Bible. Many of the other leaders here would say the same thing. I believe this because it is the only thing that makes sense. Jesus is no liar and certainly no legend.

There was a time when I didn't know that Jesus was God. And a time I knew very little about Jesus. Lots of people have tried to prove that Jesus isn't God, but interesting things happen to these people.

C.S. Lewis was a professor at Oxford University. He did not believe there was a God. But after he spent a long time reading a lot of books, talking to a lot of people and searching for himself, he eventually came to the conclusion that Jesus was God.

Josh McDowell set out to disprove that Jesus existed. His work was published in a book called *Evidence that Demands a Verdict*. In the end Josh decided that he was wrong and that there really is a God.

Two very famous people gave their opinions of Jesus. Einstein said: "I am a Jew, but in the luminous presence of the Nazarene I stand enthralled." Einstein was one of the cleverest people who ever lived and he said that Jesus is amazing.

Napoleon said: "I know men and this is more…" Napoleon was a great general, and he was convinced that Jesus was definitely more than an ordinary man.

Throughout time, people who are honest always come to the conclusion that Jesus is God. There are lots of proofs that Jesus is who he says he is, but the only way to be sure is to invite Jesus to come and be part of your life. Then it really doesn't matter what others may say. When you know Jesus, you know he is God. Even if nobody believes you, you know you're right.

• STORY – The Adventures Of Zoë And Oliver (3)

"Wake up!" shouted Zoë frantically. "Oliver, wake up!"

Oliver opened his eyes and saw his sister's big, round eyes looking down at him. "What is it, Zoë?" he grunted. "Is the house on fire? Or is it Christmas Day?"

"Neither," answered Zoë. "I just saw a spaceship landing in the field."

Oliver turned his head to look at the clock. It was four o'clock in the morning. He pinched himself to see if he was dreaming, and, no, he wasn't dreaming. Then he looked back towards his sister. He had been fairly sure for quite some time now that Zoë was a little crazy and now he was absolutely sure. His sister was crazy! His mum and dad shouldn't be too shocked. He had told them lots of times that she was, but they never seemed to believe him.

"Go back to bed, Zoë. You've gone nuts." But Zoë was having none of it. She tugged Oliver's blankets off and jumped up and down, making such a noise that eventually Oliver was forced to sit up and listen. He wasn't going to believe her, though, whatever she said – she was clearly insane, as he had long told everyone.

"I saw a bright light flying through the sky and then I saw a big explosion. It came from space, I'm telling you. It landed over in the trees, just behind where we built our den last summer."

If Oliver hadn't been so tired he would have laughed. As it was, he smiled and pulled the blankets back over his face, mumbling: "I can't wait to tell everyone this story tomorrow in school."

Zoë thought she would go and tell her parents instead. She was sure they would believe her. She went in and began to shake them and call out: "Mum, Dad, wake up! There's a spaceship in the woods."

Mum opened her eyes and then nudged Dad and whispered: "Your turn. I went to the last bad dream." Dad sighed. He pulled himself out of bed and picked up his little girl.

"OK, sweetheart, everything's fine. The dream has gone away now."

"But it wasn't a dream!" Zoë shouted.

Dad stroked her hair and said: "I'm sure it didn't seem like a dream, but I don't think we would have spaceships landing outside. That doesn't really happen." And with that he tucked a very cross Zoë back into her bed and went back to bed himself.

At breakfast time Zoë had to sit through a whole pile of Oliver's nasty comments and jokes: "Oh, look, Zoë! A spaceman!" School was worse. Zoë was amazed by how quickly Oliver managed to tell everyone about the incident of four o'clock that morning. Her so-called friends kept walking up to her pretending to be space people, and Oliver's friends kept rushing passed her pretending to be flying saucers.

By lunchtime Zoë had had enough of the teasing and crept out of the school gates and went home. She couldn't be in school with all this teasing any longer. She knew she would be in trouble, but she didn't care.

When she arrived home, everyone was out. She went to her room, switched on the computer and went on the Internet. She typed in "spaceships". She had been on the computer lots of times and this wasn't difficult for her. Lots and lots of suggestions came up. If she could just find one the same shape as the one she saw...

She spent ages looking at strange-looking space people and even stranger-looking human people. She saw lots and lots of different-shaped spaceships, but none of them looked like hers, and, anyway, they all looked as if someone from reception class had drawn them.

Eventually she clicked on a site that was titled "NASA". She had heard of NASA but wasn't sure what it did. There, flashing on the front page in big letters, was a notice: "MISSING NASA SATELLITE – LAST SEEN OVER EUROPE – INFORMATION NEEDED". Zoë clicked on the link below and there it was: a picture of the spaceship she had seen! Well, not a spaceship, as she quickly read, but a satellite. She clicked on the next link and it opened up a link to e-mail NASA. So Zoë did. She wrote:

> At 4am last night I saw a big flash in the sky and then a bang. The thing you have missing landed behind my den that my brother and I made. If you want it back, it is there. Nobody believes me here; they think I am crazy or had a dream. Zoë (aged 5).

Zoe then happily logged off the computer and went back to school. The children kept on making fun of her, but she just smiled and ignored them. They'd see soon enough.

That afternoon, when Mum arrived home from school with Zoë and Oliver in the car, the whole house was surrounded by white vans. And there were men in suits everywhere. They all sounded American. Mum went to talk to them after telling Zoë and Oliver to stay in the car, but Zoë jumped out and ran over and shouted: "I'm Zoë! Have you come to see me?"

The Americans smiled and the man in charge replied: "We have. We got your e-mail." Mum was confused. But when Zoë led the way to the den and then to the crashed satellite behind the den, Mum realised that Zoë had been right all along. And Oliver realised that he was in big trouble.

Zoë was given a very special reward by the men from NASA: they gave her four tickets to go to Disneyland in America and they gave her tickets to fly there.

You see, Zoë was right. And when you are right, you don't have to worry too much when people don't believe you. Eventually they might. We know that Jesus is God and we will keep trying our best to explain to others that he is not a legend or a liar but he's God himself. But even if they don't believe us, we know that we're right.

That night, Zoë and Oliver were lying in their beds. Oliver said sorry to Zoë. He did feel a little sorry, but he really wanted to go to Disneyland and thought Zoë wouldn't let him if he didn't say sorry. Zoë simply said: "Well, Disneyland is going to be great."

Oliver answered: "It will. I'm so excited."

Zoë added: "Me too. I'm taking me, Mummy and Daddy and... Bunny." There was silence. Oliver hoped she was joking, but was very nice to her for the next couple of days, just in case.

For Us And For Our Salvation

he came down from heaven;
by the power of the Holy Spirit he became incarnate of the Virgin Mary, and was made man.
For our sake he was crucified under Pontius Pilate; he suffered death and was buried.

	Programme	Item
Section 1	**Welcome**	
	Rules	
	Prayer	
	Introductory Praise	
	Game 1	Bravery Challenge (for boys)
	Praise	
	Fun Item 1	
	Game 2	Bravery Challenge (for girls)
	Fun Item 2	
	Bible Text	John 15:13
	Announcements	
	Interview	
Section 2	**Worship Time**	
Preaching	**Bible Lesson**	The Cross
Time	**Illustration 1**	Interesting Lives
	Illustration 2	Amazing Things
	Illustration 3	Sacrifice
	Story	The Adventures Of Zoë And Oliver (4)
	Prayer	

Some people have very interesting lives; others do amazing things; some give up their lives for others. Jesus did all these things.

Bravery Challenge (for boys)

PREPARATION	A bowl of chocolate Angel Delight (to represent mud) per team and some flumps – five in each bowl.
PLAYERS	Five boys per team.
SET-UP	The players line up in relay formation at A. The "mud" is placed at B.
OBJECT	The children are told that the bowls contain mud. They also contain worms, spiders and probably a lion! They run one at a time, put their heads in and pull out a flump. No hands are to be used.
WINNING	The first team to recover all the flumps and eat them wins.

Bravery Challenge (for girls)

PREPARATION	A bowl of chocolate Angel Delight (to represent mud) per team and some flumps – five in each bowl.
PLAYERS	Five girls per team.
SET-UP	The players line up in relay formation at A. The "mud" is placed at B.
OBJECT	The children are told that the bowls contain mud. They also contain worms, spiders and probably a lion! They run one at a time, put their heads in and pull out a flump. No hands are to be used.
WINNING	The first team to recover all the flumps and eat them wins.

PreachingTime

THE CROSS

"The greatest way to show love for friends is to die for them." (John 15:13)

Today's creed extract:

> For us and for our salvation he came down from heaven;
> by the power of the Holy Spirit he became incarnate of the Virgin Mary, and was made man.
> For our sake he was crucified under Pontius Pilate; he suffered death and was buried.

And back to the Jesus Story:

If it was a surprise seeing that Jesus would leave heaven and disguise himself as a baby and then grow and choose disciples and do such amazing things, what happened after this will be absolutely startling.

He was eating supper with his disciples. Judas, who was one of the disciples, decided that he would betray Jesus to some people called Pharisees who were desperate to get rid of him. Judas told the Pharisees where Jesus would be, and now at the end of the supper they came and arrested Jesus.

Keep remembering who he is. This is God himself: God the Son – Jesus. He could have called armies of angels to come and help him, not fluffy angels that somebody made up, who sit on clouds and play harps, but real angels with swords ready to destroy God's enemies. He could have called for angels, but he didn't.

They beat him up, they placed a crown of thorns on his head and they made him carry a heavy cross. Then at the top of a hill, a hill called Golgotha, they took some nails and they nailed him to the cross. He died on that cross, so that all the wrong things we had ever done, or would ever do, could be forgiven.

He could have called for angels to come. He didn't. He suffered on a cruel cross so that we could have the chance of going to heaven when we die.

It is a Friday. It is 12 noon, and the sky turns black – black in the middle of the day. It stays dark for three whole hours. People are getting a little worried, particularly the people who nailed Jesus to the cross. This is worrying. At 3pm Jesus takes one last breath and calls out, "My God, my God, why have you abandoned me?" And then he dies.

The creator God dies. On a cross of wood Jesus dies.

Interesting Lives

Object needed: *A big red book (and some pictures for the OHP or video projector showing one of the leaders growing up: his or her baby pictures, school photos, wedding photos, etc.)*

There is a programme on the television that old people tend to watch. It is called *This Is Your Life*. It involves the presenter sneaking up on somebody famous and saying to them: "This is your life."

The presenter then takes them to a studio and shows them lots of photos from their life and introduces them to friends from the past who talk about the person. At the very end the presenter gives the person a big red book that contains all the information about their life.

For example, if we were to try and do this with *(choose a leader)*, we would call him up and say "*[Leader]*, this is your life." Then we would show horrible pictures of when he was a baby... like this one *(show a baby photo – it really does work best if the leader has no idea they were going to be chosen. Work through the rest of the photos)*.

You see, lots of people have interesting lives. Some people have lives even more interesting than *(insert name of leader)*. The programme presents people who started huge companies, people who were prime ministers, people who were in televisions or films for many years.

But I think none of them had a life as interesting as Jesus. He was born in a stable in Bethlehem; he was visited by shepherds and wise men. He had a completely sinless life – he never did anything wrong. He loved all people and was incredibly kind to all. He really did live an interesting life.

Amazing Things

Object needed: *None.*

Some people do amazing things. There was a woman who sailed around the world single-handed, a man who was the first person to climb Mount Everest, the first man to land on the moon...

I can think of lots of people who do the most amazing things. But I don't think any of them did anything as amazing as Jesus. He healed people who were blind, and lame, and paralysed. He raised people from the dead. He calmed storms. He really did do some amazing things.

Sacrifice

Object needed: *A picture of the cross.*

Some people sacrifice themselves for others. That is, they give something up for others. I read of a woman who worked in a nursery school who stood in front of a man with a sharp knife; she got cut to stop the man hurting the children. I heard of a man who rushed into a burning building to try and rescue some trapped children. We often hear the stories of soldiers who give up their

lives to protect our country and our way of living.

People who give up their lives for others or for their children; people who give up their lives or get hurt to save those they love; soldiers dying so that we can be kept safe. These are examples of sacrifice.

But Jesus sacrificed as well. He gave up his life also. He gave it up not for one or two people. He gave up his life not just to protect a whole country. He gave it up for the whole of the world. Jesus died on a cross so that you and I and everyone we know and everyone in our country and everyone in our world and everyone who has ever lived and everyone who is alive now and everyone who is yet to be born has the opportunity to go to heaven when they die and to live for Jesus when they are alive.

He really did sacrifice.

• STORY – The Adventures Of Zoë And Oliver (4)

Oliver came rushing home from school very, very excited. Matthew's dad had dropped him and Zoë off. "Mum, Dad, come quick!" he called. Mum and Dad came in obediently. "Our class trip this year is skiing in France. Can I go? It's only £500. Can I go?" Mum and Dad looked at each other.

Seconds later Zoë walked in. "Mum, Dad," she began, "my class is going on a trip to London to the Victoria and Albert Museum. Can I go? It's only £100. Can I?" Mum and Dad looked first at Oliver, who was standing there holding his invitation in his hand, and then at Zoë, who was waving hers in the air.

"We'll talk about it over dinner," Mum answered, hoping to buy herself some time to have a chat with Dad first.

Both children rushed towards the stairs to get changed out of their school uniforms, leaving Mum and Dad to begin discussions. But Oliver was a little sneakier than Zoë and when Zoë rushed up the stairs to get changed, Oliver hung back to listen to what his parents were saying. Mum and Dad looked at each other, and Dad shook his head first.

"We can't afford this, can we?" he began.

"No, we can't," Mum agreed. Then she added, "Well, that's not absolutely true. We could afford for one of them to go, but that wouldn't be fair on the other. We have some money set aside for school trips, but not £600 worth.

Oliver didn't want to listen any more. He was devastated. He walked upstairs very quietly, changed into his play clothes and walked out to the garden and sat on the swing. Zoë joined him and she chattered and played as she always did. She teased the cat and threw acorns up to the squirrels. But Oliver simply sat and swung backwards and forwards, saying nothing, but thinking very hard.

He was watching his little sister and remembering the time that he had gone to the Victoria and Albert Museum in London – it had been his first ever school trip and he remembered how excited he had been. And now Zoë wouldn't be able to go on her trip and he wouldn't be able to go on his. He swung a little more. He really did enjoy his first trip, though.

Then a strange thought entered his head. It was strange because it wasn't the way he usually thought. He tried to force the strange idea out of his head but it wouldn't go away. In the end he gave in. "Fine!" he said out loud. "I'll do it."

"Do what?" asked Zoë. But Oliver didn't answer.

Dinner time came and they all sat down. The meal was served and they began eating. Mum and Dad looked very sad. Then Mum started to say: "We have some bad news for you both… " but Oliver jumped in and said quickly: "No, you don't, Mum. I was listening and I heard what you and Dad said, and it doesn't need to be bad news for us both; I've already been to the Victoria and Albert Museum when I was five and it wouldn't be fair if Zoë didn't get to go because of my ski trip, so I won't go so that Zoë can go to the museum."

He said all this without taking a breath. Mum and Dad were amazed. They sat there with their mouths open. Zoë took a while to work out what was going on but when she did, a big tear ran down her face. "Oliver, you are the kindest brother in all the world," she stated.

"I know," said Oliver, "but please don't tell anyone. I have a reputation to keep up." Everyone laughed and finished their meal, but Mum and Dad couldn't help but be impressed by how kind Oliver had been.

It's never easy giving something up for someone else, but sometimes it really is worth it. Jesus gave up his life so that we might have the chance to live for him and go to heaven when we die. It was a great sacrifice, but Jesus thought you were worth it.

Zoë and Oliver were tucked up in bed when Mum walked in. "Are you asleep?" she asked.

"Nearly," replied Oliver.

"No," answered Zoë. "I was thinking how wonderful my brother is."

"Well," began Mum, "I have some great news. I was just on the phone to Gran and I was telling her what a kind thing Oliver had done and how excited Zoë was about the trip, and Gran was so impressed with you, Oliver, that she has offered to pay for you to go on the ski trip." Oliver was so excited he fell out of bed. Then he jumped in the air and shouted, "YES!" at the top of his voice. Zoë was pleased too. Mum kissed them both and left.

"Thank you for being so kind, Oliver," Zoë began. But Oliver wasn't listening. He was imagining himself flying down the ski slopes, waving to the people as he passed.

On The Third Day He Rose Again in accordance with the Scriptures; he ascended into heaven and is seated at the right hand of the Father.

	Programme	Item
Section 1	**Welcome**	
	Rules	
	Prayer	
	Introductory Praise	
	Game 1	Burial
	Praise	
	Fun Item 1	
	Game 2	Resurrection
	Fun Item 2	
	Bible Text	Matthew 20:19
	Announcements	
	Interview	
Section 2	**Worship Time**	
Preaching	**Bible Lesson**	The Resurrection
Time	**Illustration 1**	Jesus Wasn't Dead?
	Illustration 2	The Disciples Stole The Body!
	Illustration 3	He Really Did Rise From The Dead
	Story	The Adventures Of Zoë And Oliver (5)
	Prayer	

There are lots of ideas surrounding the resurrection. Did it really happen? Did Jesus really die? Did the disciples steal the body? We'll take a look at the theories in this lesson.

games

Burial

PREPARATION	None needed.
PLAYERS	Six players and a (light) leader per team.
SET-UP	The leader lies on the floor at A with all six of the players.
OBJECT	The players must carry the leader from A and "bury" them by placing them at B.
WINNING	The first team to complete the object wins.

Resurrection

PREPARATION	The leader remains in burial position at B.
PLAYERS	Three per team.
SET-UP	The players line up in relay formation at A. They represent three days.
OBJECT	The first player runs to B and touches the leader and returns to A. Day 1 has passed. The next player then goes and returns (Day 2). After the third player has gone (Day 3), the "buried" leader jumps up and runs back to join the rest of the team.
WINNING	The first team to bring back their leader wins.

BIBLE LESSON THE RESURRECTION

"... and then they will hand him over to foreigners who will make fun of him. They will beat him and nail him to a cross. But on the third day he will rise from death." (Matthew 20:19)

Today's bit of the creed says:

> On the third day he rose again in accordance with the Scriptures;
> he ascended into heaven and is seated at the right hand of the Father.

And back to the Jesus Story:

God the Son is dead. How can that be? It seems to his friends that everything has gone wrong. The disciples all run away and hide. Everyone is afraid.

And then on Sunday morning some women go to the tomb to make sure Jesus has been buried properly. In those days, they buried people by placing them in caves and rolling huge stones across the entrance. But when the women get there, the stone has been rolled back and Jesus is missing. The women are very concerned and start to panic, thinking somebody has stolen the body.

Then two angels appear. They tell the women to stop looking here for Jesus, because he's no longer dead – he's alive.

You see, you and I remembered all along that this was God the Son. I think maybe these women and the disciples had forgotten.

The women are rushing to go and tell the other disciples, when suddenly they run into Jesus himself! They are amazed and excited and delighted and surprised all at once. He tells them to tell everyone else that he will meet them in Galilee.

And so God the Son came, died, was buried and rose from the dead. He then spent some time teaching his disciples and then, in case the disciples hadn't seen enough amazing things, Jesus ascended back into heaven. As the disciples stood on a hillside and watched, Jesus started to rise into the air until he disappeared through the clouds. Wow!

Jesus had gone back to be with his Father in heaven.

Jesus wasn't dead?

Object needed: *A magnifying glass and three cards saying:*
1. *Jesus wasn't really dead*
2. *The disciples stole the body*
3. *Jesus rose from the dead*

Imagine with me for a few minutes that you are a detective. And that you live in the same time and place as Jesus. You've just been called in by the man in charge of Jerusalem and he's told you something amazing: "There's this man called Jesus and he is supposed to have risen from the dead. Go and investigate and find out the truth."

So off you go with your magnifying glass. You're going to look at all the evidence and find out what really happened. But you know the answer is one of three things.

The more you can play the part of the detective, the better. If you can wear a police uniform and conduct the investigation it will seriously enhance this lesson. Ask a child to hold each of the three cards as you come to them:

1. Jesus wasn't really dead
2. The disciples stole the body
3. Jesus rose from dead

You, the detective, begin to look at each of the options one by one. You begin to think about number 1... But then you remember. Hey, Jesus was whipped, he was beaten, they placed a crown of thorns on his head, they made him carry his own cross and by then he was too weak to carry it far. They nailed his ankles and his wrists to a wooden cross. And then after allowing him to hang from the cross for such a long time they stuck a spear into his side and the Bible says blood and water came out – doctors will tell you this is a sure sign he was dead.

If we don't believe that he was dead, then we have to believe that, after all this, he was still strong enough to move a giant stone and escape from his own tomb.

I don't think so.

Tear up the first card.

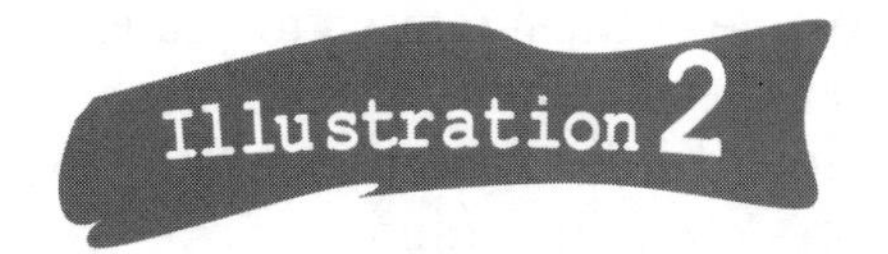

The Disciples Stole The Body!

Object needed: *A picture of a Roman soldier.*

So, imagining you are a detective, you come to number 2: The disciples stole the body. Let's think about this one.

These are the same disciples who ran away when Jesus was arrested. They clearly were not the toughest guys in the world. And what we have to remember is that Jesus' tomb was guarded by a crack squad of Roman soldiers, and they really would be doing their job well – if they didn't, they would be killed, so they would do their job very well.

So, we have to ask ourselves this question: Do we really think that these disciples were up to stealing away Jesus' body from this squad of Roman soldiers?

No, I don't think so.

Tear up the second card.

He Really Did Rise From The Dead

Object needed: *None.*

We are left with one option: Jesus really did rise from the dead, just like the Bible says.

You know, if we leave our detective business back in Jerusalem, there are more reasons why I am convinced that Jesus rose from the dead. One is the way his followers behaved afterwards. I really don't think if the disciples thought that

Jesus was dead they would have been so courageous.

All of them (except one) were arrested and given the following deal: "If you deny that Jesus really rose from the dead, then your life will be saved. If you don't deny it, then you will be executed." Every one of them refused to change their story. They were all completely convinced that Jesus rose from the dead and they would do anything for him – even die for him.

Things have not changed. Many years after the disciples had died, there were many others who refused to deny that Jesus rose from the dead, and many of them were killed also. And still today there are men and women around our world who would rather die than deny that Jesus rose from the dead.

I've looked at all the evidence and there really is only one answer: Jesus really did rise from the dead.

• STORY – The Adventures Of Zoë And Oliver (5)

"Hello, bright sun," shouted Oliver. "Hello, puffy clouds." Oliver couldn't remember a time when he had felt so happy. He was out in the meadow flying his kite.

And then he saw it – the sight that was to ruin his day. There on the other side of the hedge his five-year-old sister Zoë was giving his mother a daffodil, and in return his mother gave Zoë a big hug. Suddenly it seemed to Oliver as if a dark cloud had crept into the sky. Zoë seemed to be getting a lot of hugs lately, a lot more than he was. He hadn't really been keeping count but he was sure she was getting more hugs than him.

"She's stealing all the love," he said to himself. "Soon there won't be any left for me!" So Oliver decided he'd be a dark cloud in Zoë's day.

"Guess what?" Oliver said to Zoë as soon as his mother had gone. "Mum loves me the best!"

Zoë's face turned red. "No she doesn't. She loves us the same."

"Poor Zoë," sighed Oliver. "I wish Mum could have two favourites, but favourite means one, and one means me."

Zoë was getting very cross and then she had an idea. "Why don't we have a contest?" she said. "Whoever gets the most hugs from Mum and kisses from Mum before supper time will be the winner." Oliver wasn't sure he was going to win, but he really had no choice now. "Well, all right," he muttered.

Zoë rushed into the house to win her first kiss. "I'll do the dusting for you, Mum," she said. "You sit down and rest your feet."

Mum gave Zoë a delighted kiss. "You are very thoughtful, Zoë."

"I can do better than that," Oliver told himself. "I'll make Mum a soothing footbath." And he made his way to the bathroom to find the right ingredients. He mixed some pink bubble bath with some orange bubble bath and some blue bubble bath. He added some of his own special bubble bath from his Thunderbirds holder – it was green. He added some bath salts and then looked in the cabinet under the sink and added some bits and pieces he found there. He then added the hot water. The steam started to swirl up into the air and, rather unusually, Oliver thought, the water had turned green. He carried the bowl downstairs.

His mum seemed delighted and he was sure he would get many hugs and kisses for this. Mum took off her shoes and socks and placed her feet into the bowl. All seemed fine. Mum looked very relaxed. Then suddenly her feet began to burn. She gave a scream and kicked out! The bowl fell over and spilt green gunge all over the carpet. What was worse – Mum's legs and feet had gone green. She looked like the Incredible Hulk and she was not happy. Oliver ran for it, out through the back door and into the garden.

So, with a heavy heart, Oliver walked up and down the garden wondering what he could try next. Then to his astonishment he heard music coming from the house. He gazed in through the living room window to see his sister, the hug thief, playing piano for Mum.

If Zoë was going to play piano, Oliver was going to do something even more wonderful. He was going to make Mum his own amazing music box.

He got to work at once. He went to the shed to collect an old box, some glue and some paint. He then put the box together, finishing it off with a lovely coat of purple paint. There was just one thing missing – the music. But Oliver had an idea for this. He spent the next two hours rummaging around in the grass near his house until he had collected 20 or so grasshoppers. He then placed them in his box and closed the lid.

The grasshoppers hopped around and rubbed their legs together, making the click-click sound that grasshoppers make. Oliver thought it sounded like wonderful music and took it in to his mum. This time he was going to win. He was sure to get many hugs and kisses for this one.

He walked into the house. "Sorry about

earlier, Mum," he shouted, "but I've made it up to you." And, with that, he pulled out his musical box. Mum was impressed, but just as Oliver was passing the box to his mum, the bottom fell out and 20-or-so very angry grasshoppers started to jump all over the house. Oliver scurried around trying to catch them. His mum screamed and jumped on a chair. Oliver knew it was no good and ran back towards the garden.

He flopped onto the ground underneath one of the trees. "Not a single hug all day," he mumbled to himself. He gazed up into the sky. It had seemed such a nice day. And now it was ruined. But what was this above his head, in the tree? Of course, peaches. He would take his mum some peaches.

He went to the shed and collected the ladder. It was quite an old ladder, but he wasn't very heavy and he'd be able to reach. He positioned the ladder in front of the tree and began to climb. He went up five steps, but just as he put his foot on the sixth step, the sixth step snapped. But he was fine; he just fell back one step. He stepped over step six and began climbing higher and higher. He was nearly there. One more step and he was there. He began to gather peaches and put them in his pockets. Five peaches, six peaches, seven peaches, then... SNAP!

The top step broke and Oliver came tumbling down. The peaches lay on the ground squashed, and next to the peaches lay a very squashed Oliver. He began to cry loudly. Their neighbour, Uncle Edmund, saw the whole thing and rushed round to Oliver's aid. After checking to see if anything was broken he picked up the little boy and carried him quickly into the house.

"Nothing too serious!" yelled Edmund as he came in. "Just a lot of bruises and scrapes." In seconds Mum had ice packs and a blanket and a bowl of soup for her poor, wounded boy. Oliver was getting more hugs and kisses than Zoë could count.

"Oliver really is your favourite!" Zoë began to scream. Mum looked confused. "All day long Oliver has messed everything up," Zoë went on. "He ruined the carpet, he turned your feet green, he let bugs run free in the house and he fell out of a tree. And he still gets all the love."

Mum picked Zoë up and rested her on her knee, right next to Oliver. "Zoë," Mum began, "you are my favourite Zoë, and Oliver is my favourite Oliver. I don't love you because of what you do for me. I love you just because you're my children." Then she gave them both a special hug.

God works pretty much the same way. He doesn't love us any more or any less for what we do for him. He loves us because we are his children. Christ came, he died, he rose again because he loves us. He could not love us any more; he could not love us any less. He loves us absolutely.

(This would be a good point in the series to invite the children who have never given their lives to Jesus to do so – but you know the children you are with, so feel your way sensitively.)

That night, as Zoë and Oliver were lying in their bunk beds, Zoë said, "I'm glad Mum loves us both the same. It would be sad if she only loved one of us."

"Yes, it would," Oliver answered.

The silvery moon shone into the room as the stars twinkled against the dark sky. Zoë was just drifting off to sleep when Oliver added: "Too bad Dad loves me best, eh?"

He Will Come Again In Glory to judge the living and the dead, and his kingdom will have no end.

	Programme	Item
Section 1	**Welcome**	
	Rules	
	Prayer	
	Introductory Praise	
	Game 1	Thief In The Night (for girls)
	Praise	
	Fun Item 1	
	Game 2	Thief In The Night (for boys)
	Fun Item 2	
	Bible Text	1 Thessalonians 5:1–2
	Announcements	
	Interview	
Section 2	**Worship Time**	
Preaching	**Bible Lesson**	The Second Coming
Time	**Illustration 1**	Embarrassed
	Illustration 2	The Race
	Story	The Adventures Of Zoë And Oliver (6)
	Prayer	

This is a subject not often touched on in many children's gatherings. It is here to remind us that one day Jesus is coming again and the emphasis in the Bible is "Be ready".

games

Thief In The Night (for girls)

PREPARATION	A square is drawn at B and filled with tennis balls. A leader is placed in the middle of the square.
PLAYERS	Five per team.
SET-UP	The players line up in relay formation at A.
OBJECT	The players run one by one from A to B. At B they must take a tennis ball from the square. If they are touched by the leader, they must put the ball back. If they take the ball after they have been touched the whole team is disqualified. They must then return with the ball to A.
WINNING	The team with the most balls after three minutes wins.

Thief In The Night (for boys)

PREPARATION	A square is drawn at B and filled with tennis balls. A leader is placed in the middle of the square.
PLAYERS	Five per team.
SET-UP	The players line up in relay formation at A.
OBJECT	The players run one by one from A to B. At B they must take a tennis ball from the square. If they are touched by the leader, they must put the ball back. If they take the ball after they have been touched the whole team is disqualified. They must then return with the ball to A.
WINNING	The team with the most balls after three minutes wins.

Preaching Time

BIBLE LESSON THE SECOND COMING

"I don't need to write to you about the time or date when all this will happen. You know that the Lord's return will be as a thief coming at night."
(1 Thessalonians 5:1–2)

This is the part of the creed for today:

> He will come again in glory to judge the
> living and the dead,
> and his kingdom will have no end.

And to the Jesus Story:

If the Jesus Story wasn't exciting enough already, there is even more. So far we have seen Jesus, before time began, creating the universe; we have seen him creating us; we have seen him disguising himself and coming into the world as a baby, growing, living a perfect life, being killed on a cross, rising from the dead and going back up to heaven to be with God the Father.

The Bible tells us something else about Jesus. It tells us that he is coming back again – not as a baby this time, but in all his wonder and power. He's coming back to wind the whole thing up. He started time off when there was nothing at all, and one day he will come and stop the whole thing and we will live with him for ever in heaven.

The Bible teaches us not only that Jesus has come, died on the cross, risen again, and ascended back to heaven to his Father, but also that Jesus will come back again.

We do not know when. But the Bible isn't trying to show us when. The Bible is telling us, "Get ready!" We have to live in such a way that if Jesus came tonight we wouldn't be doing anything we'd be embarrassed about.

Embarrassed

Object needed: *A picture of a rock star.*

I have a friend whom I was in college with and he's a little bit wild. When he was younger he was even more wild and always doing crazy things. He was often getting embarrassed by the things people caught him doing.

One day when I was in college, there was some really loud music playing. It took some of us a while to work out where the music was coming from, but eventually we followed the sound and it led to my friend's door. It really was incredibly loud.

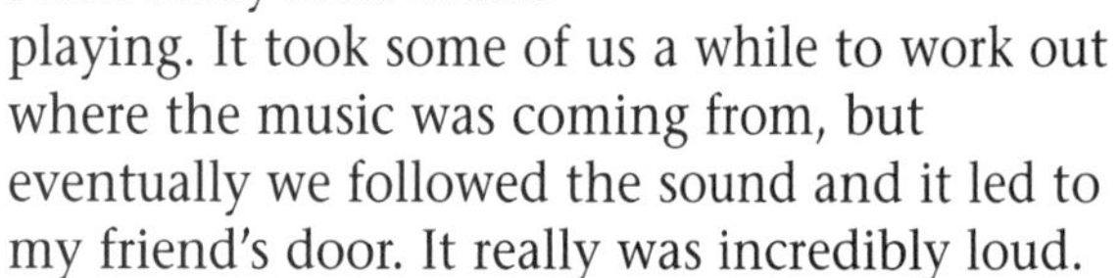

By the time I'd got there, there were lots of people standing outside the door ready to complain about the noise. They all looked at me. I was supposed to be his friend. They had knocked on the door several times, but obviously the music was so loud he couldn't hear the knocks. So it fell to me to open the door and see what was going on. I reached out my hand to the handle, and turned it very slowly.

You have to understand, our rooms in college were not very big. They had a desk, a chair, a bed and a cupboard, and that was it. So I turned the handle and pushed.

And there he was – my friend – standing on the chair, his hair pushed back with gel, a brush in his hand that he was using as a microphone, and he was dancing and singing into the mike, with his eyes tightly closed. It took him a while to realise that his door had opened and by then there were at least 20 people watching him sing and dance. It was very funny!

On another occasion we had all come round to his house for a surprise birthday party organised by his mum. We had all piled into the living room while he was upstairs and his mum then called him down and switched off all the lights.

We all went very quiet, waiting for him to come. Eventually he walked into the room calling "Hello". We all waited. Then he switched on the lights and we all shouted "Surprise!" But it was us who got the real surprise. He had been in such a rush to come down and find out what his mum wanted that he hadn't put any trousers on! There he stood in front of all his friends in just his underpants. It was very funny.

But these things would not have happened to my friend if he'd been ready, if he'd been prepared.

They are all very funny things. But Jesus tells us that he is coming again and that we should be ready. Wouldn't it be terrible if Jesus came again and we'd stopped going to church, or praying to him or, worse still, we'd started deliberately doing things that we knew were wrong? We would be surprised and we would be very embarrassed.

And the Bible teaches us that Jesus is indeed coming again.

The Race

Object needed: *A picture of a runner.*

Imagine it's the Olympic Games. The best runners in the world are lined up for the 1,500 metres. They're looking strong and very fast – all except one, that is.

The athletes have spent the last four years training as hard as they could. They were up very early; they ran long distances. They practised running quickly; they practised running for a long time. They practised using weights. They made sure they ate the right food; they made sure they had plenty of sleep. They made sure they didn't get injured. All the athletes are ready for this race – all except one, that is.

One of the athletes has decided that even though he did really well in the last Olympics he didn't want to spend any time training and he certainly didn't want to be going to bed and getting up early. And there was no way he was eating the food they said he had to eat.

So, instead, he hasn't trained. He has been eating pie and chips every day. He has been up until midnight every night and has stayed in bed until 11am every morning. His tummy is looking very big as it hangs over his shorts. He looked out of breath just walking to the starting line.

Do you think he is going to win? Absolutely not! He has not spent the time preparing. He has not spent the time getting ready.

It does take time to get ready, and if Jesus were to come today, would we be ready? Would he look into our hearts and find them clean? Would he see that we do things to show that we love him? Would he?

● STORY – The Adventures Of Zoë And Oliver (6)

It was springtime and this was a great time for playing outside. Oliver loved it. He would come home from school, dump his school bag down, take his lunch box to the sink, run upstairs, put his play clothes on and be out in the garden in minutes.

He loved to play on the swing. He loved to see how high he could go. He loved to kick his football about, and he loved to terrorise his little sister, Zoë. That was probably his favourite part. He would pretend he had a spider and chase her round the garden with it, or maybe instead throw water at her from the pond.

Then Mum would call them in for dinner. Oliver would eat very quickly. He really wanted to be back out in the garden as fast as he could. But before he could leave the table Mum would ask him the usual question: "Do you have any homework to do?"

Well, actually, tonight he did. Tomorrow was the big test. If he failed it, it would mean a letter home to Mum and he would be grounded. But he also knew that if he told Mum about the test he wouldn't be allowed out. So he said: "No, Mum. Just a little bit of reading that I can do at bedtime."

So Oliver rushed back into the garden. In the back of his mind he was sure he could do his reading for the test before he went to sleep. So he rushed outside. He was very excited to be back out. For the longest time he ran round and round the garden as fast as he could. Then for a while after that he played jumping the stream. He was very good at this by now, and unlike his sister, who was always falling into it, he never got wet.

Then it was as if all his dreams came true. He saw a toad, a big ugly toad. It wasn't that Oliver liked playing with toads. It was just that Zoë hated them. So Oliver picked up the toad and ran with it towards Zoë, who was on the swing. She saw him coming and screamed and ran away as quickly as she could. Oliver chased after her laughing; Zoë ran away from him screaming. In the end when Zoë was too tired to run she burst into tears and ran indoors to Mum. Mum did tell Oliver off for that, but it was so worth it.

It began to get dark and Oliver and Zoë were called in for their bath. They washed. They cleaned their teeth. Dad came to read them a story, but Oliver said he would like to read his own book tonight, so Dad just read to Zoë. Oliver was looking for a chance to look at his work for the test. He started to read through it, but he was so tired after all the running about that he began to close his eyes. He decided that he would sleep and get up extra early in the morning to do it.

Dad finished the story, kissed Oliver and Zoë and then turned out the lights. Oliver was sleeping before Dad reached the bottom of the stairs. He didn't feel as if he had slept at all when Mum called him to wake up. He turned over and looked at the clock. "Oh no! I have to be on the bus in 20 minutes and I haven't looked at the test!"

He rushed downstairs and ate his breakfast, thinking all the time that he could read through the test stuff on the way to school. But they got to school so quickly and Mum kept asking him what he was doing and there was no way he could own up.

He thought he could read through the test stuff over lunch and then he would be just fine. But, to his horror, when he sat down at his desk, there was a piece of paper turned over in front of him. His teacher announced: "I've decided that we should do the test this morning. I hope nobody minds. Then we can have the afternoon for more pleasant things."

The tests were turned over and Oliver began to read the questions. He tried to do three out of the ten but he knew that he was guessing even those. He hadn't prepared and he was going to be in big trouble.

Some people behave a little like Oliver. They know that Jesus is going to come again soon. But they keep thinking that they can do bad things and be unkind to others and ignore God and they'll have

plenty of time to put everything right before Jesus comes. They could be very wrong. It is a very big chance to take. The Bible teaches that only those who are ready will be going to heaven. That really is worth knowing.

Sure enough, by the end of the week the test results were out and Oliver was in big trouble. He was grounded for a whole week so that he could catch up with everyone else who had prepared. When he thought about it he realised that he hadn't been so clever. He now had to miss out on seven nights of play when he could have learnt the test in one night.

That night Zoë whispered up to his bunk bed: "Good night, Oliver. I'll say hi to your toad friend when I see him, because you won't be coming out for a while."

We Believe In The Holy Spirit,

the Lord, the giver of life, who proceeds from the Father and the Son.
With the Father and the Son he is worshipped and glorified.
He has spoken through the prophets.

	Programme	Item
Section 1	**Welcome**	
	Rules	
	Prayer	
	Introductory Praise	
	Game 1	H.O.L.Y.S.P.I.R.I.T
	Praise	
	Fun Item 1	
	Game 2	F.I.R.E
	Fun Item 2	
	Bible Text	Acts 1:8
	Announcements	
	Interview	
Section 2	**Worship Time**	
Preaching	**Bible Lesson**	Acts 2
Time	**Illustration 1**	Teacher
	Illustration 2	Policeman
	Illustration 3	Strongman
	Story	The Adventures Of Zoë And Oliver (7)
	Prayer	

Overview The Bible teaches that we all receive the Holy Spirit when we give our lives to Jesus. There are various doctrinal debates as to whether there is a separate experience of the Holy Spirit after this time. We are not going to look at that, but instead focus on what the Holy Spirit does.

Game 1

H.O.L.Y.S.P.I.R.I.T

PREPARATION	Cut out the individual letters H.O.L.Y.S.P.I.R.I.T.
PLAYERS	Five per team.
SET-UP	The letters are placed at B in order. The players line up at A in relay formation (i.e., one behind the other).
OBJECT	The first person runs from A to B, collects the first letter and returns to A. At A they begin to construct the sentence while the second player starts running. They keep going until all the letters are collected.
WINNING	The first team to construct the sentence wins.

Game 2

F.I.R.E

PREPARATION	Cut out the individual letters F.I.R.E.
PLAYERS	Four per team (this is kept very simple for the younger players).
SET-UP	The letters are placed at B in order. The players line up at A in relay formation (i.e., one behind the other).
OBJECT	The first person runs from A to B, collects the first letter and returns to A. At A they begin to construct the word while the second player starts running. They keep going until all the letters are collected.
WINNING	The first team to construct the word wins.

Preaching Time

BIBLE LESSON **ACTS 2**

"But the Holy Spirit will come upon you and give you power. Then you will tell everyone about me." (Acts 1:8)

This week's section of the creed is:

We believe in the Holy Spirit,
the Lord, the giver of life, who proceeds
from the Father and the Son.
With the Father and the Son he is
worshipped and glorified.
He has spoken through the prophets.

And the Jesus Story continues:

I'm about to describe to you the event that some call the "birthday of the church". It is the day of Pentecost – a special Jewish festival – and Jerusalem is full of people. The disciples are all together in an upper room.

The disciples think that maybe Jesus has gone and that's the end of that. But Jesus promised them something. He said if he went back to heaven, then God the Holy Spirit would come.

Keep remembering: God is God the Father, God the Son and God the Holy Spirit – all God. I know it's confusing, but it's true. Now the Holy Spirit can do something that Jesus couldn't. When Jesus was walking the planet, he chose to be human. The Holy Spirit doesn't do that. He can be absolutely everywhere.

And that's what happens: Jesus returns to heaven and the Holy Spirit comes. This is what happens:

It's the day of Pentecost. All the disciples are together in one place. Suddenly there's a noise from heaven like the sound of a mighty wind. Then they see fire moving in all directions until the fire settles on each of the disciples. Then the Holy Spirit fills everyone and they start to speak in languages that they have not learnt.

The disciples run out and start talking to people, and all the people, even though they are from different places, hear them speaking in their own language. But not only do they speak in strange languages, but something else has also happened. The Holy Spirit has filled them with power, just like Jesus said. And they start preaching and telling everyone about Jesus. And they're not so frightened. God the Holy Spirit is with them.

Teacher

Object needed: *A picture of a teacher.*

It would be useful to prepare the three pictures mentioned in the illustrations and have them all displayed at the front from the start.

The Holy Spirit is God, but he has many jobs that he does that are distinctly his. Let me explain a few.

When I was in school I had good teachers and bad teachers. I had teachers who taught me about history and geography and mathematics and English and computers and things like that. But I also had teachers who taught me how to behave: how to be kind to people, how to show respect to people, how to be honest.

It's the second kind of teacher that the Holy Spirit is like. The Bible says that the Holy Spirit leads us into all truth. He shows us how to behave and helps us understand Jesus more.

The Holy Spirit is a teacher.

Policeman

Object needed: *A picture of a policeman.*

You might find this hard to believe, but there have been times in my life when I have done things wrong! This is true especially when it comes to my driving, and especially when it comes to my driving on motorways. For a while I used to spend lots and lots of time on the motorway, going from one place to another. And I was usually late. So because I was late I would go very fast – sometimes very, very fast.

One day while I was going very, very fast I heard a strange noise behind me. I didn't know what it was. Then my whole car was full of a flashing blue light and I was convinced that I was being kidnapped by space aliens. When I looked in the mirror I wished it *had* been space aliens, for there behind me was a police car. The policeman made me stop and then he asked me to come and sit in his car. It really was a very cool car with buttons everywhere. It did look a little bit like a spaceship.

He told me that I had been going too fast and because of that he was going to give me a fine. I would have to pay £60. That was a lot of money for just going a bit fast, but the policeman knew that if I went too fast, I was a danger to myself and to everyone else on the road. He wanted to keep me safe.

The Bible says that the Holy Spirit is a little bit like a policeman. It says that the Holy Spirit convicts us regarding sin. That means the Holy Spirit inside us reminds us when we are doing wrong things and tries to steer us back to Jesus.

The Holy Spirit is a policeman.

Strongman

Object needed: *A picture of a strongman.*

It's not on television much any more, but when I was little I used to watch a cartoon called "Asterix". It was very funny to watch and had all sorts of very interesting characters. There was Asterix, who was chief of the village, and there was Getafix, who was in charge of the medicine. It was his job to make up a special drink that all the villagers would drink; it made them super-strong. Getafix would make up the drink in a huge barrel. The villagers needed to be super-strong because they were always being attacked by Roman soldiers.

Another of the characters – and perhaps my favourite character – was called Obelix. Obelix was never allowed to drink the special drink that Getafix made because when Obelix was a baby, he had fallen into the barrel of drink and he'd drunk so much of it before they pulled him out that now he was permanently super-strong. The drink had turned him into a strongman all the time.

In the old part of the Bible, the Holy Spirit would come to people in much the same way as the villagers would drink the special drink. The Holy Spirit would come to people, make them strong, or wise, or know something about God, and then the Holy Spirit would leave them again. This happened to Samson. You remember: the Holy Spirit comes on Samson and makes him strong and then leaves him again; later, when Samson needs God again, the Holy Spirit comes back.

After the bit in the Bible that we read today, the Holy Spirit doesn't do that any more. He comes and lives in us. He wants us to be permanently strong, like Obelix. But not strong in the sense that we have big muscles and we win every fight. No! Strong in the sense that we can stand up for Jesus and tell people about him, and strong enough to read our Bibles each day and be strong for God.

The Holy Spirit makes us strong.

● STORY – The Adventures Of Zoë And Oliver (7)

Dad was very tall and very strong. But he was nowhere near as strong as Uncle Frank. He really was strong. Uncle Frank worked in the forest just outside the village. He cut down trees and carried them to the sawmill.

He could pick up Oliver in one hand and Zoë in the other hand and lift them both up over his head. Whenever Uncle Frank came round for dinner it was always great fun for everyone – well, nearly everyone. It did mean that Mum had to spend a lot of extra time in the kitchen making a lot of extra food. Uncle Frank could eat enough for 30 people in one meal and still have room for dessert.

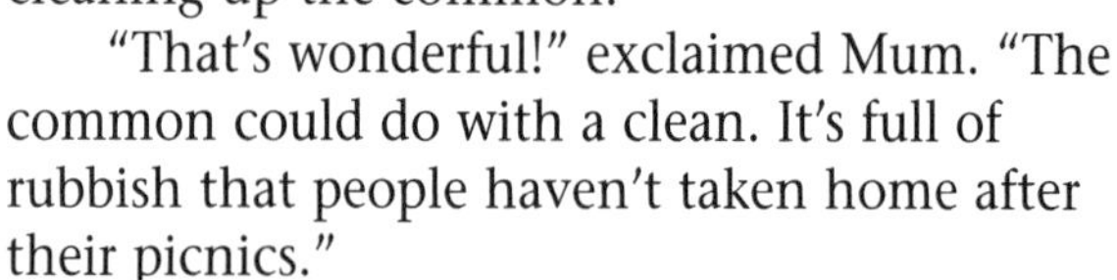

Today's dinner with Uncle Frank had been the usual round of jokes and fun. But it soon became obvious to everyone that Oliver wasn't laughing as much as he usually did. Uncle Frank asked him: "Hey, Oliver, what's up?"

Oliver looked down and then he explained: "I have volunteered to be in charge of cleaning up the common."

"That's wonderful!" exclaimed Mum. "The common could do with a clean. It's full of rubbish that people haven't taken home after their picnics."

"I know," said Oliver. "That's what I told my teacher and I told her that somebody should clean it up and she said 'You're right' and I said 'I know I'm right' and she said 'Good' and I said 'Good' and then she said 'You can do it; I'll get you some helpers' and before I could stop her she was announcing to the class that I was organising a clean-up on the common on Monday after school and they had all better be there to help or instead she would be giving extra homework and the whole class sighed and nobody is very happy with me.

"So, tomorrow after school," Oliver continued, "I have to stand on the common and organise everyone to clean up the mess."

"Well, I'm very proud of you, nephew," said Uncle Frank. "You'll do a great job, I'm sure."

"But, Uncle Frank," Oliver began, "nobody is going to listen to me, are they?"

"You never know until you try," prompted Dad.

All the dinner things were packed away and Uncle Frank went outside to play ball with Oliver and Zoë.

Oliver didn't sleep well that night. He was very worried about the following evening. Nobody seemed particularly keen on talking to him in school either. They didn't want to be cleaning up the common after school; they wanted to be playing PlayStation games.

But at 4pm that afternoon Oliver stood on the bandstand in the middle of the common and called everyone to come closer. They eventually did. The whole class had turned out – but only to avoid homework.

Oliver started to tell people what to do. "Right, if you four start on that side, and you four start on that side..." But nobody was listening. They were talking to each other. Some of them even had their backs to him and were looking away into the distance. They might have been forced to be there, but that didn't mean they had to listen. And if they didn't listen, then they wouldn't know what to do, and if they didn't know what to do, then they wouldn't have to clean up the rubbish.

Oliver tried again: "Can you four start at that corner by the trees, and can you four..." Suddenly everyone stopped talking and stared intently at Oliver. For some reason he suddenly had everyone's attention. "Now that's better," he announced. "OK, if you four can go to that corner and work your way in, and if you four can..." And to his absolute amazement everyone started doing what they were told. He suddenly had awesome authority.

He finished giving out the instructions and then turned to see how much rubbish there actually was. As he turned he saw why everyone had gone so quiet. There, standing behind him as tall as a giant (well, he seemed that way) and as wide as a car, was Uncle Frank.

"Thought I'd come and see how you were doing," he chuckled.

That is what it's like when you know that God the Holy Spirit is with you. It's like having your own personal Uncle Frank standing behind you all the time. You feel bold and you speak with authority because there is someone with you who is powerful beyond your wildest imagination. That's what it is like when the Holy Spirit is with you.

The common was cleared in no time. Surprisingly, when Oliver's class saw how nice it looked without the rubbish, they were very pleased with themselves and thanked Oliver for being such a good organiser.

Oliver was very sleepy that night. He hadn't slept well the night before and he'd worked quite hard. But, before he could drop off, Zoë couldn't resist her little comment: "Good night, Oliver the rubbish man."

We Believe In One Holy Catholic And Apostolic Church.

We acknowledge one baptism for the forgiveness of sins. We look for the resurrection of the dead, and the life of the world to come. Amen.

	Programme	Item
Section 1	**Welcome**	
	Rules	
	Prayer	
	Introductory Praise	
	Game 1	Church-building 1
	Praise	
	Fun Item 1	
	Game 2	Church-building 2
	Fun Item 2	
	Bible Text	Matthew 16:18
	Announcements	
	Interview	
Section 2	**Worship Time**	
Preaching	**Bible Lesson**	The Church
Time	**Illustration 1**	Church 1
	Illustration 2	Church 2
	Illustration 3	Church 3
	Story	The Adventures Of Zoë And Oliver (8)
	Prayer	

This last part of the creed could in itself become a series. We are going to restrict ourselves to the opening lines regarding the church and talk about the church as a gathering of people who believe in Jesus.

Church-building 1

PREPARATION Building blocks (as many as you can lay your hands on) divided between the three teams at B.

PLAYERS Three players per team.

SET-UP The blocks are placed at B and the players are in relay formation at A.

OBJECT The players run from A to B, collect a block at B and return to A to start construction of the "church". The next player sets off.

WINNING When all the blocks are gone, the best "church" wins.

Church-building 2*

PREPARATION None needed.

PLAYERS One leader per team.

SET-UP None needed.

OBJECT The leader must choose children and other leaders and by placing them "gently" on top of each other – on shoulders, backs, etc. – he must build a "church".

WINNING The leader who builds the best "church" wins.

THE CHURCH

"I will build my church, and death itself will not have any power over it."
(Matthew 16:18)

The final section of the Creed:

> We believe in one holy catholic and apostolic Church.
> We acknowledge one baptism for the forgiveness of sins.
> We look for the resurrection of the dead,
> and the life of the world to come. Amen.

And the last part of the Jesus Story:

Let me tell you what's happened so far.

Jesus has created the world; he's created Adam and Eve, he's created every new life; he disguised himself and came to live on the planet for a while; he lived a perfect life, but was still nailed to a cross and killed; he rose from the dead, and returned to heaven; from heaven he sent the Holy Spirit to give us all power to speak from God. And now Jesus is in heaven praying for us and waiting for the time when he will return to the planet in power and might.

All that is what we as a church believe. This is the main reason the church exists, to let the whole world know how amazing Jesus is and to give everyone a chance to become his followers. It is a great church, and it is here to show how amazing is the God we serve: God the Father, God the Son and God the Holy Spirit.

* Please be careful in Game 2. It can be a lot of fun and is hysterical when the construction begins to wobble, but there should be enough leaders on hand to keep it all controlled.

Illustration 1

Church 1

Object needed: *Lots of pictures of churches in your area (this will work best if you can find pictures of churches old and new).*

When we think of "church" these are probably the things that come to mind. This is the church down the street, this is the church across the town, and this is the church some of the leaders normally go to.

They are all quite different, but they are all what we think of when we think of church. Some of them are very new – built only several years ago; some are very old – many hundreds of years old. But they are what we usually think of when we think of church – we think of buildings.

Some of them are really beautiful with stained-glass windows and enormous steeples. Some are built to be more usable and have playgroups and nurseries in them during the week.

But they have all been built by people.

Illustration 2

Church 2

Object needed: *Lots of pictures of people inside churches. Again, if photos can be taken in the local area, all the better.*

Now these are pictures of some of the people in some of the churches in our area. Some of them are pictures of people who are talking about the Bible in somebody's home. Some of them are pictures of people singing songs at a service in the local school. This is the amazing thing. This is actually what God calls "church". You see, church isn't really about bricks and stuff, although buildings are useful things to meet in. God talks about *people* when he talks about church. And when God says "church", he doesn't just mean the group who meet in the home, or the group who meet in the school, or the group who meet in that old building we usually call a church. God means all those people who love him and gather together in his name to pray to him and sing their songs of praise to him and learn more about him. That's why the Creed says, "We believe in one Church". It is a church that is made up of people who meet in all these different types of building, people who meet all over the world, people who speak all sorts of different languages; but they are *all* church. They are all "one church".

It really is very exciting when you think about it. It means that the church isn't just ten people in a house or 100 people in a building or 1,000 people in a large warehouse, but the church is billions of people who love Jesus.

Church 3

Object needed: *A picture of your children's group. If you have the technology to take a photo on that day or evening and show it to them in enlarged form or on the screen it will be all the more effective.*

I want to show you just one more picture of the church. Now remember: the church is not buildings; the church is people who love Jesus. And the church is made up of all sorts of people – people from England and Ireland and Wales and Africa and India and France and Switzerland and Australia and everywhere else you can think of. The people who make up church are all different: some are rich, some are poor, some live in huge houses, some live in igloos, some in tents or caravans. Some live in one place all the time; some move about.

And get this bit: some of them are really old – like the leaders here – and some are very young. Actually, I have one more picture of church. Let me show it to you *(display the picture)*.

Yes, that's you. The church is people who love Jesus, who gather together to learn about him and to sing their songs of praise to him – just like we do. You guys are church. You and I and the other leaders, we are church.

The church is not buildings, but people who love Jesus. Our story of Zoë and Oliver has one more thing to show us about church.

• STORY – The Adventures Of Zoë And Oliver (8)

Most of the time, Zoë and Oliver managed to get along. Sometimes they had little arguments and sometimes Oliver was mean and chased Zoë around with a toad in his hand. Sometimes Oliver was particularly mean to Zoë and she then did what all five-year-olds do when they are being treated badly by their older brother or sister. They go and cry to Mum.

Well, this afternoon after school, Oliver and Zoë had been playing in the garden as they liked to do, when Oliver found a spider. He showed it to Zoë, who screeched as usual and ran away. Now if Oliver had stopped there, everything would have been just fine. But he didn't stop there. He knew he should, but he didn't. Instead he ran after Zoë and put the spider down her back.

She screamed so loudly that Mum thought there must be a poisonous snake in the garden or something. When she got to the garden Zoë was shaking her jumper, and eventually the spider fell out. But Zoë was so upset she couldn't stop crying and instead she sat on the ground, sobbing.

Mum was furious. She looked at Oliver. He was trying his best to look upset but was sure he was going to laugh any minute, that is, until Mum announced: "Oliver, go to your room. You are not to come outside for the rest of the week."

Now it was Oliver's turn to cry and to shout things about how unfair it was and to stomp off in the direction of the stairs. He stomped up every step and sat on his bed. At dinner time he said nothing at all and after dinner he stomped back upstairs again. He sat on his window seat and looked outside. It was now beginning to rain heavily. Oliver was feeling very upset indeed. He watched the puddles forming outside and then he decided: "That's it, I'm running away. They are all so mean to me here, I'm leaving."

He could hear everyone else downstairs, so he crept down, grabbed his coat, put on his wellies, got himself a packet of crisps, opened the door and stepped out into the night. He had no idea where he was going, but he was going.

The wind was blowing hard. The rain kept falling. Now there was thunder and lightning. Oliver was wet through. It was very dark. The wind made strange sounds through the trees. His red coat was wet through and so was his T-shirt – by now it was so wet it stuck to his skin. His trainers were making squelching sounds and his jeans had become so tight it was getting very difficult to walk.

By now he'd reached the path that led into the woods. He took it and kept walking. The rain kept falling and Oliver walked on. He walked for about an hour before he realised that he had left the path. He tried walking back to find it, but the woods looked so different in the dark. He was beginning to get a little frightened. Running away didn't seem like such a good idea now.

Write up the following adjectives and phrases quickly as you come to them.

He felt *lonely* and *lost.* He felt that *nobody loved him,* that *nobody cared for him.*

He walked further still but by now had no idea where he was going. He wanted to go home now. He wanted to go back to his warm, cosy bedroom. But he was lost. What would happen to him? It was getting cold and he was very wet, and now... now there was a sound coming towards him. Oliver couldn't see who or what it was but he was getting out of there as quickly as possible. He began to run as fast as he could and then, suddenly, something stepped out in front of him, but he was running so fast and the ground was so slippery he couldn't stop. BANG! – he ran straight into it. Oliver closed his eyes, not daring to look at whatever had got him. It picked Oliver off the ground and held him in the air. Oliver opened his eyes slowly. To his total relief he was looking into the face of Uncle Frank.

"I thought you might have come in here. Your mum and dad have got half the village out looking for you. What were you thinking?"

"But they made me sad, Uncle Frank," Oliver said in his defence.

"Well, from what I hear you didn't exactly make Zoë happy yourself. Fancy putting a spider down her back. You are a little tinker sometimes." Uncle Frank smiled, and Oliver breathed a sigh of relief. It had seemed a good idea at the time to run away but when you're in the middle of the woods and it's dark and wet it doesn't seem so smart.

Uncle Frank took Oliver home, and everyone was very pleased to see him. He had to take a long bath before bed and Mum and Dad were so relieved to see him they didn't even tell him off (although Mum did mention that he was still grounded for what he did to Zoë).

Oliver lay in his bed. Now he felt some very different feelings.

Write the following words down opposite the other words.

He felt *secure* and *loved* and *cared for.* He felt *special* and *happy.* He felt that *he belonged.*

These are the feelings we have when we are in a family. Having told you what the church isn't, and hopefully having told you what the church *is*, maybe I should add that the church is also a family. When we love Jesus we are also told to love each other, so we should feel loved and cared for and secure and special and happy and belonging when we meet with other people who love Jesus. These should be the things we feel when we meet at our children's club.

Zoë whispered: "I'm glad you're back, Oliver. I really did miss you. I forgive you for putting the spider down my back. I do love you, Oliver."

Oliver whispered back: "Thank you, Zoë. I love you too." Then he added: "But I wonder if you'll still love me tomorrow night after I put a worm down your back."

Zoë said "Urghhh" and rolled over to sleep, wondering why God had given her a brother anyway!

HUDSON TAYLOR

A Series in Six Parts

Introduction

Title	Themes covered
1 Getting Ready 1: The Skills We Need	**Preparation**
2 Getting Ready 2: Protection	**God protects**
3 Getting Ready 3: We Start At Home	**Missions home and abroad**
4 The Journey Begins: Leaving Things Behind	**Travelling light**
5 Problems To Be Faced	**Overcoming**
6 Over To You	**Playing our part**

This whole series has a major emphasis on world missions. It is worth preparing for this well in advance. Contact your denomination's headquarters and ask for a list of missionaries and where they are based (this is essential for Game 2 in Lesson 2). If during the "Interview" slot you can invite a missionary, this will enhance the presentation. Alternatively, invite someone with a world-missions emphasis – maybe your church missions director.

The aim of the series is to show children that God has a plan for the whole world, that he wants to reach different people-groups all over our world. To this extent the story revolves around Hudson Taylor, missionary to China; and the Bible Lessons involve Daniel, who himself was a missionary in a foreign land (Babylon), albeit not of his own choosing.

The series is designed to give children an insight into world missions and to explain basic principles such as the need to prepare for missions, God's provision

and protection in missions, etc. It is my hope that through this series children might themselves be inspired to seek God with regard to world missions. After all, most of our modern missionary heroes felt called to foreign lands when they were children, for example, Amy Carmichael, Hudson Taylor, Gladys Aylward...

Another prop that might help you in your presentation is a timeline, onto which you could mark up Hudson Taylor's birth date and the date of his death, and then add various aspects of his life as you tell the stories – this is included in Appendix 2.

1 Getting Ready 1: The Skills We Need

	Programme	Item
Section 1	**Welcome**	
	Rules	
	Prayer	
	Introductory Praise	
	Game 1	UK Jigsaw
	Praise	
	Fun Item 1	
	Game 2	China Jigsaw
	Fun Item 2	
	Bible Text	Jeremiah 29:6
	Announcements	
	Interview	
Section 2	**Worship Time**	
Preaching Time	**Bible Lesson**	Daniel
	Illustration 1	Holidays
	Illustration 2	Sports Skills
	Illustration 3	Learning: Why?
	Story	Hudson Taylor (1)
	Prayer	

It came as no surprise to Mr and Mrs Taylor when their son announced that he felt God calling him to China. But the call of God was not enough; there was preparation needed before he could set off.

games

UK Jigsaw

PREPARATION Cut the map of the UK in Appendix 4 into ten pieces.

PLAYERS Five players from each team.

SET-UP The jigsaw pieces are placed at B. The players line up in relay formation at A.

OBJECT The first person races from A to B, collects a piece of the map and returns. This continues until all the pieces are collected. The jigsaw is then constructed.

WINNING The first team to construct the map wins.

China Jigsaw

PREPARATION Cut the map of China in Appendix 4 into ten pieces.

PLAYERS Five players from each team.

SET-UP The jigsaw pieces are placed at B. The players line up in relay formation at A.

OBJECT The first person races from A to B, collects a piece of the map and returns. This continues until all the pieces are collected. The jigsaw is then constructed.

WINNING The first team to construct the map wins.

Preaching Time

BIBLE LESSON **DANIEL**

"Increase in number there; do not decrease." (Jeremiah 29:6, New International Version)

When Jehoiakim was king of Judah, the king of Babylon decided to invade. He fought against Jerusalem and captured it. He took many things from the city back to Babylon, and he also took with him some of the young men who lived there. One of these men was Daniel.

We will be talking about Daniel over the next couple of weeks at the same time as we will be talking about a man called Hudson Taylor. When we first encounter Daniel he probably isn't feeling very happy. He's in a foreign land, he's lost his parents and he doesn't know what will become of him. He is probably very afraid.

Daniel could have easily buried his face in his hands, cried a lot and felt sorry for himself. But Daniel believed in God – Daniel believed in a God who would look after him. Daniel knew that even in a foreign land he could serve God well. Daniel knew that God had called him to be more than just a Babylonian slave, but while he was waiting to become what God had called him to be, Daniel began to learn. He learned everything the Babylonians would teach him, but all the time stayed faithful to God. He learned their language and many other languages; he read their books and began to understand their customs and culture. Daniel was convinced that God could use him, so he began to prepare himself. He would be everything he could; he would be ready for God to use him.

Daniel had probably heard of the words of Jeremiah the prophet. He might have known Jeremiah's command to increase and not to decrease. God wanted his people to grow strong and learn and be prepared, wherever they were.

Daniel played his part well and prepared himself well. Very soon, Daniel was called before the king of Babylon. He proved to be better than all the other slaves. God had called him, he had done his best to prepare himself, and now it began to happen.

Daniel, through God's plans, became the prime minister of Babylon.

Being chosen by God to do something is not enough; we need to prepare ourselves for the work God has called us to do. But preparing ourselves is not enough either; we need to find out what God wants us to do as well. We only do this by spending time with God.

Holidays

Object needed: *A suitcase and assorted holiday items.*

Packing for holidays is never easy. You've made your list: suntan lotion, swimming trunks, skis, underwear. You think you have everything. You have prepared as best you can to go on this holiday. You spent hours and hours persuading your mum and dad that this would be the best place to go. You showed them the pictures of the water slides and the amazing obstacle course. You showed them the really cheap price. Eventually they went for it.

You wake up early in the morning – 2am – so that you can get to the airport in plenty of time. You carry your case. It seems really heavy, but it certainly isn't as heavy as your mum and dad's. Your sister has brought her silly doll to ride on the aeroplane. This is going to be a great holiday. You go to check in at the desk; your mum hands over the tickets. They tell you which terminal you are to leave from. You are ready to go. Two weeks in the sunshine!

You arrive at the terminal; the man there asks for your passports. Your mum looks desperately at your dad; he searches desperately in his pockets... The passports are not there. You can't go. You weren't properly prepared. What a disaster!

Sports Skills

Object needed: *A video of a famous sportsman in action.*

Play a clip of the video.

He's good, eh? You know what? He used to be rubbish. He used to be so bad that even my granny could beat him. After he'd been rubbish for a while he became average, and then a bit later on he became fairly good, and then good and then very good. A few years later he became excellent. Now he's one of the best in the world.

But it was no accident. When he was rubbish he practised and practised until he got better. He was preparing for the day when he would be the best, the day when he would be playing in one of the best competitions in the world. Even when he was very good he kept practising. He was going to be the best. To be the best takes major preparation.

Some people think that they can become a Christian and then go off and do anything that God wants. That isn't how it works. God prepares people. And people who want God to use them also prepare themselves.

Before we can do some things for God we need to prepare ourselves properly. If we feel God wants us to go to another country and tell people there about him, then maybe we need to learn the language of that country and find out as much as we can about that country. There's always preparation involved. Whether it's going on holiday, learning a sport or serving God, there is always preparation to be done.

Learning: Why?

Object needed: *A school book.*

Replace some of the illustration with your own personal experience.

My worst subject in school was French. I was really bad at it. The teacher didn't like me much and I wasn't too keen on her. I just couldn't learn all those words. I really couldn't see the point. But when it came to computers I was brilliant. I really liked computers and was sure that this was important. Soon everyone would be using a computer.

I learned the things I thought were valuable. I learned the things I thought I should know. I think that was smart. Some people refuse to learn anything in school. It isn't that they are stupid – they just don't want to learn. That's not so clever. No matter what we eventually do, we need to prepare, and school is a great place for preparation.

I did make a major mistake though! I spend a lot of time in France now; I wish I could speak that particular language. The key is this: you need to learn as much as you can. Your preparation may help you with the things that God wants you to do.

• STORY – Hudson Taylor (1)

"Dear God, if you should give us a son, grant that he may work for you in China."

So prayed James and Amelia Taylor. On May 21st 1832 they did have a son. They named him James Hudson, although he preferred to be called just Hudson. Seventeen years later, many people would have thought the Taylors' prayer of no consequence. Maybe God hadn't heard it, or, if he had, certainly by now he would have forgotten it.

But God always hears our prayers and the only thing he forgets is our sin – the junk and garbage in our lives – when we come to him and ask for forgiveness. God hadn't forgotten Mr and Mrs Taylor's prayer. God watched over Hudson as he grew. He watched as Hudson fell sick and then as he recovered. He watched as Hudson spent long nights wondering if God existed at all. God watched. And then at the age of seventeen Hudson finally decided to give his life to God. He asked God to forgive his sins and committed himself to being used by God. Then God began to speak to Hudson.

God watches us today, waiting for that point when we will give our lives fully to him, waiting for that point when he can begin to use us for his glory. Some of you may need to give your lives to Jesus today.

It came as no surprise to James and Amelia when their son announced that he was going to China. They knew that God would call him to go there. They simply thanked the God who always hears and answers prayers.

But being called by God to go to China wasn't enough. Hudson was sure that God wanted him to go there, but there was work to do. Hudson was convinced that God had placed it in his heart to go to China, so he would spend much time praying for the people there. But Hudson knew that it wasn't enough simply to pray; he needed to be prepared. So Hudson spent much time learning as much as he could about China. He studied maps, read books and talked to those who had been there. He spent time learning the incredibly complicated language and worked hard at deciphering the strange words that made up the Chinese language.

Hudson learned a skill that he would need in this unusual country: Hudson studied as a doctor. When our story really begins, Hudson is 20 years old and has travelled to London to continue training to be a doctor.

Hudson was sure that God wanted him to go to China. He was clear that God wanted him to tell the people there about God, but he was also sure that God wanted him to prepare. We must be ready to prepare for what God wants us to do.

There were other things that Hudson had to learn before he could set off for China. We look at them next week, but for now we must think: How can I best prepare myself for what God wants me to do?

2 Getting Ready 2: Protection

	Programme	Item
Section 1	**Welcome**	
	Rules	
	Prayer	
	Introductory Praise	
	Game 1	Noodles 1
	Praise	
	Fun Item 1	
	Game 2	Noodles 2
	Fun Item 2	
	Bible Text	Isaiah 43:2
	Announcements	
	Interview	
Section 2	**Worship Time**	
Preaching	**Bible Lesson**	Daniel In The Lions' Den
Time	**Illustration 1**	Fire And Water
	Illustration 2	*The Cross And The Switchblade*
	Story	Hudson Taylor (2)
	Prayer	

Overview We all have to learn certain lessons. Some of us learn them when we are young; some of us learn them a bit later. But we all have to learn that God provides for us and that God protects us before we can walk with him with any certainty and confidence.

Noodles 1

PREPARATION	A bowl of noodles and a pair of chopsticks per team.
PLAYERS	Four per team.
SET-UP	The bowl is placed at B along with the chopsticks. The teams line up in relay formation at A.
OBJECT	To run from A to B, eat as many noodles as possible within two minutes using the chopsticks and return to A.
WINNING	The team that eats the most noodles wins.

Noodles 2*

PREPARATION	A bowl of noodles and a pair of chopsticks per team.
PLAYERS	Four per team.
SET-UP	The bowl is placed at B along with the chopsticks. The teams line up in relay formation at A.
OBJECT	To run from A to B, eat as many noodles as possible within two minutes using the chopsticks and return to A.
WINNING	The team that eats the most noodles wins.

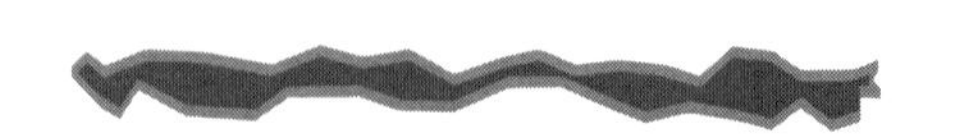

BIBLE LESSON

DANIEL IN THE LIONS' DEN

"When you walk through fire, you won't be burnt."
(Isaiah 43:2)

Remember: Bible Lessons can be presented using a video clip, as a drama sketch, asking the children to act out the lesson, as a story with visuals or as plain narrative.

Daniel had prepared himself well and now held a position of great prominence in Babylon, but this hadn't made him very popular. Lots of other men had wanted his position. They desperately wanted to find a way to get Daniel into trouble. But this wasn't easy. Daniel loved God and lived his life to please God, so he didn't do anything wrong. But the jealous men were determined to try and find a way to get Daniel into trouble.

Every day before breakfast Daniel would pray to God; every day before dinner Daniel would pray to God. And after supper, he prayed to God. Three times every day Daniel would pray to God. Now these jealous politicians really were trying their hardest to get Daniel into trouble, but he never seemed to do anything wrong. He never broke any of the laws of the country. So the politicians decided to ask the king to make a law banning people from praying to God. They suggested this to the king, and the king thought it was such a good idea that he made it a law straight away: "No person is allowed to pray to anyone except me from now on."

The politicians were delighted. Now Daniel would be in trouble. But still every day before breakfast Daniel prayed to God, and before lunch he prayed to God, and after supper he prayed to God. The politicians went straight to Darius the king and said: "Daniel's praying, and not to you but to God."

The king was furious and went straight to see Daniel. "Daniel," he said, "if you don't stop praying to God, I'll throw you to the lions."

Next day after breakfast Daniel prayed, and before dinner and after supper. King Darius was furious. "Bring me Daniel right now!" he

* When a game tastes this good it would be a crime to only do it once.

ordered. So Daniel was thrown into the lions' den.

The lions roared and licked their lips, but just as the lions were about to eat Daniel, God shouted: "STOP! Nobody eats Daniel. He's my friend." The lions were very disappointed, but they didn't dare disobey God.

The next day the king and the politicians came back very early to see the dead body of Daniel. The politicians were excited, but the king was actually really sad. He liked Daniel and he knew that the politicians had tricked him to find a way to get Daniel into trouble. When they reached the cave the king couldn't believe his eyes. There was Daniel, without a mark on him!

The king told Daniel to come out of the cave and instead the king threw the politicians to the lions. Daniel did what God asked, and God protected him in the lions' den.

Fire And Water

Object needed: *Some lighter fluid in a baking tray and a jug of water – it may be worthwhile having a fire extinguisher at hand, but I have used this illustration many times and there has never been a problem.*

Restate the rules at this point. If you don't, the illustration will cause so much excitement that nobody will be listening.

I think we should explain today's Bible Text or some of us could be in all sorts of trouble. The whole verse says: "When you cross deep rivers... you won't drown. When you walk through fire, you won't be burnt."

Now if we misunderstand what this verse means, then we might just be foolish and try walking through fire *(light the lighter fluid)* or we might try living underwater without breathing equipment *(pour some of the water into a cup)*.

Fire represents danger. Even when this verse was written, thousands of years ago, people knew very well the danger of being caught in a fire. They also knew about shipwrecks and how serious it would be to be lost at sea. Water represents danger.

God wanted his people to know that even though they faced danger they would be kept safe. Even though all sorts of bad things would come near them, he would protect them. Now let's be sure we understand this properly. God never said that his people would never be in danger – God's people are often in danger. But he did promise to be with us always. There are many stories of people who have been amazingly protected by God in very dangerous situations. On other occasions God has chosen to allow people to die so that they can come and be with him. We are often in danger, but God is always with us. Whether in life or death, God is with us.

Pour the water onto the fire.

The Cross And The Switchblade

Object needed: *A knife.*

The Cross And The Switchblade is quite an old book now. But it still makes exciting reading. It tells the story of David Wilkerson. God spoke to David and told him to go and tell teenagers who belonged to various gangs in New York City about Jesus. These gangs were full of teenagers who had committed no end of serious crimes. They had stolen, they had damaged property, they had beaten people up and many of them were murderers. But still God loved them and sent David Wilkerson to tell them about him.

One of the most dramatic moments in the book is when David finds himself surrounded by one of the most vicious gangs of all and face to face with the gang leader, Nicky Cruz. Nicky had killed several people and would think nothing of killing David Wilkerson. David had started to tell the gang about God and about Jesus dying for them. But Nicky didn't want to listen. He pulled out a knife and was intent on killing David Wilkerson.

If you ask anyone who has read the book, they'll all remember this part. You see, God doesn't keep us out of danger; he protects us *in* danger. Nicky Cruz walked towards David Wilkerson with his knife in hand. David looked straight into Nicky's eyes and said these words: "Nicky! You could cut me into a thousand pieces and each piece would cry out 'God loves you'."

Nicky had never known love. He put the knife away. This was the start of Nicky Cruz's journey to becoming a Christian.

● STORY – Hudson Taylor (2)

Hudson Taylor faced many dangers in his time as a missionary.

He faced incredible dangers on his journey to China, a voyage that lasted a total of 23 weeks. He boarded his ship, called the *Dumfries*, on September 19th 1853. The ship nearly ran onto rocks off Holyhead and then again it was nearly shipwrecked off the coast of France. But through it all Hudson held on to God. He trusted the God who would keep him safe and protect him.

On another occasion Hudson had travelled deep into the heart of China to tell the people there about God, but his servant had been unfaithful and had stolen his luggage and run away. Hudson, with no clothes except those he wore and no money to pay for accommodation, had to sleep on the stairs of a Buddhist temple. In the middle of the night he heard a man approach him and shouted, "Be on your way!" The man walked off. Later, some more men crept up behind Hudson to do him some mischief, but again he commanded them to go and, even though they could easily have overpowered him, they too ran off into the night.

There were many times when Hudson was in danger in China, but always he knew that God would protect him and look after him. Hudson knew that God could do this because of an incident that had happened to him long before he left for China. In 1852 Hudson had been training to be a doctor. In the middle of an exam he pricked his finger with a needle, and a deadly virus entered his body. He quickly developed a very high temperature. A doctor came to examine him and rapidly came to a decision: "Hudson, there is no doubt in my mind that you will die before the night is out. Use this time to make preparation for your death."

Can you imagine hearing news like that? Hudson was horrified. What was he to do? He began to pray and then very firmly announced to the doctor: "Sir! I have it on good authority that I will go to China and proclaim my God there. I will not die. God has said." And, sure enough, even though Hudson was very ill for some time, he did recover. He returned to his preparation to proclaim God in China.

The key is this: it is important to learn that God will always protect us before we leave for countries that God may send us to. Not only do we need to prepare, we also need to understand and preferably experience the protection of God.

Later when Hudson was in China he would witness a horrific scene: Hudson had met a young Chinese man who went by the name of Peter. Hudson and Peter were travelling on a boat down a very deep river. As Hudson stood in his cabin he heard an almighty splash outside. He rushed onto the deck to see Peter in the water. The current was fast and Peter was soon pulled under.

A strong wind was pulling Hudson's boat away from the drowning man. Hudson quickly let down the sail to stop his boat moving and then shouted to people on the bank of the river. They were fishermen and Hudson shouted: "Please will you help me rescue my friend?" Peter by now was drowning.

But the fishermen shrugged their shoulders: "Why should we help?" they said. Hudson couldn't believe what he was hearing. Eventually he persuaded the fishermen to help by offering them all he had. Then slowly they paddled into the middle of the river and started to search. They pulled Peter out, but by this time he was dead.

Later, when Hudson was thinking about the sadness of his friend's death, he came to this conclusion: "Weren't those fishermen guilty of Peter's death? They had the means to help, but did nothing."

Christians can be like that. Sometimes we have the means to help, but do nothing. Whether it's helping an old lady across the road, carrying some shopping, painting a fence or telling people about Jesus, we need to do what we can to help.

We must learn that God will always look after us and be with us, but we must do what needs doing. We have to do what God wants us to do. God doesn't keep us out of danger, but he will always be with us.

3 Getting Ready 3: We Start At Home

	Programme	Item
Section 1	Welcome	
	Rules	
	Prayer	
	Introductory Praise	
	Game 1	Table Tennis 1
	Praise	
	Fun Item 1	
	Game 2	Table Tennis 2
	Fun Item 2	
	Bible Text	Acts 1:8
	Announcements	
	Interview	
Section 2	Worship Time	
Preaching	Bible Lesson	Daniel
Time	Illustration 1	Target
	Illustration 2	Being Witnesses
	Illustration 3	From Here To There
	Story	Hudson Taylor (3)
	Prayer	

Overview We often think that missionary work only happens abroad, but missionary work begins where we are. Someone once said that mission begins with the sinner who is closest to us and ends with the one who is furthest away.

games

Table Tennis 1

PREPARATION A table-tennis bat and a table-tennis ball per team.

PLAYERS Four per team.

SET-UP The teams line up in relay formation at A with the front person holding the bat and ball.

OBJECT To run from A to B while bouncing the ball on the bat, and return to A. The bat and ball are then swapped and the next player sets off.

WINNING The team that returns first wins.

Table Tennis 2

PREPARATION A table-tennis bat and a balloon per team.

PLAYERS Four per team.

SET-UP The teams line up in relay formation at A with the front person holding the bat and balloon.

OBJECT To run from A to B while bouncing the balloon on the bat and return to A. The bat and balloon are then swapped and the next player sets off.

WINNING The team that returns first wins. If a team bursts their balloon they are disqualified.

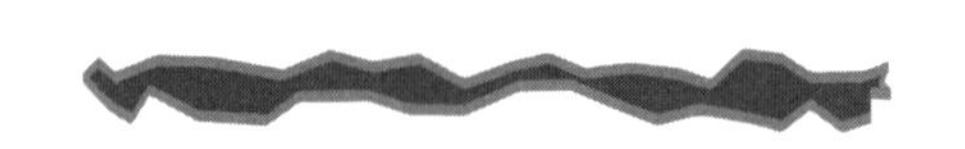

BIBLE LESSON DANIEL

"... you will receive power when the Holy Spirit comes on you; and you will be my witnesses in Jerusalem, and in all Judea and Samaria, and to the ends of the earth." (Acts 1:8, New International Version)

Daniel, as we know by now, is a long way from home. He is serving God in Babylon and, because he trusts God, God has placed him in a very important position.

This is a great way to be a witness – a witness is someone who shows people the love of God. Daniel has been placed in a position of responsibility and he is using this position to show the love of God. He is making sure that the things that God sees as good, such as love, kindness, doing the right thing, etc., happen.

Daniel had literally been given the job of prime minister in Babylon. But Daniel used his position to stand for God, to stand up for the things that are important to God.

One day we too might be in important positions, and we too can use these positions to make sure that things that God sees as important are the things that happen. You may become teachers, magistrates, church leaders, politicians – one of you may even become prime minister. God wants us to use these positions for good.

Before you get old enough to have a job you might still hold positions of responsibility in your school; you might be a class leader. In your club you might be a junior leader. It's very important that we use all these positions for God.

Illustration 1

Target

Object needed: *A map of your city.*

Today's Bible Text isn't trying to tell us all to catch an aeroplane to Jerusalem. Instead, God wanted to tell his disciples something very

important. He wanted them to know that even though they would start their work in Jerusalem, i.e. exactly where they were, he didn't want them to stay there. He wanted them to start there, but make sure that they told everyone outside of there as well. So they were to show people in Jerusalem the love of God, but they were to also show his love to people in Judea and Samaria and to those all over the world.

There is something else we need to see. The verse doesn't mean that we start in Jerusalem and then when we go to Judea we stop telling people in Jerusalem. It means that we start where we're at, but make sure we tell as many people as possible about God.

So what does that mean for us? Here's a map of our city/town/village. We are to tell people about God here where we live. But we don't just tell people here; we could later tell people about God in different parts of the country. We make sure that we tell people here, and then in other parts of our country and then in other parts of Europe, and then maybe all over the world.

Being Witnesses

Object needed: *A picture of Mother Teresa.*

Showing the love of God to those at home and those in other countries isn't just about preaching and telling others about Jesus. There are many ways to show people the love of God. Mother Teresa spent much of her life in Calcutta, India, feeding the poor. She looked after children who had no parents and cared for people who needed help. Many people became Christians – they gave their lives to Jesus – not because someone told them about Jesus, but because they saw the love of God through Mother Teresa and the other nuns who worked with her.

It's not just about us telling people about Jesus. It's about us showing the love of God. We do this when we help others out, when we volunteer to mow the lawn in an old person's garden, when we offer to wash a disabled person's car. There are many ways to be witnesses for Jesus.

Some of the missionaries we've talked about run orphanages, some work with street children, some run colleges; there are many different ways to show God's love. It's important to use as many as possible.

From Here To There

Object needed: *A sign with the words "You are now entering the mission field" and a map of the world.*

Display the sign.

One church used to have this sign above the doors of the church, on the inside. It was there to remind people of something very important. It was there to remind them that mission isn't just what happens in countries far away. It is also something that should happen as soon as we leave the church. One person put it like this: "Missions start with the nearest person who doesn't know Jesus and end with the furthest person away who doesn't know Jesus."

Display the map.

So here it is. We are to be witnesses for Jesus to the person who is closest to us who doesn't know Jesus. Now that could be a person in this building, or a person in the house next door, but that's where missions begin. Now where would be the furthest-away person? I guess for us it would be someone in New Zealand or Australia. But all these countries in between also have people who need to hear about the love of God and see the love of God.

So there's the deal: to show Jesus to the person who is closest and to the person furthest away, and everyone in between.

● STORY – Hudson Taylor (3)

Long before Hudson Taylor ever left to go to China he had started to be a witness for Jesus – he had already begun telling and showing others the love of God.

Hudson had learnt very early on to trust God for everything he had – including money – but this wasn't always easy. Sometimes it's not easy serving God, or showing others the love of God.

When Hudson was in his late teens he came to the point where he had only one coin left in the whole world. Let's say it was a £2 coin – although the money he used was different from ours. It wasn't much, but it would probably buy him some food for the next day or two. It was a Sunday, so he attended church in the morning as he always had done and then, as had become his habit, he spent the afternoon and evening holding church services in the poorer parts of Hull. Just after he had finished his final church service, about ten o'clock, a man who was obviously very poor came to Hudson and asked him if he would come and pray for his wife, for she was dying. Hudson, although feeling tired, agreed readily. He began to follow the man into the poorest parts of Hull.

On the journey Hudson asked the man why he hadn't gone to his own minister, and the man responded that he had done that, but his own minister wouldn't come without payment and he didn't have any money. Hudson then asked the man why he hadn't gone to the authorities. The man responded that he had done that also, but they would not come until the morning, by which time he was sure his wife would be dead.

Hudson thought about the £2 coin in his pocket and wondered if he should give it to the man, who was obviously in need. Then he remembered his own empty cupboards at home. If he gave away the coin, how would he eat tomorrow? The situation seemed even worse when they turned into one of the roughest parts of Hull. Hudson had been there before and had tried to tell the people about Jesus. They had responded by driving him out of the area, ripping up his books and telling him that if he ever came back, he would be seriously hurt. Hudson followed the man deeper into the town.

Eventually they came to a rundown house and together the two men climbed the stairs into a wretched home. The man opened the door. There stood five frightened children, relieved to see their father home. But Hudson noticed that their cheeks were drawn with constant and prolonged starvation. He looked to the corner where the mother lay. Beside her, moaning, was a newly born baby. Hudson felt the £2 coin in his pocket and knew he could help this family by giving it. But instead he began to speak comforting words about God and how much he loved them.

You see, there are times to speak, but there are also times to help people practically. And this was not a time for words.

Hudson continued to speak, but all the time he was feeling more hypocritical and bad. He then proceeded to pray for the woman and the child but all the time he knew that this family needed more than his prayers. Eventually Hudson stood to leave and the man thanked him for being so kind as to come; he was sure now that his wife would die in peace and go to be with God. Hudson felt a lump in his throat. He reached his hand into his pocket and slowly pulled out the coin. He handed it to the man. As he handed the man the coin, Hudson said this: "Sir, you probably think that I am rich and passing you this coin is of no importance to me. You are wrong; this is my last money. But God wants you to have it because he really does love you."

The man took the coin and Hudson left. The guilt had gone. He felt nothing but joy inside, despite the fact that he had nothing to buy food with. Hudson began to sing a song of praise to God as he walked. And before he went to bed that night he asked God to forgive him for being so slow to part with the coin.

The story could end there, but I guess you, like me, would like to know what Hudson did for food the next day, now that he had nothing.

The following morning Hudson got up to eat his last bowl of porridge. As he was eating, a knock came at the door. Hudson went and took delivery of a package. As he opened the package he found a pair of gloves. "Who is sending me gloves?" he thought. He tried to read the label, but he couldn't work out who had sent the parcel. But as he began to open the package, there onto the floor fell a coin – a coin worth four times what he had given to the poor family.

If we learn to be missionaries for God both here and abroad, then God will look after us. He always will. We just need to do what God wants.

The Journey Begins: Leaving Things Behind

	Programme	Item
Section 1	**Welcome**	
	Rules	
	Prayer	
	Introductory Praise	
	Game 1	Numbers
	Praise	
	Fun Item 1	
	Game 2	What To Take
	Fun Item 2	
	Bible Text	Philippians 3:13
	Announcements	
	Interview	
Section 2 Preaching Time	**Worship Time**	
	Bible Lesson	Daniel
	Illustration 1	Baggage
	Illustration 2	Travelling Light
	Illustration 3	Memory
	Story	Hudson Taylor (4)
	Prayer	

Overview Even when it was eventually time for Hudson to leave, it wasn't easy. Hudson had to say goodbye to a lot of things. He had to say goodbye to his mother and his sisters; he had to leave many important things behind, things he loved. It was time to travel light.

games

Numbers

PREPARATION Photocopy a list of 20 numbers, for example, 20, 7, 30, 12, 4, 18, etc.

PLAYERS Four players per team.

SET-UP Players stand at A. The numbers are placed at B.

OBJECT The team runs from A to B in relay formation. The player collects a number and then returns. The players can go as often as they want. There is a two-minute deadline. At the end of the two minutes the numbers collected by the team are added together.

WINNING The team with the score closest to 100 wins. However, if a team exceeds 100, the team is disqualified. The point is this: it was the numbers that were left behind that helped the team win.

What To Take

PREPARATION Items you might need for the Sahara, Antarctica, etc. For example, a woolly hat, a set of skis, a sun hat, sun cream, a mosquito net.

PLAYERS Three players from each team.

SET-UP The items are placed at B. The players stand at A.

OBJECT The Games Master shouts the names of various countries. The players decide which items they need in that country and collect them from B. Include places such as Greenland and Iceland just to make things difficult.

WINNING The team to get the most right wins.

Preaching Time

BIBLE LESSON DANIEL

"I forget what is behind, and I struggle for what is ahead." (Philippians 3:13)

Remember: Daniel was taken away from his home when he was only a boy by the Babylonian army. Three times every day Daniel would come to his room in Babylon. He would open his windows in the direction of Jerusalem and he would kneel and pray. Every day Daniel would think of the country where he was born. He might have remembered the streets he used to play in as a boy. He might have thought of his mother and his father. He might have remembered his home so far away.

You can imagine what Daniel felt, how he would have longed for his home. But even though Daniel thought about his home, he knew that he had work to do in Babylon. The apostle Paul said today's Bible Text. He was determined not to spend his time looking into the past; instead he would keep going forward to discover all that God had for him. Daniel too looked forward. He remembered where he had come from, but he pushed on to be everything God wanted him to be. He would do whatever God wanted in this strange land.

Illustration 1

Baggage

Object needed: *A suitcase.*

Once when I was a student I had come home for half term, and now it was time to go back to college. I'd had a brilliant idea. I was going to take all my weightlifting gear back to college with me. So I collected my college clothes and packed them into a suitcase. I put all my weightlifting stuff into a sports bag, put my weightlifting bar – a two-metre bar – over my shoulder, and set off.

Now it was 200 miles to the college. I went two miles in a bus and then changed to another bus. I went another nine miles on a different bus. I then caught a train and changed trains in three different stations. I then got to a bus station and travelled another fifteen miles to a little village quite close to the college. The whole way, I'd been carrying my weights and my suitcase and my metal bar. I was exhausted.

I had three miles left to go to get to the college and I was feeling very tired. To make things worse, there were no buses left. I had to walk the last part. I walked for two miles and my legs were aching, my shoulder was sore, my arms felt stretched and I couldn't go any further. I had to hide all my things behind a tree and walk to the college. When I got to the college I had to ask someone with a car to drive back and collect my things.

There was no way I could complete the journey while I carried all those things. There was no way Daniel could be used by God if he only thought about Jerusalem. Hudson Taylor would never be any good in China if he didn't give up some things. And you too may have some things that you need to give up, perhaps some habits that you may have which you know are wrong. It's time to drop the things that stop us being and doing what God wants.

Illustration 2

Travelling Light

Object needed: *A person dressed in athletic gear but carrying two suitcases.*

This is a sight you don't see in too many athletic stadiums. Who knows that this person is not going to win too many races? He's carrying too many things he's not supposed to have.

"Hey, mate! If you would like to have a chance of winning the race, you have to leave those things behind."

It's not the things that we take with us that allow us to win the race. Sometimes it's what we leave behind.

Memory

Object needed: *A picture of a brain.*

Our memories contain all sorts of amazing things. I suppose if we could dig way back into them we might even be able to remember being born. Our memories contain all sorts of nice things: our best birthday parties, picnics in the park, games on the beach. But it's also possible that our memories contain all sorts of bad things: the first time we felt sad, the first time we had an argument with our best friend.

What we must learn is that our memories remember things from the past. And while that's a good thing – we are supposed to learn from our past – we cannot live in the past.

Paul, who wrote today's Bible Text, understood this. That's why he said we had to forget what is behind and press on towards what is ahead. What we are going to do should be more exciting and more amazing than what we have already done. If you are a Christian, that's definitely what should be happening – we will do greater things for God today than we did yesterday – God always leads us forward and doesn't make us live in the past.

● STORY – Hudson Taylor (4)

You will need two L-shaped pieces of card to help tell this part of the story.

Finally, on Monday September 19th 1853, the little three-masted clipper *Dumfries*, weighing less than 500 tons, slipped quietly out of Liverpool harbour with Taylor aboard, bound for China. He was just 21 years old. He had spent time praying with his mother before the ship set off. She had tried to be strong for the sake of her son, but just as the ship was about to leave she had burst into uncontrollable crying. She waved goodbye to her son and then he was gone.

The *Dumfries* took quite a battering on its way round the coast but eventually the ship reached calmer water and Hudson, for the first time on his hectic journey, was able to think. Two main thoughts would have come into his mind, two thoughts he would have to consider and deal with before he reached China. These two **L** shapes will help us to share Hudson's thoughts.

The first **L** is for love. Hudson would think about those he loved. Hudson would have thought of his mother, whom he had left crying on the shores of England, and also he would have thought of Marianne Vaughan. Hudson had fallen in love with Marianne when he first heard her playing the piano. He wanted to marry her; he had spent some time getting to know Marianne, and eventually asked Marianne's father for permission to marry his daughter. Hudson was surprised by the response: "Hudson, I would gladly allow you to marry my daughter, if you weren't going to China." So Hudson didn't marry Marianne – he went to China instead.

He had to leave all his **L**oves behind *(throw the first* **L** *away).*

This second **L** isn't an **L** at all. If I turn it slightly, any Australian could tell me what this is. Yes, a boomerang. Does anyone know the special thing that boomerangs do? Yes, they always come back. Hudson would have thought to himself: "I will probably never see England again. I may never come back."

Hudson had to drop this **L** as well *(throw the second* **L** *away).*

To do what God wanted him to do, Hudson had to leave behind those he loved and all his chances of coming back. But still he went.

To serve God we need to leave behind things that hold us back.

Problems To Be Faced

	Programme	Item
Section 1	**Welcome**	
	Rules	
	Prayer	
	Introductory Praise	
	Game 1	Keep Going
	Praise	
	Fun Item 1	
	Game 2	Piggyback Race
	Fun Item 2	
	Bible Text	Philippians 3:14
	Announcements	
	Interview	
Section 2	**Worship Time**	
Preaching	**Bible Lesson**	Daniel
Time	**Illustration 1**	William Booth
	Illustration 2	Rugby
	Illustration 3	Mount Everest
	Story	Hudson Taylor (5)
	Prayer	

Once again we come to one of the most important themes of scripture: perseverance. When all else is stripped away, the difference between greatness and mediocrity is simple – mediocre people quit just a bit too early.

Keep Going

PREPARATION	You will need an assortment of objects such as tennis balls, basketballs, footballs, uni hoc sticks, etc.
PLAYERS	One player per team.
SET-UP	Player stands at A. All the equipment is at B.
OBJECT	The player runs from A to B and collects an item – given to them by their team leader. They then return to A and then back to B for another item. As soon as they drop an item, they are out.
WINNING	The team left in at the end wins.

Piggyback Race

PREPARATION	None.
PLAYERS	Two players from each team.
SET-UP	The lighter person must "piggy-back" the heavier.
OBJECT	The pair race from A to B and then back. They keep going for ten laps.
WINNING	The first team to complete ten laps wins. If a player is dropped, the team is out.

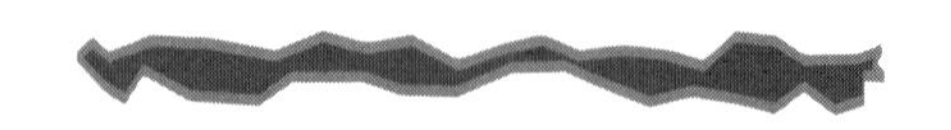

BIBLE LESSON DANIEL

"I press on towards the goal to win the prize for which God has called me."
(Philippians 3:14, New International Version)

In Daniel chapter 10 there is a very unusual account. Daniel meets face to face with a man, but clearly he is more than a man; he is an angel. Here's a description of him. He was...

> ... dressed in linen and wearing a solid gold belt. His body was like a precious stone, his face like lightning, his eyes like flaming fires, his arms and legs like polished bronze.

The angel unfolded to Daniel a strange story. The angel told Daniel that as soon as Daniel had prayed he had set out from God with an answer to his prayers. But on the way he had been prevented from continuing by an angel of the devil – called the prince of Persia. The angel told Daniel that he was unable to proceed until God sent Michael, a warrior angel, to move the prince of Persia aside.

Daniel might have thought that God wasn't hearing his prayers. But that wasn't the case; his prayers had been heard, but the answer was slow in coming. Daniel might have chosen to give up, thinking no answer would come. But Daniel wasn't like that. He kept on praying and asking God until the angel eventually brought the answer.

Now we may not be visited by an angel, but we to need to learn to keep going, to persevere.

William Booth

Object needed: *William Booth's words on acetate.*

Evangelism takes a "courageous patience" and a settled persistence of vision. Such was the battle cry of William Booth. He said this:

> While women weep, as they do now, I'll fight. While little children go hungry, as they do now, I'll fight. While men go to prison, in and out, in and out, as they do now, I'll fight.
>
> While there is a poor lost girl upon the streets, while there remains one dark soul without the light of God, I'll fight.
>
> I'll fight to the very end.

This is the sort of person God is looking for. He wants people like William Booth who will keep going, no matter what.

Rugby

Object needed: *A clip of a piece of sport footage where the underdogs win. Adapt the account.*

The following is an account of a rugby game between Wales and England played in March 1999.

> England came storming back, and a strong forward movement resulted in the Welsh being caught offside, and Wilkinson made the kick from just outside the 22-yard line. The score became England 31, Wales 25.
>
> But England, who had looked so dominant in the early part of the game, began to creak, however, with Howarth and Jenkins sending England back into their half with some superbly angled kicks.
>
> After another impressive penalty from Wilkinson, Jason Leonard was then shown the yellow card for a late tackle on Howarth.
>
> With just 15 minutes of the match remaining and the score still at England 31, Wales 25, England moved a quick ball from left to right, and Matt Perry seemed certain to put the match beyond Wales' reach, until he dropped the ball just five yards from the line.
>
> Only six points behind, Wales undoubtedly sensed victory, running every opportunity they had – only to be confronted by a wall of white shirts... That is, until Scott Gibbs tore through the England defence in a remarkable solo break to touch down just to the right of the posts. The score was now England 31, Wales 30. It left Neil Jenkins the unenviable task of having to convert the final kick of the game.
>
> Welsh fans need not have worried. The Pontypridd man, who then boasted more than 750 international points, never looked like missing.
>
> And when the final whistle blew it was England 31, Wales 32. All of Wales celebrated.

It's important for us to learn that even when things look as if they are over, even when we think we've lost, if we keep going, it might just happen: we *can* win.

Mount Everest

Object needed: *A picture of Mount Everest.*

George Leigh Mallory was a famous explorer and mountain climber. He was the man who, when asked why he wanted to climb Everest, responded: "Because it's there". He had tried to climb Everest on several occasions, but the huge mountain had always managed to beat him.

On one occasion Mallory was asked to make a speech at a special dinner. The dinner was to commemorate the brave men who had died trying to climb the mountain. During the end-of-dinner speech, Mallory looked at the pictures of Mount Everest on the walls. As he looked at them he said these words: "Everest, you have beaten us once, and, Everest, you have beaten us twice, but, Everest, you need to know that there will come a time when we will beat you. For, Everest, you can't get any bigger, but we can."

Mallory knew that as long as we keep learning and trying, we will eventually win.

● STORY – Hudson Taylor (5)

Hudson experienced some exciting things on his first visit to China. He saw people come to know Jesus, he found a wife and he explored much of the undiscovered part of the country. His first two children were also born there.

He also experienced some great difficulties. The people who sent him didn't send him enough money to survive, many of the other missionaries didn't like Hudson's custom of dressing like the Chinese, and the way he wore his hair with a pigtail at the back caused them immense annoyance. Some of Hudson's friends had died of diseases contracted in China, his good friend Peter had drowned in front of his very eyes, and the wife of his good friend Dr Parker had died of cholera. The sister of Hudson's wife Maria had also died.

Hudson had also contracted a disease which left him very weak. By 1860 Hudson was too weak to remain in China and he and his new wife, Maria, had to return home. It had cost Hudson greatly to go to China and speak of Jesus. But he went as God had asked. Sometimes we have to pay a great price to serve Jesus – but still we go.

Six years after he came back to England, on May 26th 1866, Hudson, his wife Maria and their four children returned to China, taking 26 new missionaries – people determined to tell the Chinese about Jesus – with them. It seems amazing that the place where Hudson had seen so many difficulties, the place where Hudson had seen so much death, was the very place that he was quick to return to. And not only did he return, but he brought 26 other missionaries to help. The missionaries called themselves the China Inland Mission, and so they journeyed to tell the Chinese about Jesus.

The same pattern would quickly begin to emerge. They would find great things taking place. People were giving their lives to Jesus, new churches and hospitals were started, the great things that God was doing through Hudson Taylor and the people of the China Inland Mission affected many lives. But there were also difficulties.

Many of the other missionaries still didn't approve of Hudson's habit of dressing in Chinese robes and particularly didn't approve of him letting women do the frontline work of missionaries. But Hudson remained strong in his purpose. Two of the missionaries who had travelled to China with Hudson were Lewis and Eliza Nicol. They too had received criticism for their habit of wearing Chinese dress, and they too had faced many difficulties.

Lewis Nicol and a Chinese man who had given his life to Jesus – Tsiu Wen-li – had started to take church services in a place called Siashom. They had moved onto the streets to tell the people about Jesus. But one evening the town leader and 50 soldiers barged into the Nicols' home. Seizing Tsiu, they beat him, hit him with whips and rods and left him half dead on the ground. They then turned to Lewis and announced: "If you are not out of here by tomorrow you will be beheaded."

Hudson Taylor and Lewis Nicol both faced difficulties doing what God had called them to do. They were both criticised, they were both threatened and they both watched loved ones experiencing great pain. Hudson knew that God had called him, he knew what he should do, and with raw perseverance and courage he kept going. Two years after their arrival, the Nicols went back home!

Will we be like Hudson Taylor or will we be like Lewis Nicol? Will we be bold enough to do what God has called us to do, or will we go back?

Hudson Taylor kept going so that he could see the great things that God would do in China.

6 Over To You

	Programme	Item
Section 1	Welcome	
	Rules	
	Prayer	
	Introductory Praise	
	Game 1	Relay Race
	Praise	
	Fun Item 1	
	Game 2	Relay Race Connect
	Fun Item 2	
	Bible Text	Matthew 28:18
	Announcements	
	Interview	
Section 2 Preaching Time	Worship Time	
	Bible Lesson	Daniel
	Illustration 1	God's Hall of Fame
	Illustration 2	Baton
	Illustration 3	If Not You, Who?
	Story	Hudson Taylor (6)
	Prayer	

Overview Hudson Taylor did an amazing job in China. Through his life and ministry many people came to Jesus, but there came a point when his life was nearly over. Who would continue what he had begun? Hudson had no fear; he had trained many missionaries to continue the work.

games

Game 1

Relay Race

PREPARATION	A relay baton per team (a banana or cucumber will do).
PLAYERS	Five players per team.
SET-UP	Players stand at A, the first player holding the baton.
OBJECT	The game takes the form of a straight relay race. The first person runs from A to B and then back. On their return they pass the "baton" to the next player.
WINNING	The team that returns first wins. But if the baton is dropped, the team is disqualified.

Game 2

Relay Race Connect

PREPARATION	As for Game 1, but each team will need four batons (bananas or cucumbers).
PLAYERS	Five players from each team.
SET-UP	As for Game 1, except that the first four will need batons.
OBJECT	The first person races from A to B holding the baton. On their return the next player takes hold of the baton and then sets off from A to B and back. On their return, the next player holding a baton connects – and so it continues until all five players run round together.
WINNING	The first team back wins.

Preaching Time

BIBLE LESSON DANIEL

"Therefore go and make disciples of all nations." (Matthew 28:19)

God showed Daniel some amazing things that would happen on the earth and Daniel did some amazing things in his life. But at the end of his life Daniel asked God what would become of him. God said to him, "You will rest, and at the end of time you will rise from death to receive your reward."

Daniel would join his ancestors. He was not unique. He had served God. He had done some amazing things for God, but he was only a part of the line. Since the dawn of time amazing people had done amazing things for an amazing God. People like:

- Abraham, who left his home and began an amazing journey because God said so
- Noah, who built a huge boat before the world had ever seen rain*
- Joseph the young dreamer, who became the commander of Egypt
- Moses, who led an entire nation to the Promised Land
- Ruth, who served God so well she became the great-great-great...gran of Jesus
- Joshua, who fought bravely for God and won the Promised Land
- Deborah, who led and commanded Israel to great victory
- Samson, who was the strongest man who ever lived
- David, the man after God's own heart, who loved God greatly

And the line wouldn't end with Daniel. The list continues:

- Jesus, who died to take away our sins
- Peter, who walked on water
- Paul, who planted churches all over the world

---

* According to my belief in the "canopy theory" – you can check it out on the Internet or purchase a book on the flood to explore this theory.

God's Hall of Fame

Object needed: *Pictures of the following people, if possible.*

The list of God's great people doesn't end there. It continued with people like:

- David Livingstone, who travelled to Africa to tell the people there about a God of love
- Amy Carmichael, who left her home in Ireland to tell the children of India about a God of love
- Gladys Aylward, who also went to China to tell the Chinese about a God of love

The list continues right up until today. Will the list end? Or are there people here who will join this long, exciting line of amazing people, who will do amazing things for an amazing God?

Baton

Object needed: *A picture of an athlete – maybe carrying a baton.*

The 4x400 metre relay race is one of the highlights of the modern Olympics. Four runners take it in turns to run for their country: Americans, Russians, Chinese, French, British. The first runner for each country stands at the starting line. The gun goes off; the race commences.

The first runner runs the first 400 metres, at which point they pass the baton to the next runner. The next runner hands it to the next and so it continues to the final runner. The first team to the finish line wins the gold medal. But of course there is a rule, a rather special rule. If at any point the baton is dropped, then the race is over.

God too has a set of "runners", each one with a job to do, a role to play. Each one is commissioned to run. They have a specific task that God has given them, and their purpose at the end of the race is to pass the role on to the next person. But the same special rule applies: if the baton is dropped, then it's all over. Our job right now is to get hold of that baton. Let's find out what God wants us to do and run with it. Then in times to come it will be our job to pass it on to the next runner.

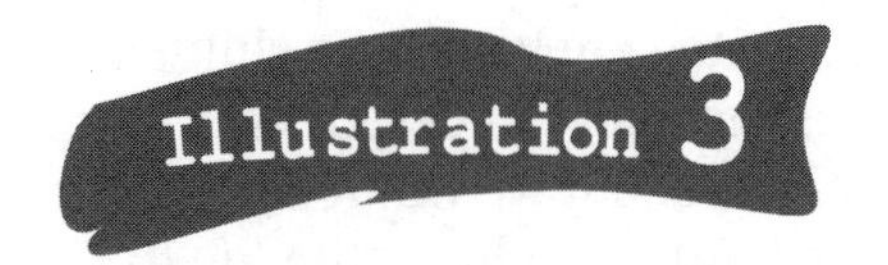

If Not You, Who?

Object needed: *A picture of Tiananmen Square.*

In 1989 the world stared in disbelief at an incident which took place in China, the Tiananmen Square protest. It was the culmination of a series of student-led demonstrations in China. The Chinese government refused to listen to the students, who simply wanted to be heard. They wanted every person in China to be allowed to vote for their own leaders – much as we do in this country. The government threatened violence. But one student stood in front of the rest and said these now famous words: "If not us, then who? If not now, then when?"

On May 4th 1989, approximately 100,000 students and workers marched in Beijing. The protesters continued their demonstrations during a visit by Soviet premier Mikhail Gorbachev later that month. On May 20th, the government ordered troops to Tiananmen Square. On June 3rd 1989, the People's Liberation Army brutally crushed the supporters, killing hundreds of students, injuring another 10,000, and arresting hundreds of others.

Many died, but the students struck a strong blow against the way the Chinese government treated people. They were a radical group of young people willing to do anything. That's what God wants. That's what God is asking you: If not you, then who? If not now, then when? We're looking for people who will take the baton and do what God wants.

● STORY – Hudson Taylor (6)

By the late 1880s, Hudson Taylor's vision had begun to ignite imaginations all across the world. In 1888 Taylor visited Canada, and, wherever he preached, young people offered themselves as missionaries to China. Taylor had been opposed to the idea of establishing a branch of the China Inland Mission in North America but now grew convinced that it was God's will. By the time his visit was finished, over 40 men and women had applied to join the CIM.

Just after Taylor died, a young Chinese evangelist looked upon his body and summed up Taylor's most important legacy: "Dear and venerable pastor, we too are your little children. You opened for us the road to heaven. We do not want to bring you back, but we will follow you."

Hudson Taylor had given his entire life to telling people in China about Jesus, so it was probably only fitting that he be buried there among the people who lived there. Over a hundred years have passed since Hudson started his amazing work, but many people in China are still desperate for people to go and tell them about a God who loves them – and not just in China but also all over the world. Who will go? Who will tell them?

Probably the first person to give his life to Jesus on hearing Hudson in China was a man named Nyi. Hudson had been preaching and telling people about Jesus for quite some time and it seemed as if nothing was happening. The Chinese were happy to listen, but they were very reluctant to believe. And then one day, after Hudson had been talking about Jesus for several years without seeing anyone turn to God, a man stood up in one of his meetings and announced: "I have spent many years searching for the truth, but never found it. I have tried Confucianism, Taoism, Buddhism and many other religions, but have never found the truth. But tonight I have heard the truth for the first time."

The man was Nyi, and that night he gave his life to Jesus. He proved how serious he was because several days later he stood in a Buddhist temple to tell the other Buddhists what he had done. Hudson was overjoyed at seeing Nyi becoming a Christian, but something Nyi said disturbed Hudson greatly. One day Nyi asked: "Hudson, how long have you had the truth in your country?" Hudson knew that there had been Christians in Britain for well over a thousand years, and explained this to Nyi.

"Well then, Hudson," Nyi asked, "why has it taken so long to bring the truth to us? If you had come earlier, my grandfather and my father could have heard the truth before they died." Hudson didn't have an answer. He just knew that he must take the truth to every part of China.

If you are a Christian today, then you have this truth. Who will be the new missionaries to touch our world for Jesus? Will it be you? You see, many missionaries who eventually went out to serve Jesus decided they were going to do it at a very young age. Now listen to the whispers from ages gone by. People like Hudson Taylor who went to China, David Livingstone who went to Africa, Amy Carmichael who went to India... Their voices are whispering to us from the past. Who will go now? Who will go now?

When Hudson Taylor died he left 800 CIM missionaries working alongside 2,000 Chinese pastors, teachers and evangelists in China. His was a life that counted!

FIG LEAF PHIL

A Series in Five Parts

Introduction

Title	Themes covered
1 Risks	**What risks are worth taking and what risks are not**
2 The Value Of A Life	**We sometimes forget how valuable we truly are; Purchased at such a great price.**
3 The Test Of A Person	**We never really know what a person is like until they are under pressure or things are going wrong. It's quite a test.**
4 God Heals	**We serve a supernatural God. We must keep emphasising this in our secularised world.**
5 A Job To Finish	**God started a work in us that he intends to finish; however, he also wants to give us a job that he wants us to finish.**

We have spent some time looking at Paul in a previous series ("The Example of Paul", *Fusion*, Volume 1). This series homes in on a more specific period in the life of the apostle and focuses on his shipwrecked adventures in Malta. It opens up a wide variety of teaching themes and also allows us the scope to run sideline themes for crafts with desert-island ideas, and also to decorate the venue in desert-island style.

The Story looks at a man by the name of Captain Philip, who later becomes Fig Leaf Phil.

1 Risks

	Programme	Item
Section 1	**Welcome**	
	Rules	
	Prayer	
	Introductory Praise	
	Game 1	Wheelbarrow Races
	Praise	
	Fun Item 1	
	Game 2	Piggyback Races
	Fun Item 2	
	Bible Text	Ephesians 5:16
	Announcements	
	Interview	
Section 2	**Worship Time**	
Preaching	**Bible Lesson**	Paul Is Shipwrecked
Time	**Illustration 1**	Risk And Reward
	Illustration 2	We Take These Risks...
	Illustration 3	Blomgren And The Wheelbarrow
	Story	Fig Leaf Phil (1)
	Prayer	

What risks are worth taking and what risks are not? Jesus asks us to take a risk and follow him, but is this really a risk? When we look at the person asking us to follow him, he can be trusted and therefore there is no real risk.

Wheelbarrow Races

PREPARATION	None needed.
PLAYERS	Three per team and a leader.
SET-UP	The players line up at A.
OBJECT	The leader takes the legs of the first player and "wheelbarrows" them from A to B and back. The players then swap.
WINNING	The first team to complete the game and sit down wins.

Piggyback Races

PREPARATION	None needed.
PLAYERS	Three per team and a leader.
SET-UP	The players line up at A.
OBJECT	The leader "piggybacks" the first player from A to B and back. The players then swap.
WINNING	The first team to complete the game and sit down wins.

Preaching Time

BIBLE LESSON PAUL IS SHIPWRECKED

"Making the most of every opportunity, because the days are evil." (Ephesians 5:16, New International Version)

Paul was an apostle, a servant of Jesus and a very good man. However, because he lived at a time when some people hated Christians he had been arrested. Simply for believing what he believed, he was being sent to Rome to be tried by the Roman emperor in a court.

Paul had never done anything particularly wrong. He had only stood up for Jesus. He had only proclaimed that Jesus was the Son of God. He had simply told people the truth.

Sometimes, standing up for the truth is not easy. And sometimes giving your life to Jesus is also not easy. It takes courage. Although most of us will never be arrested for being a Christian, there is often a price to pay.

Friends may mock, people may not understand, even some of your parents may not understand. Being a Christian is often difficult. Paul had been placed on a ship and, although he was being treated kindly, the ship itself was being tossed and turned and thrown all over the place by enormous winds. The ship was going to lead Paul into an adventure – an adventure he would never have had if he wasn't a Christian.

And that really is the balancing fact. Sometimes being a Christian can be difficult, but it is always exciting.

Illustration 1

Risk And Reward

Object needed: *Two chairs and the soundtrack of* Who Wants To Be A Millionaire?*

Play a brief version of your chosen quiz game.

Whenever I watch this programme it always puts me on the edge of my seat. The contestant has already won so much, they are so incredibly better off than they were at the start of the show, and now they have to make a decision. Do they walk away with all that cash, or do they risk it all on the outcome of the final question? "What part of the body does the term 'cardia' refer to?" "Who was the tenth king of England?" "Where are the Niagara Falls?"

If the person gets it right, then they take a huge amount of cash away. If they get it wrong, then they walk away with nothing. We take big risks because we believe there will be big rewards if we do so. The key is to know when to take the risk, when to take a chance. Unfortunately, that choice is always up to the contestant.

This evening I may be asking you to take a risk. Whether you take it or not will be up to you.

We Take These Risks...

Object needed: *An OHP showing the words "We take these risks not to escape life but to stop life escaping us."*

I have these words written on my Bible. They are taken from a series of posters called "No Fear". They show men jumping off huge cliff faces into the waiting sea below; they show women climbing up sheer cliff faces; they show countless people on surfboards riding inside waves. They are full of amazing people doing amazing things. They are full of people taking risks.

Today I want to tell you that there is a God who loves you passionately and unconditionally, a God who sent his own Son Jesus to die on a cross to be punished for the wrong things you have done. A God who wants to forgive all the wrong things you've done, a God who will give you a reason to live if you just ask him.

But when it comes down to it, you have to take a risk. You have to take a chance. Are you going to take a chance of asking God to forgive the wrong things you have done, or are you not?

Blomgren And The Wheelbarrow

Object needed: *A picture of a wheelbarrow.*

Blomgren wavered on his tightrope, then he regained his balance. He had done it so many times. The great Blomgren continued to the other side. He had walked on his tightrope back and forth across the Niagara Falls on various occasions. But today he was going to do a new thing: the world-renowned Blomgren was going to walk across the falls with a person in a wheelbarrow in front of him.

Eventually a volunteer came forward, He reluctantly stepped into the wheelbarrow and now Blomgren walked towards the tightrope. They were more than halfway across now and everything was going very well. The man in the

---

* The particular quiz programme is not important. Any can be inserted as long as they offer the contestant a choice of taking the prizes/money or risking it all for a bigger bet prize/money.

barrow felt very relaxed. Men and women on the other side had been making bets, and money had been changing hands. Several people had bet a lot of money on Blomgren and his new-found assistant toppling out of the barrow to their deaths below. However, when it looked as if Blomgren would undoubtedly make it, one of the gamblers took matters into his own hands and cut through one of the holding ropes. The tightrope was no longer tight and began to swing wildly. Blomgren and his companion swayed this way and then the other. The man in the barrow panicked and started to scream.

Then Blomgren, his voice like thunder, commanded the man to be quiet. The expert who had crossed this rope would do it again. He said to the man, "Take my hand. If you want to live, take my hand. Step out of the barrow." The man did as he was told and the barrow toppled to the rocks below, shattering into a thousand pieces.

"Now look at me," said Blomgren. The man fixed his eyes on Blomgren. There they stood, two men thousands of metres above the rocks.

"Now walk with me," ordered Blomgren. "Walk when I walk, stop when I stop, be one with me and we will make it."

The expert began his journey. The man copied his step, his eyes locked on the master. One step after another they walked. They would make it across because the man trusted the expert, he trusted the one who had walked this route before.

It is a risk to follow Jesus, but not a great risk. You are trusting in someone who will never let you down, someone who will stand with you in every difficult situation, the author of life, the creator of the universe.

To trust in Jesus is a worthwhile risk.

• STORY – Fig Leaf Phil (1)

Captain Philip Anthony Luke John Hogwash had been captain of the *Jolly Jim* for the last ten years. He had sailed the seven seas. He had carried prime ministers and kings, he had carried dukes and earls and princes and presidents. He had gathered buried treasure and even discovered some countries that had never been visited before.

But right now Captain Philip was in trouble. He was in the most serious storm of his entire life and he was alone. His crew had been in a rowing boat visiting a nearby harbour when the storm had blown up – seemingly from nowhere – and the anchor had broken and the ship had been swept out to sea. Captain Philip had battled hard to steer the ship in some sort of direction. The rain hammered down on him, the wind seemed determined to throw him overboard and eventually he had given up; the ship was being pushed by the wind towards... who knew where.

There was a bright flash and then a crack. Lightning had struck the main sail pole and the pole was toppling towards the ship below. Captain Philip tried to jump aside but he was too slow. He was trapped by the mast.

The ship was heading for some rocks, but Captain Philip was stuck. The ship looked as if it would sink and take Captain Philip with it. He had to do something. He pulled and pulled at his legs, but it wasn't looking good. Then he got out his dagger and began to cut off his lovely leather shoes. He managed to slide his legs out, but the ship was getting closer to the rocks. Captain Phillip stood on the edge of the deck. The rain continued to hammer down, the wind howled and eventually it happened: the ship hit the rocks.

Captain Philip was thrown to the edge rail. He stared into the water below. He had to jump; if he didn't he would go down with the ship. He had to take a risk. If he jumped into the water he might hurt himself, but if he didn't he was sure to drown. Captain Philip jumped. He hit the water very hard. The waves threw him towards the island, where he rolled onto the beach. He was very wet and very cold, his clothes were ripped to shreds and his arm had a nasty gash. But he was alive.

Sometimes we have to take the right risk.

(Next time we'll find out about this strange island.)

2 The Value Of A Life

	Programme	Item
Section 1	**Welcome**	
	Rules	
	Prayer	
	Introductory Praise	
	Game 1	L.I.F.E.
	Praise	
	Fun Item 1	
	Game 2	Giant Smarties Find
	Fun Item 2	
	Bible Text	Romans 5:8
	Announcements	
	Interview	
Section 2	**Worship Time**	
Preaching	**Bible Lesson**	Paul Is Shipwrecked
Time	**Illustration 1**	Albanian Life
	Illustration 2	Lines And Circles
	Illustration 3	What Price A Life?
	Story	Fig Leaf Phil (2)
	Prayer	

We sometimes forget how valuable we truly are, how we were purchased at such a great price by the Son of the King of the universe. Life is one of God's most precious gifts and should be appreciated.

games

L.I.F.E.

PREPARATION	Sheets of paper per team with the following letters written on them: L.I.F.E.
PLAYERS	Four per team.
SET-UP	The players line up at A with a sheet of paper each.
OBJECT	The players are to run from A to B and then place their paper on the floor. The players must then assemble the word "LIFE".
WINNING	The first team with all the sheets lined up to read "LIFE" wins.

Giant Smarties Find

PREPARATION	Five Giant Smarties per team are hidden in a bowl of jelly per team.
PLAYERS	Five per team.
SET-UP	The players line up at A, with the jellies at B.
OBJECT	The team in relay runs from A to B; at B the player gets a Smartie out of the jelly using just a spoon. When the Smartie is rescued the player can return to A.
WINNING	The first team with all the Smarties gone wins.

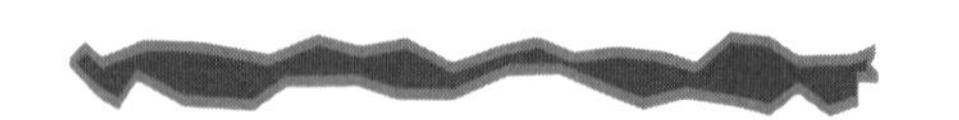

PreachingTime

BIBLE LESSON **PAUL IS SHIPWRECKED**

"But God showed how much he loved us by having Christ die for us, even though we were sinful." (Romans 5:8)

> We went along the island of Cauda on the side that was protected from the wind. We had a hard time holding the lifeboat in place, but finally we got it where it belonged. Then the sailors tied ropes around the ship to hold it together. They lowered the sail and let the ship drift along, because they were afraid it might hit the sandbanks in the gulf of Syrtis.
>
> The storm was so fierce that the next day they threw some of the ship's cargo overboard. Then on the third day, with their bare hands they threw overboard some of the ship's gear. For several days we could not see either the sun or the stars. A strong wind kept blowing, and we finally gave up all hope of being saved.
>
> Since none of us had eaten anything for a long time, Paul stood up and told the men: "… I belong to God, and I worship him. Last night he sent an angel to tell me, 'Paul, don't be afraid! You will stand trial before the Emperor. And because of you, God will save the lives of everyone on the ship.' Cheer up! I am sure that God will do exactly what he promised. But we will first be shipwrecked on some island." (Acts 27:16–26)

Because God valued Paul so much, he would save the whole ship.

Albanian Life

Object needed: *A football.*

(Hold the football up.) This looks harmless enough, doesn't it? You know, God values life very highly indeed. The difficulty is that we

don't value life as much as God does. Some people don't value life at all.

Some people who were working with children in Albania told me this true story: A teenage Albanian boy was playing football in his garden. He kicked the ball too high and it went over the fence and bounced on the windscreen of a Land Rover that was passing by. A father and son were in the Land Rover. They slammed on the brakes and jumped out. The matter was made worse by the fact that the boy whose football it was had already been accused by the father and son of stealing from their fishing nets. The father, the son and the teenager who kicked the ball started to shout at each other.

Then, without warning, the father reached into his Land Rover, grabbed his gun and shot the teenage boy dead. The teenage boy's father saw what happened and rushed to grab his own gun as fast as he could.

The father and son tried to jump into their Land Rover and drive off, but they were too slow. The dead boy's father had got his gun and run to the Land Rover. He shot the two people inside dead.

This tragedy was all because of a football – all because some people have no idea how valuable life is.

Lines And Circles

Object needed: *A piece of string and a hula hoop.*

(Hold the string out.) Some people's life is like this string. It had a beginning and it will have an end. They are born and they will die.

(Hold out the hoop.) Some people's lives are like this hoop. It may have a beginning but it has no end. Some of us were born, but we will live for ever.

What is the difference? People who have asked Jesus to forgive the wrong things they've done, who have given their lives to Jesus – these people will live for ever. They are like the hoop. Those who haven't given their lives to Jesus will not live for ever. They are like the string.

What Price A Life?

Object needed: *Three people with various price labels on each: one saying £100, another saying £10,000 and another saying £1,000,000.*

What is a person really worth? If it were just a case of working out the chemicals inside each person, then it wouldn't come to very much indeed. We'd all be worth about £3.77. But I'm sure you'd all agree that we're all worth more than £3.77. But how much *is* a person worth.

Is Person 1 the right amount? £100 is a lot of money.

Is Person 2 the right amount? £10,000 is definitely a lot of money.

Or maybe Person 3? £1,000,000 is a huge amount of money.

The interesting thing is this: we don't really work out how much a person is worth by what price tag we put on them. We can maybe work out how much a person is worth by finding out how much someone is prepared to pay for them. So, any bids on this first person? Hands up if you want to make a bid!

Lots of answers! Some of them very interesting. But God showed us the real value of a life when he allowed Jesus to die on a cross for the wrong things you've done. God valued you so much he let his only Son die for you. My word, you are more valuable than any amount of money.

I hope you realise how valuable life is, and I hope you realise how valuable you are.

• STORY – Fig Leaf Phil (2)

Captain Philip lay on the sand, trying to catch his breath. Waves still rolled over his body. His trousers were now torn shorts and his shirt was in shreds with no buttons left. He wondered where he was. He tried to sit up, but his body was still very battered and bruised.

Then from the beach he heard some screaming. He turned his head slowly so as not to attract attention. He could just about make out several men chasing a woman across the beach. The woman was dressed in complete contrast to him: she wore a jewelled skirt and a brightly coloured top. The men chasing her, in contrast, wore sandy-coloured clothes that merged in with the sand and each had a round hunter's hat on his head. Each man carried a gun, but nobody was shooting; they wanted to catch this woman alive.

Phil looked on with horror as one of the men threw a net towards the woman, who tripped over and was captured. More men then came, not as well-dressed as the first but certainly not wearing tatters; Phil guessed that they must be the men's servants. The men quickly took the net off the woman and pushed her roughly into a wooden cage. The servants then picked up the cage and set off.

Phil dragged himself to his feet and set off to follow the young woman. His bones ached, his muscles were strained, but he was determined to find out where they were taking her. He dragged himself through thick jungle, twisting his ankle and adding to his pain. In the process, he narrowly escaped being bitten by what was clearly a very poisonous snake that the hunters had disturbed. As night-time fell, he only just stopped himself from falling over a cliff that he hadn't seen. But still he followed the men.

As the darkness began to grip the island the men came to a camp. A high bamboo fence surrounded it, and the gate that marked the entrance was guarded by more of the men's servants. Phil watched from his hiding place, wondering what he could do. If he went down there to that camp, then he could be caught. He had already been through a whole range of dangers to get here in the first place. What a day he was having – shipwrecked and now about to risk his life again to save a woman he had never met!

Phil understood something that many people never do: he understood the value of a life. He understood that all life is important and special. He understood that everyone has the right to live, and he was going to make sure that the woman down there got to live. Life is so incredibly important; don't forget that.

Phil waited until all was quiet and then he made his way down to the camp. Slowly and methodically he began to dig his way under the bamboo until there was a hole big enough for him to drag himself through. He hid in the shadows, moving very slowly and very stealthily for a man with so many bruises. He caught sight of the woman and couldn't believe it: she was completely unguarded. He crept over. She turned her head and was about to scream when Phil lifted his finger to his lips and said: "I've come to save you. Be quiet or we both die."

She obeyed. She didn't know who he was, but he seemed to be her only chance. Slowly, very slowly, the ropes were untied and the pair began to creep back towards the hole. Phil couldn't believe how easy it had been. But the thought came a little too early. As Phil was lowering the woman into the hole he heard an enormous BANG! Pieces of bamboo near his left ear came splintering off, and blood was pouring from his shoulder. Phil had been shot, but it wasn't serious. He dropped into the hole and climbed quickly up the other side. By now the camp was a buzz of activity, all the lights were on, all the men were out and the gates were opened. The men would search all night if necessary.

Phil and the woman ran into the forest as fast as they could. They ran and ran until they could run no further, then they climbed the tallest tree they could find and sat as still as statues. It wasn't long before the men came. They stopped below their tree and looked around. They stood for what seemed like an eternity but eventually they walked on.

Phil and the woman sat on a branch of the tree, shaking. Phil looked at her. "What's your name?" he asked. "And why did those men take you?"

"My name is Tuesday", she responded, "Princess Tuesday. And the men want to capture me because I know the secret."

Phil was too tired to ask what she meant. His shoulder was leaking blood, his bones were aching, he had bruises on his bruises.

And all because he knew the value of a life.

He was on a desert island with Princess Tuesday, who knew "the secret". Men dressed in camouflage were hunting him and his ship was at the bottom of the ocean. With his mind swirling, his thoughts overloading, he passed out and fell out of the tree.

(To be continued…)

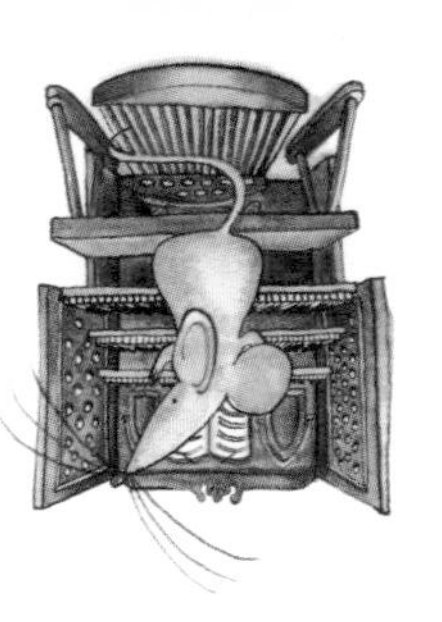

3 The Test Of A Person

	Programme	Item
Section 1	Welcome	
	Rules	
	Prayer	
	Introductory Praise	
	Game 1	Goal
	Praise	
	Fun Item 1	
	Game 2	Headers
	Fun Item 2	
	Bible Text	1 Samuel 16:7
	Announcements	
	Interview	
Section 2 Preaching Time	Worship Time	
	Bible Lesson	Paul Reveals A Snake
	Illustration 1	Diamonds And Coal
	Illustration 2	What's Inside Comes Out
	Illustration 3	Flash Or Burn
	Story	Fig Leaf Phil (3)
	Prayer	

We never really know what a person is like until they are under pressure or things are going wrong. Then it's quite a test.

games

Goal

PREPARATION	A football per team, a set of goals (or two made-up posts), and a goalkeeper.
PLAYERS	Five players per team.
SET-UP	The five players line up in relay formation at A with the front player with the ball. The goals are set up at B with the goalkeeper in position.
OBJECT	To dribble from A to B, and shoot at goal, collect the ball and return to A.
WINNING	The team that scores the most goals after three minutes wins.

Headers

PREPARATION	A football per team and a leader per team who can head the ball.
PLAYERS	Five players per team.
SET-UP	The five players line up in relay formation at A with the front player with the ball. The leaders are at position B.
OBJECT	To run from A to B, and throw the ball to the leader, who heads it back, collect the ball and return to A.
WINNING	The team that gets the most headers after three minutes wins.

Preaching Time

BIBLE LESSON **PAUL REVEALS A SNAKE**

"People judge others by what they look like, but I (God) judge people by what is in their hearts." (1 Samuel 16:7)

Paul and his colleagues had crashed their ship on the shores of Malta. All the sailors were wet and cold after their ordeal, so they lit a fire and tried to get warm. Paul went to collect firewood; he collected bundles of wood – or at least what he thought was wood. It wasn't until he started to put some of the pieces onto the fire that he found out what one of the "sticks" really was.

It's not until we face times of pressure that we find out what we're really like. Or sometimes when things are really tough we find out what our friends are like.

Paul tried to throw what he thought was a stick onto the fire. But the "stick" was a snake and as soon as it felt the heat of the fire it lunged at Paul and bit his arm. We all reveal what we're really like when things get hot, when things are hard. And some of you are like the snake; when things are hard you become nasty.

The amazing thing was that even though the snake was poisonous, God protected Paul and he never even got ill.

Diamonds And Coal

Object needed: *A diamond and a piece of coal.*

These two items are made of exactly the same stuff. They're both made of carbon. They're both made in exactly the same way: they are underground and subjected to massive pressure. The difference between the two is the amount of pressure pushing down on them.

Some people can cope with a small amount of pressure; others can cope with a huge amount of pressure. Some of us get angry and rude and horrible if things get tough or hard; others are able to cope. Some people become nasty under pressure; they're like coal. But diamonds can handle a lot more without being crushed.

Are you like the diamond? Or like the coal?

What's Inside Comes Out

Object needed: *Three cups, one containing blackcurrant squash, one containing orange squash and one containing water.*

Here are three containers full of three different liquids. This one contains blackcurrant squash. When I pour it out, what comes out? Obviously, blackcurrant squash. What's inside is what comes out.

This one contains orange squash. When I pour it out, what comes out? Obviously, orange squash. What's inside is what comes out.

If you tell me you're a Christian, then I expect when things go wrong or when things go right, what comes out of you is something Jesus would be proud of. For example, if someone swore at you, you would respond as Jesus responded.

Last week I explained to you that we have the Spirit of Jesus inside us. What comes out of you is what's inside you. If I see you always fighting and swearing and being rude and horrible I know that, no matter what you say to me, you're not really a Christian. Because what's inside comes out.

This cup contains water. When I pour it out, what comes out? Obviously, water. What's inside will eventually come out. No matter how hard we try to hide it, what's inside will eventually come out.

What's inside *you*?

Flash Or Burn

Object needed: *Ordinary paper, Flash Paper* and matches.*

These two pieces of paper may look exactly the same. They may both look like ordinary pieces of paper, but you can tell what they're really like when you place them near fire.

Let's pretend the fire represents a bad thing that has happened to us. Maybe somebody just took our seat in children's church. What are we going to do? What will we be like?

Some of us will come near to the fire... but we will deal with it calmly *(bring the ordinary paper close to the match, then take it away).*

Some of us will come near to the fire... and we will explode, probably lose our temper and hit someone *(bring the Flash Paper close to the match; it will burn fiercely).*

Which one do you think Jesus wants us to be? When the pressure is on, let's react like Jesus.

● STORY – Fig Leaf Phil (3)

Captain Philip was on a desert island with Princess Tuesday, who knew the secret. Men dressed in camouflage were hunting him and his ship was at the bottom of the ocean. With his mind swirling, his thoughts overloading, he passed out and fell out of the tree.

When Phil next opened his eyes he was looking up into the face of Princess Tuesday. She was mopping his head with a damp cloth and speaking to him very softly. The memory of the night before came rushing back to him. He jumped up quickly – and wished he hadn't. He was left holding his spinning head.

When Phil began to focus he realised that there was somebody with Princess Tuesday. "Who are you?" Phil enquired, surprised by how strong his voice was now sounding.

The man, who was quite short, with a tummy that hung over his tight trousers, answered: "I am Shalam. I am the friend of the king and of Princess Tuesday. I have come to help you bring the princess back home."

* Flash Paper is available from www.tricksfortruth.com

Phil listened and then got to his feet and shook hands with Shalam. "Well, I have no idea where the princess lives or how to get there," he said, "but we had better get going before those hunter people come back."

The three walked for what seemed like hours, but all the time Shalam kept whispering to Phil: "We can't trust the princess. She will lead us into a trap. She has been under much stress, and being captured has affected her. The princess, she is very confused." Flies buzzed around their heads and the sun beat down on them. Phil was feeling very uncomfortable but they kept walking. He figured that they must be heading towards the palace where the princess lived. He would never have guessed that the island was as big as it was. They came to a point on the path where it branched into two different directions.

"Which way now?" asked Phil.

But both Princess Tuesday and Shalam seemed to have different ideas about which way they should go. They began to argue, then to shout. Princess Tuesday shouted: "Shalam, why do you want us to go down that way? You know that is a dangerous way! It is longer and the hunters go there!"

Shalam for his part was shouting: "You see, Fig Leaf Phil! [that is what Shalam called Phil on account of his ripped clothes] She does not know what she is saying!" Phil looked from one to the other, from Princess Tuesday to Shalam. How was he to decide? He looked at the princess, but he remembered the words of Shalam in the back of his mind: "She is tired, Fig Leaf Phil. She is very stressed."

Phil grabbed the princess's arm and dragged her in the direction that Shalam had indicated. "You have chosen well, Phil," Shalam mumbled. But, as they turned the corner, hunters surrounded them. They seemed to come from all directions, emerging from behind the trees and the bushes. All had their guns aimed at the three people.

"Well, Shalam," Phil began, "we have still ended up trapped." Shalam began to laugh, then he walked away from Phil and Princess Tuesday and joined the hunters. He pulled a round hat out of his bag and placed it on his head.

"Phil, you are so easily led. Let me introduce you to my friends." Then, turning his attention to Princess Tuesday, he whispered, "And tomorrow, Princess, you and your secret will die for ever."

Phil couldn't believe it. How could he have been so stupid? He believed Shalam when he knew nothing about him. He had been fooled completely. Shalam looked as if he would be his friend, but when trouble came it was clear he was not a friend at all.

We need to be careful. Not everyone who looks like our friend is. Not everyone who claims to be a Christian is. But when things get difficult, it's usually quite easy to see.

Phil would have a lot of time to think about these things. He was about to spend the night trapped in a bamboo cage with Princess Tuesday.

(To be continued...)

God Heals

	Programme	Item
Section 1	Welcome	
	Rules	
	Prayer	
	Introductory Praise	
	Game 1	Casualty
	Praise	
	Fun Item 1	
	Game 2	Bandaged Heads
	Fun Item 2	
	Bible Text	Mark 16:18
	Announcements	
	Interview	
Section 2 Preaching Time	Worship Time	
	Bible Lesson	Paul Is Unharmed
	Illustration 1	Ford
	Illustration 2	The Creator
	Illustration 3	Call For The Doctor
	Story	Fig Leaf Phil (4)
	Prayer	

We serve a supernatural God. We must keep emphasising this in our secularised world.

games

Casualty

PREPARATION	Lots and lots of bandages.
PLAYERS	Five per team and a team leader.
SET-UP	The players line up at A with the pile of bandages. The leader is at B.
OBJECT	The players – in turn – run from A to B, where they have 30 seconds to wrap their leader up in bandages. The players then return.
WINNING	When all the players have gone, the team whose leader looks most like a casualty wins.

Bandaged Heads

PREPARATION	One head bandage per team.
PLAYERS	Five per team.
SET-UP	The players line up at A, with the first player wearing a head bandage.
OBJECT	The first player runs from A to B. On their return they take off the head bandage and the next person runs off wearing it.
WINNING	The first team back wins.

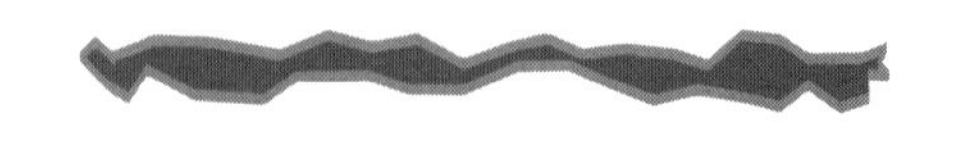

BIBLE LESSON **PAUL IS UNHARMED**

"They will also heal sick people by placing their hands on them." (Mark 16:18)

Paul shook the snake off into the fire and wasn't harmed. The people kept thinking that Paul would either swell up or suddenly drop dead. They watched him for a long time. When nothing happened to Paul the people with him were very surprised. God was able to protect Paul.

> The governor of the island was named Publius, and he owned some of the land around there. Publius was very friendly and welcomed us into his home for three days. His father was in bed, sick with fever and stomach trouble, and Paul went to visit him. Paul healed the man by praying and placing his hands on him.
>
> After this happened, everyone on the island brought their sick people to Paul, and they were all healed. The people were very respectful to us, and when we sailed, they gave us everything we needed. (Acts 28:7–10)

Paul was not the person who was doing the healing; God was healing people through Paul.

Ford

Object needed: *A picture of a vintage car or, better still, a man dressed as a mechanic (telling the story in the first person).*

When cars were very rare, there was a certain man who had managed to save enough money to buy one. The car was a Ford. It was one of the very first motor cars and it had been invented and developed by a man named Henry Ford.

One day this certain man was driving his car

along the road when the car started spluttering and a strange grinding noise could be heard from under the bonnet. The man pulled into a nearby lane and lifted the bonnet (the front of the car). He checked that there was enough petrol and then he looked at the engine and the other components, but he really was at a loss as to what the problem could be.

Then, strolling towards him, came an old English gentleman, complete with tweed cap and coat and a walking stick, which he was swinging around. The man was disappointed. A mechanic would have been nice, but what help was an English gentleman going to be?

"Can I help?" enquired the gentleman.

"No!" came the abrupt answer. "I need a mechanic, not a gentleman." But the gentleman insisted on taking a look. He moved one or two leads, plugged a lead back in, cleaned out a plug; the whole time the driver kept trying to stop him, mumbling that he would only make things worse.

Eventually the gentleman finished and invited the man to try and start the car. The man was mystified when the car roared into life on the first turn of the key. However, he didn't have to stay mystified for long. The gentleman held out his hand and said: "It was good to meet you. My name is Henry Ford."

The man sat there with his mouth open. The gentleman knew exactly how to fix the car. After all, he had created it.

The Creator

Object needed: *A picture of a car and a picture of a human body.*

Display the picture of the car.

This is the thing that Henry Ford created. It's amazing, really. A car is very technical; it is an astounding invention. Henry Ford knows all about this. He knows how to fix it, how to make it go better, how to repair any serious problems.

Display the picture of the body.

This is what God created. It is a million times more complex than a car, a million times more technical, a billion times more astounding. God knows all about this. He knows how to fix it, how to make it better, how to repair any serious problems.

I don't really know why people struggle to understand how God heals people. After all, he is the creator. If you can create something so intricate, so amazing, so special – then surely you can repair it.

God really does heal people today.

Call For The Doctor

Object needed: *A picture of a doctor, or have someone dressed as a doctor.*

The interesting thing is this: whenever we are sick or one of our friends is sick, the first thing we do is call for the doctor. We grab the telephone and dial the number, or we make our parents make an appointment for us to go to the surgery.

Doctors spend a lot of time learning all about the human body. They spend a lot of time studying to find out what things help people get better. Doctors work very hard to help people and to make them better.

But, no matter how much doctors study and learn, they will never know as much about the body as God himself. God created our bodies. He made us the way we are. Maybe we need to pray and ask God to heal us before we rush to the phone and ask for the doctor. Maybe we should pray for our friends who are sick before we ask for the doctor.

God really does heal people today.

• STORY – Fig Leaf Phil (4)

Phil had spent the night trapped in a bamboo cage with Princess Tuesday. Then as daybreak arrived he could just make out the shape of the palace in the distance. He shook Princess Tuesday gently by the shoulder until she woke up. "Princess, look! They're taking us to the palace! Now everything's going to be fine. Your dad will set us free and then I can find a ship to get off this island."

Princess Tuesday began to shake her head slowly. "No, Phil, that's what the secret is. The king is not the king."

Phil looked understandably confused but Princess Tuesday explained: "My father has an identical twin brother and he is pretending to be my father and convincing people that he is really the king, but he is no king. He is the leader of the hunters and now he wants to take over the whole kingdom. I'd never have worked it out, but my dad has a scar on the back of his leg and when I saw the impostor king in the swimming pool last week, there was no scar. He saw me staring and he knew that I'd worked it out, so that's why I ran away and that's why the hunters were trying to catch me." Phil listened patiently.

Eventually the hunters arrived at the palace and Shalam commanded the men carrying the bamboo cage to go round the back and into the royal gardens. When the cage was eventually laid to rest, the impostor king was there to greet them.

"Hello, Princess, and hello, Captain. Don't looked so surprised, Captain. I saw your ship go down, and if you hadn't been in such a rush to go rescuing princesses then I would have happily helped you get back to another ship. As it is, you know too much."

Phil was about to argue, but there was nothing he could think of to say. He knew he was in a lot of trouble.

The impostor king simply smiled and commanded the guards to throw them into prison. The order was given and the next thing that Phil was aware of, he was sliding down a tube and smashing into the concrete floor of the prison far below. Seconds after he landed, there was another crash and he guessed that Princess Tuesday had landed next to him.

When his eyes eventually became used to the light he found himself in a damp, concrete room. He could see tiny, scuttling animals in the distance, which he guessed were rats. And propped up in a corner, wrapped in a blanket, was undoubtedly the shape of a man, a very thin man, but still a man.

Princess Tuesday had obviously been observing the same scene, for she suddenly exclaimed: "Father!" and ran quickly in the direction of the man. Phil followed her but kept his distance as he listened to the sobs from the princess:

"Father, what have they done to you? Father, what have they done?"

Phil came closer and looked. The man looked incredibly ill. There was perspiration running down his forehead and he was visibly shaking. Phil stared; he felt sure that the man would die. Then Princess Tuesday did something that Phil hadn't expected: she prayed.

"God, heal my dad. He's very ill and bad people have hurt him a lot." To Phil's amazement, the man stopped shaking and he looked physically better. He smiled, but was still incredibly weak.

You see, whether it's in a made-up story or in real life, God really does heal people now.

What was to happen now? The true king might have been healed but they were all still trapped and the impostor king was ruining the kingdom.

(To be continued…)

5 A Job To Finish

	Programme	Item
Section 1	Welcome	
	Rules	
	Prayer	
	Introductory Praise	
	Game 1	Marathon
	Praise	
	Fun Item 1	
	Game 2	Rainbow-maker
	Fun Item 2	
	Bible Text	2 Timothy 4:6–7
	Announcements	
	Interview	
Section 2	Worship Time	
Preaching	Bible Lesson	Paul Completes The Job
Time	Illustration 1	Farmer Who Sows Only
	Illustration 2	Marathon Man Who Stops Early
	Illustration 3	Student Who Doesn't Take The Final Test
	Story	Fig Leaf Phil (5)
	Prayer	

God started a work in us that he intends to finish. However, he also wants to give us a job that he wants us to finish.

games

Marathon

PREPARATION None needed.

PLAYERS Two per team.

SET-UP The players line up at A. Everyone will go together.

OBJECT The players are to run from A to B and back ten times.

WINNING The teams get points for completing the race, not winning. All the teams that complete it will get the same amount of points.

Rainbow-maker

PREPARATION Balloons for each team, in the colours red, orange, yellow, green, blue, purple.

PLAYERS Six per team.

SET-UP The players line up at A with the inflated balloons at B.

OBJECT The team in relay runs from A to B; at B the player collects a balloon and runs to A with it. At A they must burst the balloon before the next player goes.

WINNING All the teams that complete this will get the same points. The points are for completing the race, not winning. Reinforce this point. There are bonuses for the team that bursts the balloons in rainbow order.

PreachingTime

BIBLE LESSON

PAUL COMPLETES THE JOB

"Now the time has come for me to die. My life is like a drink offering being poured out on the altar. I have fought well. I have finished the race, and I have been faithful." (2 Timothy 4:6–7)

Paul could have stayed in Malta for as long as he liked. Publius the governor was very grateful to Paul for what God had done through him. The people there loved Paul – some of them even thought Paul was a god. He could have lived there in comfort and safety in this sunny place called Malta for the rest of his life. But that was not what God wanted him to do. God had told Paul that he would go to Rome, the centre of the extraordinary Roman empire, and stand before the emperor himself and tell of how much God loved people.

If Paul were to go to Rome, then there was a very strong possibility that he would be killed. After all, he was a Christian, and many people had already tried to kill him just for being a Christian. He could stay in Malta and live a peaceful life.

But Paul would do what God wanted him to do. He would go to Rome, even though it would mean walking a road that would lead eventually to his death.

Paul would join God's élite. These were not people who had merely started well. They were people who had completed the task. People who had done the job and not given up halfway through. These were God's best. They were nothing incredibly special; they just finished the job. People like Daniel, who overcame a den of lions and who went on to be a prime minister serving God. People like Solomon, who, the Bible says, completed all the work that God gave him to do.

What about you? Are you a good finisher or did you just start well? How many of you will finish the work God has given you to do?

Illustration 1

Farmer Who Sows Only

Object needed: *A person miming the following (dressed as a stereotypical farmer):*

A farmer has to work very hard. He has to get up very early *(the mime artist stretches and yawns. He then mimes to the words that follow).* He has to work all year round. In the springtime he has to plough the fields, make sure the soil is ready and then sow the seed.

In the summertime he protects the seed and watches it grow. He looks after it, he keeps the crows off, he makes sure everything is growing properly. Then in the autumn he gathers in the crops.

At this point the mime artist sits down and pretends to read a paper.

Then in the autumn he gathers in the crops.

The mime artist turns over the page.

Hey! Gather in the crops!

The mime artist turns over the page.

This is ridiculous. In the autumn the farmer gathers in the crops. If he doesn't, the crops are ruined. This is almost as ridiculous as people who promise to do something for God but never actually do it.

What about you? Are you a good finisher or did you just start well? How many of you will finish the work God has given you to do?

Marathon Man Who Stops Early

Object needed: *A person pretending to be in a marathon (dressed appropriately).*

On your marks, get set, go! *(the marathon runner starts jogging).* A marathon runner has to train very, very hard. A friend of mine ran a three-mile race recently and she had to train very hard. Imagine how much harder you have to train to run 26 miles. He has to focus on the run. He goes through something that they call "the wall". It's not a real wall, but it's a barrier that the marathon runner has to go through in their mind, a barrier that is trying to make them stop running.

Twenty-six miles is a long, long way. The marathon runners have to train, they have to focus, they have to take in lots of drinks so that they don't overheat. But do you know what the most important part of marathon racing is? They have to finish. If they don't cross that finish line, then it was all fairly pointless.

When we agree to do something for God, we mustn't give up halfway through. It's about finishing.

What about you? Are you a good finisher or did you just start well? How many of you will finish the work God has given you to do?

Student Who Doesn't Take The Final Test

Object needed: *Chalk and Cheese (actors or puppets).*

Cheese: Hi, everyone. It's me, the amazing Cheese. Has anyone seen the Chalk dude? He's not been around for a while. He's doing his exams.
Chalk: Hi, old chap! Did I hear you talking about me?
Cheese: Yes, I was just wondering when you're going to be back around, playing and things. I've missed you over the last couple of months. All that work you've been doing for those exams!
Chalk: Yes, it's been quite difficult. I've had to work really hard. I've got to pass three different exams and then I get this really cool certificate that says that I am really clever.
Cheese: So, you've done two and you've got the last one really soon.
Chalk: No! I've had enough now. I've been working really hard and those two exams were really long and I don't want to do any more.
Cheese: But, dude, if you don't do the last exam, then you won't get the certificate!
Chalk: That's true.
Cheese: Well, go and do the final exam!
Chalk: I don't want to; it's too much effort.
Cheese: But you've done two already; you're nearly there...
Chalk: No, old bean, I'm not going.
Cheese: But, Chalk, this is foolish!
Chalk: Yes it is, but it's not as foolish as promising to do something for Jesus and then giving up halfway through.
Cheese: Well, I know it's not *that* foolish, but it certainly is foolish.
Chalk: Well, I guess you're right. I'll do the final test. I guess I'll see you next week.
Cheese: Go for it! We can always play next week.

What about you? Are you a good finisher or did you just start well? How many of you will finish the work God has given you to do?

● STORY – Fig Leaf Phil (5)

The king had been healed, God had shown up and proved that he could do miracles, but Phil, the king and the princess were still trapped in a dungeon. They stared up at the hole they had just fallen through.

There had been no way up while the king was ill, but now that he was better there was a chance. Phil carefully stood on the king's shoulders and stretched back up to the tube he had plummeted through only a short time before. He crawled into the tube and slowly but surely began to make his way back up. Eventually he reached the top.

There seemed to be some sort of ceremony taking place in the main hall. Phil looked in briefly, only to see that it was some sort of official ceremony. It seemed that half the kingdom had gathered there. Phil crept down a long, winding staircase while everyone was distracted by the ceremony. There were no guards anywhere to be seen. Phil guessed they must all be upstairs. And just when Phil thought that it couldn't get any easier, he arrived outside the cell where the princess and the king were held, only to discover there was a simple bolt on the outside. Phil pulled back the bolt and they were free, all of them.

They began to make their way back upstairs and into the main hall. The plan had been to sneak straight out of the main gate, but just as they were about to escape, Phil clumsily knocked over an enormous vase just as the impostor king had stood to speak and everyone had gone very quiet. Everyone turned and stared and then the impostor king gave the order: "Arrest that man! He is a spy."

The guards had just drawn their swords when the real king stepped forward and proclaimed: "Not so fast. Let him go. And that man... " he said, pointing to the impostor, "is not the real king. I am."

A deathly hush fell over the whole place. The lord chancellor stared at both men and then walked up to the impostor king and looked at his leg; he then walked over to the real king and looked at his. There could be no doubt: one did not have a scar; the other did.

The lord chancellor announced for all to hear: "We have been tricked. Arrest that pretend king and throw him in the dungeon." The hunters were quick to respond; they pulled out their guns and were ready to fight it out, but they were no match for the palace guard, who quickly disarmed them and threw them onto the ground to beg for mercy. It was all over and the good guys had most certainly won.

There was a party and a lot of celebrating. The impostor and the hunters were banished from the island and the kingdom was back to normal. Phil was a hero. Without him the impostor king might have triumphed. The king instantly made Phil a knight and, of course, gave the princess permission to marry him. His ragged clothes were replaced by more fitting garments, albeit a little more brightly coloured than Phil would have liked.

So Phil was to be a knight and live on the desert island paradise for the rest of his life. He could marry the princess and live happily ever after among the palm trees and coconuts. His days would be spent swimming in the sea, having anything he wanted. Everything seemed to be going perfectly for Fig Leaf Phil.

Sometimes there are lots of things that may seem nicer than doing what God wants us to do. But in our heart of hearts we know what we should be doing. It takes courage to do what God wants. It takes great determination to finish what we started with God. But it can be done.

Phil had to admit that such a life was tempting, very tempting indeed. But Phil also knew that he was not supposed to live the rest of his life like that. He was a sea captain, an adventurer, a pioneer. He would never be happy sitting on the beach day after day. He had a job to do and he would do it. Maybe one day he would return, but, for now, his job here was done and he longed to return to the sea.

Several weeks later, when the next ship was passing the island, Phil kissed Princess Tuesday goodbye. He then turned and swam out to the ship. He would be a captain again. In years to come he would return to the little island and marry the princess, but he had many adventures to get through before then.

What about you? Are you a good finisher or did you just start well? How many of you will finish the work God has given you to do?

HEROES

A Series in Seven Parts

Introduction

Title	Themes covered
1 No Ordinary Child	We are all special. None of us is ordinary.
2 Wilderness Years	The wilderness may be hard, but we have to learn certain things before God can use us.
3 Burning Bush	God is still talking to people today.
4 Who am I?	Who am I? The Bible makes it very clear that we are the result of a direct creative act of God.
5 Miracles	We don't try to do things in our own strength. God is with us.
6 The Vital Flaw	We all have weaknesses. We must watch our flaws.
7 The Promised Land	When we are extraordinary, even when we make mistakes, there's a way back.

Moses. A miraculous birth, a supernatural calling and a vital flaw which prevented him from entering the Promised Land after many years of travelling. It is a very exciting saga with much for us to learn from on the way.

Missionaries from the past are used as the story to illustrate the principles in each story.

1ST

1 No Ordinary Child

	Programme	Item
Section 1	Welcome	
	Rules	
	Prayer	
	Introductory Praise	
	Game 1	Water Works (for girls)
	Praise	
	Fun Item 1	
	Game 2	Water Works (for boys)
	Fun Item 2	
	Bible Text	Acts 7:20
	Announcements	
	Interview	
Section 2	Worship Time	
Preaching	Bible Lesson	Moses
Time	Illustration 1	The Fight
	Illustration 2	Special
	Story	Saved For A Purpose
	Prayer	

We are all special. None of us is ordinary. But we need to remember that even though we are not ordinary, if we try to do things without God's help, we will be in trouble.

games

Water Works (for girls)

PREPARATION	Several water pistols and a row of tennis balls.
PLAYERS	Three per team and several leaders with water pistols.
SET-UP	The players line up at A. The leaders stand just before B, forming a line on each side (three each side should do it). The tennis balls are at B.
OBJECT	The first player runs from A to B. At B they collect a ball and run back. The whole time, the leaders will be squirting them with the water pistols.
WINNING	The team with most balls after three minutes wins.

Water Works (for boys)

PREPARATION	Several water pistols and a row of tennis balls.
PLAYERS	Three per team and several leaders with water pistols.
SET-UP	The players line up at A. The leaders stand just before B, forming a line on each side (three each side should do it). The tennis balls are at B.
OBJECT	The first player runs from A to B. At B they collect a ball and run back. The whole time, the leaders will be squirting them with the water pistols.
WINNING	The team with most balls after three minutes wins.

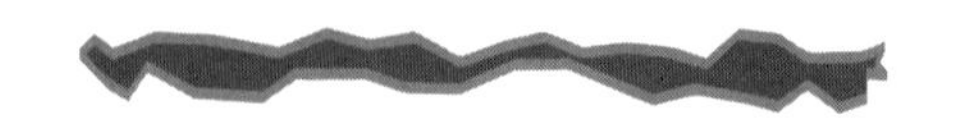

Preaching Time

BIBLE LESSON MOSES

"At that time Moses was born, and he was no ordinary child." (Acts 7:20, New International Version)

Using video footage from The Prince of Egypt *could enhance this story.*

A law had been made in Egypt because Pharaoh was worried that there were too many Israelites being born. This was the law: "If the child born is a girl, she may live; if it is a boy, he should be killed." But the Israelites didn't want to kill their babies, so they would hide them in their houses for as long as they could. One such baby was called Moses. But when his mother couldn't keep Moses hidden any longer, she placed him in a basket and hid him away in the tall grass near the river Nile.

He hadn't been there long when Pharaoh's daughter came out and found him. He really was such a beautiful child that she decided to look after him herself in the royal palace. The amazing thing is this: when it came time for the Pharaoh's daughter to find a nanny for the child, she actually chose Moses' real mother. So Moses was brought up by his real mother in the royal palace.

God was looking after Moses, and God had a special job for him to do.

The Israelites continued to grow in numbers, so Pharaoh made them work as slaves. But the slave masters were very cruel and would often beat the Israelites, who were Moses's real people. One day Moses saw a slave master beating an Israelite, and Moses got so angry he killed the slave master and hid the body.

I think Moses thought he could help his people by himself. It was true that God had a plan for him to deliver all these people from Egypt, but if Moses tried to do it without God's help, he had no chance.

Sure enough, Moses had been spotted, and Pharaoh wanted Moses killed for what he'd done. Moses had tried to help the Israelites without God's help and it had all gone very wrong. He would have to escape to the wilderness and live in the desert for many years to come, until that Pharaoh had died.

Illustration 1

The Fight

Object needed: *None.*

I once found myself in an interesting situation. My friends and I were all coming from a youth club when this big gang started to call us names. I was feeling a bit brave and decided we should go and sort them out.

We all walked towards these boys and, because I always say too much, I stood at the front and gave this gang a right telling-off. I told them that if they carried on calling us names, they were going to be in serious trouble. I was really going for it. Then suddenly I thought it was a little quiet behind me. I turned round slowly, to discover that I was all alone. My "friends" had decided that this gang had boys in it that were very big and looked as if they would be good fighters.

I found myself completely alone. I thought I was strong because of all the support I had behind me, but there was no support.

This is what it feels like when we try and do things without God. We come to a point where we realise that we are actually all alone and there is nobody there to help us. So let's make sure we do the things God wants so that he can help us in every situation.

By the way, I looked into the faces of the gang and, because I had watched *Teenage Mutant Hero Turtles* every day, I took them all on and won!! Actually, that's not strictly true. When I realised my friends had gone I turned and ran away so quickly the other gang couldn't catch me.

Illustration 2

Special

Object needed: *A lamp.*

You see, we are all very special. God created us that way. But we were designed to be at our best when we are connected to God.

You see this lamp. It's special enough, but it's designed to be connected to the power. If it isn't connected to the electricity, no matter how special it may seem, it is not as special as it should be. It needs to be connected so that it can shine bright and powerful.

We are designed to stay connected to God, to listen to him, to learn from him, to do what God asks of us. If we think we can do it without God, then we will never quite be what he intended us to be.

We must learn to get connected to God.

• STORY – Saved For A Purpose

One day, John Newton went horse riding with some of his friends. Suddenly a large bird flew up out of the grass near the trail, with such a whir of its wings that it scared John's horse. The horse reared and threw John off. He landed on his back on the ground. The thud knocked the breath out of him.

As he gasped for air, he noticed that he had landed inches from a sharp stake which could have killed him. His friends told him that he was lucky, but John remembered his mother's words: "God loves you, John, and has a purpose for your life."

Soon John forgot the lesson and went on living the way he wanted to. It is one thing knowing that we have a purpose from God, but if we decide to ignore God, he doesn't make us do his will.

A couple of years later, John and his friends decided to row down a river to see a huge warship that had docked in the harbour. They agreed to set off the following morning. But when the morning came, John slept late and the others set off without him. As they reached the harbour John's friends stood up in their rowing boat to see the warship. The waves knocked their boat and the men fell into the sea.

John was unhappy that his friends had gone

without him, until he found out what had happened. If he had been with them he surely would have drowned, because John couldn't swim. Again God was protecting John. Again John remembered his mother's words: "God loves you, John, and has a purpose for your life." But again John forgot the lesson quickly, and God would not force him. He could not fulfil God's purpose until he let God be in charge of his life.

Many years later, John was a sea captain. In the middle of the most horrific storm he cried out to God to protect him and he gave his life to Jesus. Now God could use John the way he intended. John Newton went on to become a very famous preacher. He travelled to many lands, telling people about the love of God. He was to write a very famous song, a song that goes:

> Amazing Grace, how sweet the sound
> That saved a wretch like me,
> I once was lost, but now am found,
> Was blind but now I see.

This famous song was written by a man who eventually realised that, even though he was special and God had a purpose for him, he wouldn't be able to do anything for God until he gave his life to him.

The Wilderness Years

	Programme	Item
Section 1	**Welcome**	
	Rules	
	Prayer	
	Introductory Praise	
	Game 1	Deep-sea Divers
	Praise	
	Fun Item 1	
	Game 2	Squirt!
	Fun Item 2	
	Bible Text	Psalm 139:14
	Announcements	
	Interview	
Section 2	**Worship Time**	
Preaching	**Bible Lesson**	Moses In The Wilderness
Time	**Illustration 1**	Precious Stones
	Illustration 2	Royal Marines
	Illustration 3	Gold
	Story	Training For A Young Soldier
	Prayer	

Overview Moses had to learn many things. God knew that he wasn't ready for the great things that he wanted him to do yet! He had to learn. The wilderness may be hard, but we have to learn certain things before God can use us. Moses had to be patient.

games

Deep-sea Divers

PREPARATION	A bowl of water per team, containing six coins.
PLAYERS	Six from each team.
SET-UP	Standard relay pattern at A. The bowl is at B.
OBJECT	The first person runs to the bowl, removes a coin and returns to the next player.
WINNING	The first team back and sitting down wins.

Squirt!

PREPARATION	Three lengths of hosepipe, about 1 metre each, and a T-joint to join the three lengths of pipe at a central point. Put some water into the pipes and hold up the ends so the water doesn't leak.
PLAYERS	Three players per team.
SET-UP	The three players line up, with the front member of the team holding the hosepipe on their side in their hands.
OBJECT	When the game begins the front players blow through the pipe. The players keep blowing until the water squirts out of one of the three pipes. The player whose pipe squirts out first loses and it is the turn of the next player in the team.
WINNING	The game is over when all the players in a certain team are out. The team with the most players left wins. If it is equal then it is a draw.

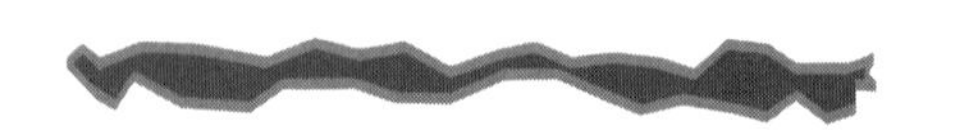

MOSES IN THE WILDERNESS

"And the fire will test the quality of each [person's] work." (1 Corinthians 3:13, New International Version)

Using video footage from The Prince of Egypt *could enhance this story.*

God did indeed protect Moses. He was rescued from the Nile by none other than Pharaoh's daughter. The child that Pharaoh tried to kill grew up in Pharaoh's palace. God had plans for this extraordinary child.

But what happened when Moses grew up was to show clearly that he wasn't ready to be used by God yet. One day Moses saw one of the slave masters beating a slave. He lost his temper and attacked the slave master and killed him. He tried to hide what he had done by burying the man, but he had been seen.

God wanted to use Moses to lead God's people away from Egypt, to lead God's people to their own land. But Moses wasn't ready for God to use yet. Moses knew that if he stayed in Egypt he would be in trouble, so he escaped. He fled into the vast desert, where he was a prince no more. Many days and nights Moses wandered in the wilderness. He had nothing to eat or drink.

The wilderness in the Bible is a place where our characters are formed – where we learn things, where we learn how to behave properly, and ultimately where we learn to trust God and become more like God.

The sand scoured Moses's body and face and he was very thirsty. Eventually he stumbled into a village and came to a well. He leaned over the well and took his first drink for some time. But no sooner had he started to drink than he heard a child's cry. "Help!"

As Moses looked up he could see shepherds pushing aside several young girls and their sheep from the well. Moses roused himself and drove the men off. Then, exhausted by the effort, he collapsed again by the well.

When he came to, he found himself in the home of a man called Jethro. And there Moses would stay; he looked after Jethro's sheep and later married Jethro's daughter. Moses would be here for the next 40 years. Here, in the wilderness, he would learn to be more like God, until the time came when God would be ready to send him back to Egypt.

Moses had to learn many things. God knew that he wasn't ready for the great things that he wanted him to do yet! He had to learn. The wilderness may be hard, but we have to learn certain things before God can use us. Moses had to be patient.

God may have to teach you certain things before you can fulfil your destiny. But remember: God lets you go through tough times so that you can learn. Don't be afraid; he'll bring you through.

Precious Stones

Object needed: *A jewel of some sort.*

Precious stones are beautiful to look at, but they don't just appear. Most precious stones are formed deep under the ground. They look like this only after great pressure has been applied to them, after they have been almost crushed by tons and tons of earth and stone and gravel.

It is the huge pressure on them that makes ordinary stones into precious stones. It is the pressure that God puts on us that makes us precious. We need to learn that when we go through hard times it's not always bad. God brings precious people out of difficult situations.

Royal Marines

Object needed: *Display a picture of a soldier / or dress up as a soldier.*

The Royal Marines are one of the fittest and best groups of soldiers in the entire world. But they didn't just suddenly appear as this élite fighting force. They didn't just turn up at their training camp just off Dartmoor and find themselves automatically excellent at everything they did.

The Royal Marines had to train. They had to learn; they had to develop. And at the end of the training they had to run 30 miles across the middle of Dartmoor, carrying their full kit, which probably weighs more than some of you. It doesn't matter what the weather is, they have to train, they have to develop, they have to learn.

They do all this because they want to be the best. We need to learn, we need to let God develop us, we need to be not afraid of the hard times. We need to learn to be everything God wants us to be, so that we too can be the best, not so that we can fight in some war, but so that instead we can be part of God's ever-increasing army.

Gold

Object needed: *Display a picture of gold.*

The best gold is produced in rather an unusual way. The gold is placed in a container and heated up. Eventually, when the heat is great enough, the gold melts. The impurities in the gold all drift to the top of the container and are scooped off and thrown away. The process is repeated and repeated until there are no impurities left.

God does much the same to us. He allows hard things and hard times to come to us, and allows us sometimes to be in situations that are very difficult for us. That is like the gold being heated up. When we are in hard situations, in our own personal wildernesses, and we deal with the difficulties right, we get better and more like Jesus.

We must learn that when we go through hard times, God can use those times to make us even more like Jesus – and then God can use us to his glory.

STORY – Training For A Young Soldier

We talked about this man a couple of months ago, but I want to look at a conversation between William Booth and his son today:

"Go home!" shouted a drunk as he leaned on the bar of the pub and shook his fist at William Booth (the founder of the Salvation Army). "And take that skinny kid with you!" Some of the others in the pub laughed and jeered; others were more interested and listened intently.

As they left the pub, William Booth turned to his thirteen-year-old son and said, "These are the people I want you to live and work with, Bramwell. The poor have nothing but these terrible pubs. But we can give them the good news about Jesus Christ. These are our people. We must tell them that Jesus can save them from the devil."

The slums of East London were a sad place to be at this time. Most of the pubs had special steps to help the children reach the counters. Children as young as five years old had become alcoholics. Some even died. But the street-corner preaching of William and Bramwell Booth worked. Alcoholics stopped drinking; gamblers stopped gambling. The pub landlords hated Booth as more and more people stopped coming to their pubs.

This was a rough place for Bramwell to grow up in, but it made him strong. When he was 16 Bramwell took over the running of the Food-For-The-Million shops that helped to feed the poor. He ran five canteens that were open 24 hours a day.

Bramwell had learnt well. He had become what God wanted him to become, and when William Booth died, aged 83, Bramwell became the leader of the Salvation Army, directing missionaries all over the world. He led thousands of people who were dedicated to serving Jesus.

Bramwell had learnt; now it was time to be everything God wanted him to be.

3 The Burning Bush

	Programme	Item
Section 1	**Welcome**	
	Rules	
	Prayer	
	Introductory Praise	
	Game 1	Water World 1
	Praise	
	Fun Item 1	
	Game 2	Water World 2
	Fun Item 2	
	Bible Text	Exodus 3:5
	Announcements	
	Interview	
Section 2	**Worship Time**	
Preaching	**Bible Lesson**	The Burning Bush
Time	**Illustration 1**	Prayer
	Illustration 2	Bible
	Illustration 3	Leaders
	Story	Then Give Me Hudson
	Prayer	

God is still talking to people today. The same God who spoke to Moses through the burning bush talks to people today. He talks through his word, through the Bible, and through other people.

games

Water World 1

PREPARATION	One empty bucket per team and a large bucket full of water. Also a paper cup per team and a couple of spares.
PLAYERS	Five per team.
SET-UP	The teams line up in relay formation at A with a cup each and the bucket of water. A team leader from each team sits at B with a bucket on their head.
OBJECT	In relay formation the children carry a cup of water to B. They must fill the bucket of their leader as full as possible in the three minutes you allow.
WINNING	The team with the most water in the bucket wins.

Water World 2

PREPARATION	A washing-up-liquid bottle full of water and a bucket per team.
PLAYERS	Six players per team.
SET-UP	Five players line up at A with the front member of the team holding the bottle. The sixth person stands at B.
OBJECT	The first person runs from A to a point about five metres before B. They then have five seconds to squirt water into the bucket (held by their teammate). A leader needs to monitor the five seconds. The player then returns to A.
WINNING	The team with the fullest bucket after five minutes wins.

BIBLE LESSON **THE BURNING BUSH**

"God replied: 'Don't come any closer... the ground where you are standing is holy." (Exodus 3:5)

Using video footage from The Prince of Egypt *could enhance this story.*

If Moses had forgotten Egypt, the Lord had not, for the Lord's memory is long. And one day, when Moses was chasing a lost lamb through the wild highlands of the Sinai, by the side of Mount Horeb, he saw an astonishing sight. Before him was a thorn bush. The bush was burning, its branches bright with flame. Yet as it burned, it was not consumed. Forgetting the lost lamb, Moses drew near.

Suddenly a powerful voice spoke from the bush: "Moses."

"Here I am," replied Moses.

"Take your sandals off," said the voice from the bush, "for the ground where you are standing is holy." Moses did as he was told, but all the time he wondered who it was who was speaking.

"Who are you?" he eventually asked.

"I am that I am. I am the God of your ancestors Abraham, Isaac and Jacob; the God of Sarah, Rebecca, Rachel and Leah."

Afraid, Moses hid his face. "What do you want with me?" he asked. And so God explained his plan for Moses to return to Egypt to lead God's people out of Egypt and to the Promised Land.

It's not so important for us today to look at what God said to Moses, but what is important is to see that God really does speak to people today. He doesn't usually speak through burning bushes, though sometimes he does use amazing things like this. But today, God usually speaks to us through three main areas. We're going to look at these three areas today.

Illustration 1

Prayer

Object needed: *A picture of a person praying.*

Cheese is pretending to pray.

Cheese: Dear Celestial Being, Creator of man's first respiratory movements. I beseech thee at this early time…

Chalk: Cheese, what on earth are you talking about?

Cheese: I'm praying. It's really difficult. You have to use big words and say "thee" and "thou" and stuff.

Chalk: Oh, Cheese, you just have to speak in English. A Christian is God's friend, so you have to talk to God in the same way you talk to a friend.

Cheese: Really?

Chalk: Yes. Just tell God how you feel. Talk about what sort of a week you've had, stuff that you would normally talk to your friends about.

Cheese: Oh! Well, that sounds easier. I'll give it a try: Hi, King Jesus. This has been a bit of a tough week. John keeps picking on me. I'm trying to be kind, but it's not easy. Help me to do the right thing.

We all get the wrong idea about prayer. Prayer is simply talking to God. And the exciting thing about talking to someone is that they also talk back. God not only wants us to talk to him in prayer, he also wants us to listen to what he says in response. God wants to talk to us, even though it isn't always with a big booming voice; sometimes he just whispers into our hearts and we know God has said something.

God can speak to me directly in my time of prayer.

Illustration 2

Bible

Object needed: *A computer manual.*

This is my computer manual. It tells me everything about my computer. It tells me how to switch it off and on, it tells me where to put the cables, it tells me what to do when things go wrong, it tells me how to load my software.

It can tell me how to deal with my computer. But when it comes to things about me, my computer manual isn't much good. Shall I steal those sweets from that shop – after all, I am hungry? Shall I be rude to the teacher – after all, she deserves it, she's always unkind to me?

My computer manual can't help me with this stuff, but God can. And he's given me a manual to help with me. This manual shows me how to live right and to do what God wants. God often speaks to me through the Bible. He tells me what to do through the words in this book.

God can speak to us through the Bible.

Leaders

Object needed: *A spanner.*

Sometimes, thankfully not too often, my car breaks down. Now I know nothing at all about cars. I know where to put the key in, where to put the petrol in, and where to put the oil and water in. But that's about it. When my car breaks down, I haven't got a clue what to do with it. I really struggle. But my dad is brilliant with cars; he takes his car apart and puts it back together quite often.

So I get my phone, and I phone my dad up and say: "Hey, Dad! My car is making a really strange grating noise. How do I fix it?" And quite often he tells me what to do.

Sometimes, when I need answers on other things that are difficult for me, I go to other people and ask their advice. When I need to know things about money, I know who to go to. And when I need to know things about computer games, I come to you guys.

Now when I need to know what God wants me to do, and I've prayed about it and feel God has given me an answer, and I've read the Bible and feel God has given me an answer, sometimes I go and talk to church leaders and ask them to think and pray about it too. You see, sometimes God speaks to me through other people, usually through leaders whom I trust.

God can speak through leaders too.

● STORY – Then Give Me Hudson

We talked about Hudson Taylor several months ago, but here's a reminder of how his great adventure with God began:

James Hudson Taylor was born in 1832 in Yorkshire, England. When he was still very young he stood at the seaside and looked out to sea. He prayed a very simple prayer: "God, give me China." Hudson wanted to see people in China coming to know Jesus.

God heard Hudson's prayer – God always hears our prayers – and spoke to Hudson. God said: "Then give me Hudson." God wanted Hudson Taylor to know that if he gave his life to God, then God would use him to affect China.

In 1853 at the age of 21 Hudson set sail for China aboard a ship called the *Dumfries*. Unlike many other English missionaries, Hudson respected Chinese ways and wore clothes like theirs and even wore his hair in a ponytail, as did most Chinese men.

His work with the Chinese helped many to become Christians. However, in 1860, while director of the London Mission Hospital, Hudson became so ill that he had to return to England. But he recovered, and, forming his own China Inland Mission, he led 800 missionaries to China. Many people became Christians as a result of his work, and the China Inland Mission continues to this day.

It all started when Hudson listened to what God said. God said: "Give me Hudson."

God wants to speak to lots of you. It's time we learned to listen.

4 Who Am I?

	Programme	Item
Section 1	Welcome	
	Rules	
	Prayer	
	Introductory Praise	
	Game 1	Apple-bobbing
	Praise	
	Fun Item 1	
	Game 2	Water Balloons
	Fun Item 2	
	Bible Text	Psalm 139:14
	Announcements	
	Interview	
Section 2	Worship Time	
Preaching	Bible Lesson	Moses (Who Am I?)
Time	Illustration 1	Chemicals And Monkeys
	Illustration 2	Purchased
	Story	The Best Jewels Of All
	Prayer	

Overview Moses' question was not unusual. Up and down our nation, and all over our world, boys and girls are asking that self-same question: Who am I? The Bible makes it very clear that we are the result of a direct, creative act of God. That makes us really special.

Apple-bobbing

PREPARATION	You will need three apples and a bowl of water per team.
PLAYERS	Three players per team.
SET-UP	Players line up at A. A bowl of water and three apples per team are placed at B.
OBJECT	The first player runs from A to B where they try to remove an apple, using only their mouth. When they are successful they return to A to tag the next player.
WINNING	The team that completes the relay first wins.

Water Balloons

PREPARATION	Six water balloons and a bucket per team.
PLAYERS	Six players per team.
SET-UP	Six players line up in relay formation at A.
OBJECT	The first person runs from A to B, throws the balloon from a distance of two metres in front of the bucket, and then returns to A where the next player begins.
WINNING	The team that has the most water balloons in the buckets wins.

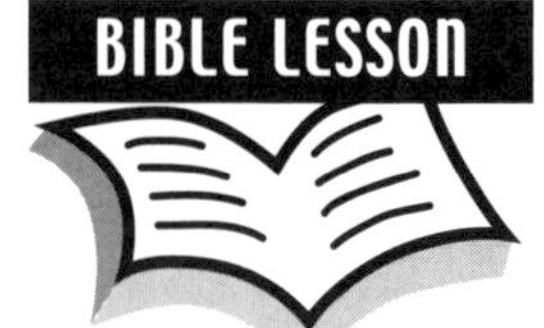

BIBLE LESSON **MOSES (WHO AM I?)**

"I praise you because I am fearfully and wonderfully made." (Psalm 139:14, New International Version)

Using video footage from The Prince of Egypt *could enhance this story.*

If Moses had forgotten Egypt, God had not, for the Lord's memory is longer than any man's. And one day, as Moses pursued one of his runaway sheep through the wilderness of Sinai, by the side of Mount Horeb, he saw an amazing sight.

Before him was a thorn bush. The bush was clearly on fire; this was not unusual – bushes often caught fire in the incredible heat of the desert. What was unusual was that the bush didn't seem to be consumed. It burned without being damaged. Moses drew nearer to look at this incredible sight. Then, as he drew very near, a voice spoke to him: "Moses! Take off your sandals; the ground where you are now standing is holy."

"Who are you?" Moses asked in a trembling voice.

"I Am that I Am", came the response. "I am the God of your ancestors and I have seen the suffering of Israel and now I shall save them. You must go back to Egypt and speak to Pharaoh."

But Moses didn't want to go back. He thought he would be killed. He started to make excuses. He said to God: "Who am I that I should go?" He was trying to say to God that he wasn't special enough to go. But the truth is that we are all special, very special indeed. And eventually, with the help of his brother, Aaron, Moses returned to Egypt.

God has a great task for you to do too. I've told you this many times. But maybe you think that you are not special enough to do things for God. You're wrong!

Illustration 1

Chemicals And Monkeys

Object needed: *Samples of the chemicals that make up our bodies. A picture of the [wrong] evolution chart of man.*

You see, when you get right down to it, how special is a person? They are only a collection of chemicals. Our body contains a lot of water, a huge amount of carbon (the stuff you use in art), some sulphur (that's the stuff in matches), varying amounts of fat... Basically we are a bag of chemicals.

So some people would have you believe that you are *nothing more* than a bag of chemicals. Others are a little bit more interesting and suggest that we are all descended from monkeys. Lots of people believe this; pictures like this are in lots of your schoolbooks. The thing is, no one has ever proved that this happened. This is one man's guess about where we came from – and, as far as I can see, it's a pretty stupid guess.

The truth is this (and I know it's the truth because God said it in the Bible): God made each and every one of us. We are unique and special creations made by God himself. He actually took the time to put you together inside your mother's tummy. He took the time to breathe life into you. God made you, and God never has made, and never will make, junk. You are God's workmanship. You are absolutely beautiful and incredibly special. You were created by the King of the whole universe.

God spoke a word and the whole universe came into being. With you, he took the time to form you, and shape you. He could have just spoken the word and you would exist, but God didn't do that; he took the time to make you special. Who's descended from monkeys? Who's a load of chemicals? What nonsense! I'm God's; he made me.

Illustration 2

Purchased

Object needed: *Choose a child.*

If I were to hold an auction here today, and the item for sale was this person (refer to the child), I wonder how much I'd get? 50p, £1, £1 million, a car, a house... I wonder how much. If I worked out how much the chemicals inside us are worth, I'd actually pay a lot less than £50.

The Bible tells us that God really did purchase people. You see, before Jesus came, we all belonged to the devil. He owned us. He owned everyone who had done things wrong, everyone with sin inside them. So God had to find a way of buying us from the devil, so that we no longer belonged to the devil, but belonged to God. God found a way.

Two thousand years ago, God sent Jesus, who, remember, is also God. He died on the cross, blood flowed from his hands, his feet, his side and his head, and the Bible actually says this: "With his blood Jesus purchased men and women from every tribe and nation."

Jesus shed his blood. He died in your place, so that you could be taken from the devil and brought to God. That's what happened. You are so incredibly special that you had to be bought with the blood of God himself.

• STORY – The Best Jewels Of All

When Amy Carmichael first went to India as a missionary, she decided to wear the Indian sari and fit into Indian culture as best she could. Although she didn't wear jewellery, Amy thought that the gold and silver necklaces, bangles, rings, anklets and earrings the Indian women wore were very pretty.

Even the members of the Starry Cluster – the group of Christian Indian women who went from village to village sharing the good news about Jesus – were adorned from head to toe with jewels. But Amy soon learned that in India a woman's jewels were a source of pride. They showed how rich her family was, how important she or her husband was, and what caste or social group she belonged to. Amy was worried – it did not seem good for Christians to care about these things. Still, she hesitated to say anything. She did not like the way missionaries made the Indian Christians adopt English clothes and English ways of doing things.

"Lord," she prayed, "if you want these women to give up their jewels, have the women themselves ask whether they should, not me."

One day, Ponnamal, a member of the Starry Cluster, heard a child say, "When I grow up, I want to join the Starry Cluster so I can wear jewels like Ponnamal does." This bothered Ponnamal; this was not the reason she wanted children to join the Starry Cluster! Ponnamal prayed and asked God what she should do. She knew that an Indian woman without jewels would be laughed at. But then God seemed to say to her, "You will be a crown of glory in the hand of the Lord." Ponnamal realised that she would be like a jewel to God, even if she wore no jewellery at all.

Ponnamal took off her jewels. One by one, the other members of the Starry Cluster took off their jewels also. People did laugh. Some mocked them. These Christians were very strange! But then people began to realise that they served each other and loved each other and others, no matter what class or social caste they were from. Many people began to join them.

And now how could people tell that they were members of this special group of Christians? None of them wore jewels. They could tell because they themselves were beautiful jewels, loved and treasured by God himself.

5 Miracles

	Programme	Item
Section 1	Welcome	
	Rules	
	Prayer	
	Introductory Praise	
	Game 1	Bucket-carriers
	Praise	
	Fun Item 1	
	Game 2	Target Practice
	Fun Item 2	
	Bible Text	1 John 4:4
	Announcements	
	Interview	
Section 2 Preaching Time	Worship Time	
	Bible Lesson	Moses And Miracles
	Illustration 1	God Is Bigger
	Illustration 2	God Is Stronger
	Illustration 3	God Is For Us
	Story	Breakfast From Heaven
	Prayer	

Moses had been in the wilderness for some time and now he was returning to command Pharaoh to "let God's people go". But he wasn't coming in his own strength. God was with him.

Game 1

Bucket-carriers

PREPARATION	One bucket full of water per team.
PLAYERS	Six per team.
SET-UP	Three team members line up in relay formation at A and three members line up in relay formation at B. The person at the front of team A has a full bucket.
OBJECT	The first person runs from A to B, and hands the bucket to the person at B. The person at B takes the bucket and returns it to the next person at A; they continue until they have all been.
WINNING	The first team to complete the race and sit down wins.

Game 2

Target Practice

PREPARATION	A water pistol per team.
PLAYERS	Five players per team.
SET-UP	A leader stands at a point five metres beyond B. Five players line up at A with the front member of the team holding the water pistol.
OBJECT	The first person runs from A to B, where they shoot the water pistol at the leader, who will desperately try to dodge it. When the leader is hit, the player returns to A to tag the next player. The game continues for three minutes.
WINNING	The team to complete the most cycles wins.

Preaching Time

BIBLE LESSON MOSES AND MIRACLES

"Because the one who is in you is greater than the one who is in the world." (1 John 4:4, New International Version)

Moses returned from the wilderness as God had commanded, and stood before Pharaoh.

"Let God's people go," Moses commanded, and, as a sign that God was powerful, Moses threw his stick onto the ground. The stick became a snake and slithered in front of Pharaoh. Pharaoh just laughed and summoned his magicians, who repeated the same thing with their sticks. But Moses' snake ate the other snakes, before turning back into a stick. God wanted Pharaoh to know that he, God, was not only powerful, but more powerful than any other god.

But Pharaoh refused to listen. He refused to let God's people go. So God again showed how powerful he was by turning the river Nile to blood. But still Pharaoh would not let them go. God performed miracle after miracle, but Pharaoh refused. Eventually, Moses proclaimed: "If you don't let God's people go, then all the firstborn males will die." But still Pharaoh refused.

God carried out his promise. The firstborn cattle and the firstborn sheep and the firstborn sons of the Egyptians all died on one evening. Pharaoh's own son died. It took this horrible act before Pharaoh eventually let God's people go.

Even then, Pharaoh soon changed his mind and sent his army to destroy God's people in the desert. But God opened up the Red Sea in front of them so that they could walk through safely on dry ground. When the Egyptians tried to follow, God closed up the sea and hundreds of Egyptian soldiers drowned.

It's important to realise that when we are on God's side he uses his incredible and amazing power to look after us and protect us, and to show others that he is God.

Illustration 1

God Is Bigger

Object needed: *The video* Veggie Tales: Where's God When I'm Scared? *available from most Christian bookshops.*

Play the Veggie Tale *video (only the first story, entitled "God is Bigger... ").*

God Is Stronger

Object needed: *Display a picture of a frog and a picture of the sun.*

God performed many amazing signs in Egypt. But they weren't just signs for no reason. The Egyptians prayed to all sorts of strange things and called them gods. The Egyptians used to pray to the sun, they used to pray to frogs, they used to worship the river Nile...

So when God performed his miracles, he was saying more than "Look how powerful I am". God was actually showing the people of Egypt that he was stronger than their pretend gods.

The people of Egypt worshipped frogs, so God showed that he had power over the frogs by sending a plague of them onto the land. Every time the Pharaoh tried to take a bath he would find his bathtub full of frogs. The people of Egypt worshipped the sun, so God showed that he had power over the sun by blocking it out so that darkness covered the land for several hours in the middle of the day. The people of Egypt worshipped the river Nile and held it as sacred, but God showed he even had power over the river Nile by turning it into blood.

God showed he had power over all the strange and unusual things the Egyptians worshipped. God is stronger than all the strange things that people worship. He is also stronger than false gods such as Vishnu and Shiva, and much, much more powerful than the devil.

Illustration 3

God Is For Us

Object needed: *A traditional picture of the devil with forked tail and horns.*

The Bible talks about the fact that "the one who is in [us] is greater than the one who is in the world". There really is supernatural power. God and God's people really can perform miracles, lay hands on sick people and see them healed, and, in a place called Indonesia, God has even allowed Christians to walk on water to show how amazing he is.

When we come right down to it, there are only two sources of supernatural power. Supernatural power comes from only two places. It comes either from God or from the devil. When Moses threw his stick before Pharaoh and it became a snake, it became a snake because of God's power. When the Egyptian wizards copied Moses, their sticks became snakes by using the devil's power. God's snake ate the devil's snakes to show that God is more powerful.

Now the magicians thought that their magic came from their god, but the devil pretends to be all sorts of different things. Some people think that the devil looks like this *(show the picture)*; I don't think so. The devil lies about who he is to trick people into worshipping him. The devil uses his power to try to make people follow him.

Whenever you see supernatural power, you must think: Is this from God or is this from the devil? It always comes from one of two places.

God gives us supernatural power to help people, to show them Jesus, to allow us to show the world how great God is. The devil wants to use his power to hurt and destroy people. Sometimes it seems that he is doing good, but really he only wants to hurt. There are only two places that supernatural power comes from: God and the devil.

• STORY – Breakfast From Heaven

"Children," said George Müller, "it will soon be time for school, so let's pray. 'Dear Father, thank you for what we are going to eat.' "

George Müller ran orphanages for very poor children, children nobody wanted and nobody would look after. He didn't receive any money from the government to run his orphanage and he didn't receive any money from other people. He just trusted God. And this was another morning in the orphanage when they were trusting God. There was no food, the children were hungry, and it was time to eat breakfast. But Müller trusted God. He had prayed, so the food would certainly come.

Just then, a knock sounded at the door, and there stood the local baker. "Mr Müller," he said, "I couldn't sleep last night. Somehow I felt you didn't have bread for breakfast, and the Lord wanted me to send you some. So I have been up since two o'clock this morning baking some fresh bread for you."

Müller thanked the baker and praised God for his care. "Children," he announced, "not only do we have bread this morning, but it is fresh bread."

Right away, there came a second knock at the door. This time it was the milkman. "My cart has broken down outside the orphanage," he said, "and I must empty it before it can be fixed. Do the children need some milk?" And so the children ate their fresh bread and drank their fresh milk. Every meal time the children and George Müller prayed, and every meal time God provided for them.

It's exciting to know that God is for you and that he has incredible power to protect you, to provide for you and to defeat your enemies.

6 The Vital Flaw

	Programme	Item
Section 1	**Welcome**	
	Rules	
	Prayer	
	Introductory Praise	
	Game 1	Water-balloon Relays
	Praise	
	Fun Item 1	
	Game 2	Water Balloons With Leaders
	Fun Item 2	
	Bible Text	1 Corinthians 10:12
	Announcements	
	Interview	
Section 2 Preaching Time	**Worship Time**	
	Bible Lesson	Moses (The Vital Flaw)
	Illustration 1	Pyramids
	Illustration 2	Football Team
	Illustration 3	Fruit Bowl
	Story	Not Good Enough
	Prayer	

Moses had led Israel faithfully. He had led them through difficult times and it seemed that he would undoubtedly lead them into the Promised Land. But Moses had a vital flaw. He had murdered the Egyptian in his anger, and it was clear that he still got uncontrollably angry. Moses loses his temper and God doesn't let him enter the land. We must watch our flaws.

Game 1

Water-balloon Relays

PREPARATION	One water balloon per team.
PLAYERS	Five per team.
SET-UP	The teams line up in relay formation at A with the front person holding a water balloon each.
OBJECT	In relay formation the children must run from A to B and back, carrying the water balloon. At B they must pass it to the next player. If the balloon bursts, the team is disqualified.
WINNING	The team to complete the relay first and sit down wins.

Water Balloons With Leaders

PREPARATION	Six water balloons and a bucket per team.
PLAYERS	Six players and a leader per team.
SET-UP	Six players line up in relay formation at A. The leader stands beside the bucket at B.
OBJECT	The first person runs from A to B, and throws the water balloon to the leader from a distance of two metres. If the leader catches it and it doesn't burst, then the balloon is placed in the bucket. Either way, the player returns to A, where the next player begins.
WINNING	The team that has the most whole water balloons in the buckets wins.

MOSES (THE VITAL FLAW)

"If you think you are standing firm, be careful that you don't fall!"
(1 Corinthians 10:12, New International Version)

Now there came a time in the desert when the people all began to complain and say that Moses and Aaron weren't good leaders. They all said that Moses wasn't doing a very good job even though he had led them for many years exactly as God wanted.

The people had run out of water and they began to blame Moses. This is when it all began to go wrong for Moses. He started by doing the right thing: he lay on his stomach and began to pray to God. God spoke to him very clearly and said: "Bring all the people together. When they are all together, speak to the rocks, and water will flow from them so that the people can see that I am for them."

Moses did as God said and assembled the people. But, as the people gathered, Moses could hear them still complaining. He had led them as best he could and still they complained. Moses had had enough. He lifted up his stick and instead of speaking to the rock as God had commanded he hit the rock again and again. He lost his temper. The water flowed out of the rock, but instead of speaking as God had commanded, Moses had struck out in anger.

Pyramids

Object needed: *A picture of a block of flats or a pyramid.*

The pyramids at Giza in Egypt are among the most famous pieces of architecture in the world. The Pyramid of Khafre was built as a tomb for the pharaoh Khafre about 2,530 years before Jesus was born. The pyramid is about 136 metres high, and was built without the use of cranes, pulleys or lifting tackle.

Nobody really knows how the Egyptians managed to build the pyramids, but one thing is for sure: one mistake anywhere and the whole thing would have come toppling down. The builders had to be sure that there wasn't a mistake. If there was, the pyramids wouldn't stand. But the pyramids were very well built and stood for many, many thousands of years.

During the late 1960s – not that long ago – people started to build blocks of flats. Some of you may live in them now. They stretch up for quite some distance, but usually not as high as the pyramids. Hundreds of people can live in them. Unfortunately, when the builders constructed many of these buildings, they made mistakes. They didn't build them properly. Many have had to be pulled down.

We have to be sure that when we build our lives, we have no flaws. We have to watch out that we don't lose our tempers easily, that we don't lie and cheat, that we don't deliberately cause trouble. We have to make sure our lives are right, or we will not stand the test of time. When trouble comes, we will let God down. We must be careful with our lives.

Football Team

Object needed: *Display a picture of a football team.*

Football is an exciting game to watch, and I know that we all have favourite football teams.

But whenever I have watched a game, it seems to me that the best teams have players who all know how to play together, who all know their positions, and who all work well together. The midfielders play in midfield; the defenders know how to defend; the attackers know how to attack. And the goalkeepers know how to save.

It is important that teams do have good goalkeepers. It's no good having a great team and having a bad goalkeeper. It doesn't work. There is a flaw. He will let the whole team down.

We can be the most talented person in the whole world, with many talents and gifts. But with one flaw we can let ourselves down. Work on that weakness. Make sure it doesn't let you down.

Fruit Bowl

Object needed: *A fruit bowl and all the fruits mentioned below.*

The Bible talks about nine fruits of the Spirit. They are all things God wants to build into our lives. This is a fruit bowl. Let's pretend it's like our lives. It's not very good right now; it's empty. But what if we begin to fill it up with God's fruit...

Here's a banana. That can be a fruit of the Spirit. We'll use the banana to remind us about self-control. Now the bowl looks more interesting, but it needs more, I think. As in our lives, self-control isn't enough. We need more.

How about a:

- **Plum** – this one could be **Love**. Our bowl's looking better and so are our lives.
- **Pear** – this one could be **Happiness**. Our bowl's looking better and so are our lives.
- **Grape** – this one could be **Peace**. Our bowl's looking better and so are our lives.
- **Orange** – this one could be **Patience**. Our bowl's looking better and so are our lives.
- **Lemon** – this one could be **Kindness**. Our bowl's looking better and so are our lives.
- **Lime** – this one could be **Goodness**. Our bowl's looking better and so are our lives.

- **Strawberry** – this one could be **Faithfulness**. Our bowl's looking better and so are our lives.
- **Apple** – this one could be **Gentleness**. Our bowl's looking better and so are our lives.

We need to make sure our lives contain all these things. When they do, then we are more like Jesus, and God can use us to do amazing things.

● STORY – Not Good Enough

Gladys Aylward sat uneasily in the headmaster's office. It was 1928, and she'd been at the China Inland Mission training school for three months. What was this meeting about?

"Gladys," the principal said gently, "your grades for the first term are... well, very poor. It would be a waste of time and money to continue."

"But," Gladys protested, "all my life I have felt God wants me to be a missionary in China."

"Besides," the principal went on, "by the time you graduate, you will be almost 30. That is too old to learn a hard language like Chinese."

Shoulders sagging, Gladys got up and began to leave. "But I can help you get a job as a housekeeper," the headmaster added helpfully. A housekeeper! Gladys was frustrated. She was sure God wanted her to go to China.

Lots of people have vital flaws. Moses' flaw was his temper; for others it might be laziness. It looked as if Gladys' flaw was the fact that she wasn't confident enough to do what God had said. She would just become a housekeeper for the rest of her life. But Gladys didn't have a vital flaw; she knew what God had said and, even though she wasn't clever enough to pass exams, she would do what God had said.

One day, Gladys walked into a travel agent's and asked how much a ticket to China would cost. There were no aeroplanes back then, so she was quoted a price of £90 to go on a ship. £90 was too much money, so Gladys asked if there might be another way. The travel agent smiled and then said: "Well, you could cross over to France and then catch a train for £40."

The travel agent smiled because the train would take weeks and weeks and, besides, the train would have to go through Russia, and they were at war with China and not letting anyone through.

But Gladys booked the ticket anyway. She didn't have enough money, so she paid something towards her ticket every week until she'd paid it all off. Then she made her way to France and got on the train. Five thousand miles and four weeks later, she arrived in Yangcheng, China. What God had told Gladys was more important than what anyone else told Gladys. Gladys didn't let her lack of confidence become the vital flaw. She did what God said.

7 The Promised Land

	Programme	Item
Section 1	Welcome	
	Rules	
	Prayer	
	Introductory Praise	
	Game 1	Water Wellies 1
	Praise	
	Fun Item 1	
	Game 2	Water Wellies 2
	Fun Item 2	
	Bible Text	2 Samuel 14:14
	Announcements	
	Interview	
Section 2 Preaching Time	Worship Time	
	Bible Lesson	Moses
	Illustration 1	It's Never Over Until It's Over
	Illustration 2	It's Never Over Until God Says
	Illustration 3	It's Not Even Over When It's Over
	Story	Livingstone's Children
	Prayer	

Overview Moses had made a vital mistake and God had stopped him entering the Promised Land. But, when you're extraordinary, there's always a way back. And Moses was no ordinary child. This lesson will conclude the series by showing us just how extraordinary Moses really was.

games

Water Wellies 1

PREPARATION	A pair of wellington boots per team and many small water balloons.
PLAYERS	Five per team.
SET-UP	Four of the players line up in relay formation at A. The fifth person wears the wellington boots and stands at B.
OBJECT	The first player runs from A to B carrying the water balloon and pushes the water balloon into the wellington boots. They then return to A, and the next person then goes. When all four people have gone, the other player runs from B back to A.
WINNING	The first team back wins.

Water Wellies 2

PREPARATION	A pair of wellington boots per team and many small water balloons.
PLAYERS	Five per team and a leader.
SET-UP	Five of the players line up in relay formation at A. The leader wears the wellington boots and stands at B.
OBJECT	The first player runs from A to B carrying the water balloon and pushes the water balloon into the wellington boots. They then return to A, and the next person then goes. When all five people have gone, the leader runs from B back to A.
WINNING	The first team back wins.

BIBLE LESSON MOSES

"But God does not take away life; instead, he devises ways so that a banished person may not remain estranged from him." (2 Samuel 14:14, New International Version)

Moses had struck the rock in anger and now he, like so many of the other Israelites, would die in the wilderness because he didn't do what God said. But the exciting thing about serving God is that it's never really the end until God says so.

Several centuries later, three fishermen were walking with Jesus. Before their very eyes Jesus became shrouded in light as bright as lightning, and two other men stood with him. We call it the "transfiguration". One of the men was Elijah – he's the person who called fire from heaven onto the followers of Baal. Guess who the other person was? None other than Moses; God hadn't forgotten him.

The Bible says that at the end of time we will all sing a song, the song of Jesus and of... yes, you guessed: Moses. You may make mistakes, you may mess up badly, but that won't stop you being an extraordinary child. It never stopped Moses.

It's Never Over Until It's Over

Object needed: *None.*

There was once a young woman who lived with her parents in Vietnam. She was just 17 years old and had always lived with her parents in their poor little village about two days' journey from the capital city. One day the girl decided that she would leave home and go to the city to make some money to send home to her parents.

She saved what little money she could until eventually she had enough money to go. She bought her ticket and was all set to leave. Her mother began to plead with her to stay: "Don't go to the city, you'll end up in all sorts of trouble. Don't go." But the girl wouldn't listen and set off.

Several days later she arrived in the city. She tried to get a job but nobody wanted to employ her. Eventually she gave up and took a job in a very bad nightclub. She got caught up in drugs and many other bad things.

Meanwhile her mother became very concerned when her daughter stopped writing to her. The mother took on extra jobs so that she could get enough money together to travel to the big city. It took her six months and eventually she set off.

On arriving in the city, she spent the last of her money in a printer's shop, where she got herself several hundred small cards printed. The cards read: "Wherever you are! Whatever you've done! Come home!" The mother wanted her daughter to know that she was prepared to love her, no matter what!

She spent the next couple of weeks putting these cards in every telephone box, in every hotel lobby and on every noticeboard in the city. Then the mother, saddened by the fact that she couldn't find her daughter, made her way home.

The daughter went from bad to worse, getting caught up in even worse things than before. Then one day she found one of the cards her mother had left. She cried and cried and then scraped enough money together and went home...

God too doesn't want to punish us for doing wrong things. He doesn't want us to be isolated from him; he wants us to come on home. Come back to him. Just because you've made a mistake, it doesn't mean it's over. It's never over until it's over.

It's Never Over Until God Says

Object needed: *A fishing net.*

Peter said three times that he didn't know Jesus! Three times he announced that he had never known Jesus. This is after he had told Jesus that he would never betray him. But on that night when Jesus was taken prisoner, the night before he would be crucified, Peter denied that he had ever even been in the same room as him. He betrayed and disowned Jesus.

Now you and I, hearing that, might think that it was all over for Peter. Jesus wouldn't want to know Peter after what he'd done. You and I may or may not think that, but Peter thought that and returned to his fishing boat.

And it was there that Jesus found him, and it was there that Jesus let him know that he had forgiven him, and it was there on the beach that Peter once again dedicated his life to serving Jesus.

It's never over until God says, and God works very hard to make sure that we always know that there's a way that we can come back to him.

It's Not Even Over When It's Over

Object needed: *A picture of a crown court.*

The Bible tells us that we die once, and after that we stand before God and are judged, in the same way that a person may stand in front of a court to be judged.

Now the way we are judged is very interesting. It's not really a case of how many bad things you've done compared with how many good things you've done. It comes down to one simple question. God will ask every person in turn: "Have you become a Christian – have you asked my Son Jesus to forgive all the wrong things you've done?" If we can answer yes, then God allows us to enter into heaven. If we can't, then God will not allow us to enter into heaven.

Even when we die, it's still not the end. God will judge everyone.

• STORY – Livingstone's Children

David Livingstone was a missionary to Africa. He loved to tell the Africans about Jesus and he loved to explore. On his second great expedition, he travelled to the Zambezi river from the eastern coast of Africa. But he became very worried about the slave trade developing in this area. Portuguese traders along the coast encouraged Africans called Red Caps to travel deep into the African jungle to buy slaves.

Livingstone knew that he would have to travel deeper into the jungle than the Red Caps, to tell people about Jesus and warn them about the slave traders. It seemed like a good plan. Using his ability to learn languages and his deep respect for the African people and their ways, Livingstone again travelled where no white person had ever gone. There were no slave traders there. He talked to people who had kept foreigners – white or black – out of their land for generations.

Then one day he came upon a group of slaves which included people from some of these tribes. After he had chased off the Red Caps and freed the slaves, he asked, "How did the Red Caps get to you? You never let outsiders into your villages!"

"They said they were with you," the people replied sadly, "so we thought it was safe to let them in."

David Livingstone was crushed. He had worked so hard to reach these tribes. Now that he was their friend, he had, without meaning to, opened the door for slave traders to come in too! It was the very last thing he wanted to happen.

He became angry, and then his anger turned to despair. What could he do? He had failed. No, it was worse than failure. He had made things worse! Many people might have quit and gone home at that point. But David knew that it was never over until God said. David Livingstone did not think of himself as too good. He knew he could fail, but he would keep trying.

Many people became Christians in Africa because Livingstone didn't quit. He campaigned to stop slavery and, fifteen years after his death, that too happened – because a man called David Livingstone never quit.

THE PIRATE KING

A Series in Six Parts

Introduction

Title	Themes covered	Hebrews 11:32
1 Discovering The Map	Adventure	Gideon
2 Delayed	Overcoming	Barak
3 Fatherless	Keeping our eyes on Jesus	Samson
4 Whom Do We Trust?	What are you holding onto?	Jephthah
5 Learning	The things we learn now...	Samuel
6 Treasure	What is truly important	David

This series will weave together three different elements to communicate the message.

The Disney DVD *Treasure Planet* will form the basis for one of the illustrations in each of the lessons. The Bible Lessons will look through the characters in Hebrews 11:32 – I have always wanted to take the time to talk about those whom the writer of Hebrews had no time to mention. And the Story to end each of the sessions is "The Pirate King" – an adventure story that I'm sure everyone will enjoy.

Themes such as adventure, learning what is important, and keeping our eyes on God are covered.

Discovering The Map

	Programme	Item
Section 1	**Welcome**	
	Rules	
	Prayer	
	Introductory Praise	
	Game 1	Pirate Jigsaw
	Praise	
	Fun Item 1	
	Game 2	Sponge Attack
	Fun Item 2	
	Bible Text	Hebrews 11:32
	Announcements	
	Interview	
Section 2	**Worship Time**	
Preaching	**Bible Lesson**	Gideon
Time	**Illustration 1**	*Treasure Planet* Video Clip
	Illustration 2	David Beckham
	Illustration 3	Give Things Up
	Story	The Pirate King (1)
	Prayer	

Overview

"You have to give some things up when you're chasing a dream." These were the words spoken to Jim Hawkins by John Silver in *Treasure Planet*. The children we are speaking to have exciting lives to live, but some of them will have to make important choices over the course of this lesson and those that follow.

Game 1

Pirate Jigsaw

PREPARATION Copy the pirate on the title page of this series onto a piece of card per team. Then cut the card into seven pieces.

PLAYERS Three per team.

SET-UP The jigsaw pieces are placed at B. The players line up at A in relay formation.

OBJECT The players run from A to B in relay order. They collect a jigsaw piece and return. When all the pieces are collected the jigsaw is constructed.

WINNING The first team with a constructed jigsaw wins.

Game 2

Sponge Attack

PREPARATION A leader per team dressed as a pirate, and a bucket of water containing pieces of sponge.

PLAYERS Five per team.

SET-UP A leader per team dressed as a pirate sits five metres beyond B. A bucket of water containing pieces of sponge is placed at B.

OBJECT The players in turn run from A to B, collect a piece of sponge and throw it at the leader. A point is scored for each hit below the neck. Any hits above the neck are discounted (make sure the children know this; the sponges shouldn't hurt, but shots to the face should be discouraged).

WINNING The team with the most hits wins.

Preaching Time

BIBLE LESSON GIDEON

"What else can I say? There isn't enough time to tell about Gideon, *Barak, Samson, Jephthah, David, Samuel, and the prophets." (Hebrews 11:32)*

Over the next six weeks we will be looking at the characters in a wonderful chapter in the Bible called Hebrews chapter 11. The chapter looks at heroes. It gives a brief account of what each of the heroes did. But at the end it says that there is no time to speak of... and it gives a list of six people. We will take the time this week to look at each of these characters. We will start today with a man called Gideon and look at a very interesting part of Gideon's life.

One night God spoke to Gideon and said: "Get your father's second-best bull, the one that's seven years old. Use it to pull down the altar where your father worships those gods which are not really gods and cut down the sacred pole next to the altar. Then build an altar for worshipping me on the highest part of the hill."

For Gideon to do what God wanted he would have to give something up – in this case he would have to give up his safety. It was fairly certain that the people wouldn't like what he had done.

Gideon chose ten of his servants to help him, and they did everything God had said. But since Gideon was afraid, he did it all at night. When the people of the town got up the next morning, they saw that Baal's altar had been knocked over, and the sacred pole next to it had been cut down. Then they noticed the new altar.

"Who could have done such a thing?" they asked. And they kept on asking, until finally someone told them, "Gideon did it." The people wanted to kill Gideon but Gideon's father protected him. God was going to ask Gideon to do many more incredible things but he had to prove that he would do what God wanted, even if it meant giving things up.

Treasure Planet Video Clip

Object needed: *A clip from the video* Treasure Planet.

Show the clip where James Hawkins has first opened the treasure planet map and they decide to undertake the adventure. At the end of the video, say:

Jim Hawkins had waited all his life for this opportunity, the opportunity to find Treasure Planet and recover all the gold. But Jim would have to leave something behind. He would have to say goodbye to his friends and family and his mother. But he was going to do it. For the sake of the adventure he was ready to leave many things behind.

David Beckham

Object needed: *A video clip of David Beckham, or a football.*

Feel free to update this lesson as necessary – I suspect David Beckham won't be famous for ever!

David Beckham was the English hero of the 2002 World Cup. His goal in the last couple of minutes of the game against Argentina guaranteed that people would be singing his praises for many years to come.

Whether it was for Manchester United or for Real Madrid or for England, David Beckham always seemed to produce what was needed. His trademark free kicks have become the substance of legends. Beckham can score goals from anywhere. He can land the ball wherever he wants; he can drop the ball at the feet of his forwards...

But Beckham wasn't born with this ability. He didn't know how to do this automatically. Like many great sportsmen, Beckham worked at it. He spent hours and hours kicking the ball. When his friends were going out to do all sorts of things, Beckham would be kicking his ball. His friends would be going to parties; Beckham would be kicking a ball. Still now, while others are off enjoying themselves, Beckham will stay and practise.

Beckham was committed. He was prepared to give something up to be what he was sure he could be.

Give Things Up

Object needed: *A picture of a hot air balloon.*

There is this little game that has been played for years and years. It works like this. You have to pretend that you are in a hot air balloon and you have with you everything that you own. The balloon is no longer going up because there is too much weight. You have to decide what you really want to keep and what you would happily throw over the side (you can't throw your little brother or sister over – that would be mean!).

So, first, what would you keep? *(Allow some of the children to respond.)*

And what would you keep? *(Allow more children to respond.)*

They are interesting answers. Over the next couple of weeks we will be showing you that God wants you to live an exciting life for him, a life of adventure. But to live that life there are things that we need to give up.

There may be many things God will ask you to give up, but the first thing is a thing that you really don't want to keep anyway. That's something called sin. Sin is the junk and rubbish and garbage in your life. God wants us to give this rubbish to him. It simply involves us praying a prayer and saying: "God, I know I have junk and rubbish in my life, the stuff the Bible calls sin. Please take this away and help me to be a Christian. Amen."

• STORY – The Pirate King (1)

Kristy sat in her classroom. She wasn't happy. So far today she'd listened to Professor Collins talking about blood and bones and then it was Professor Thomas talking about geology – something about rocks. Kristy then had to listen to Professor Sanderson, but she was fairly sure

she'd never need to know that the angles in a triangle add up to 180 degrees. And why Helen of Troy being rescued by Greeks in a Trojan horse would ever be useful, she did not know. The last hour had been spent listening to Dr Stevens explaining something about prisms – Kristy really didn't care what happened to light when it passed through a prism.

It was 200 years ago and most children didn't go to school. But Kristy did. It was one of the disadvantages of having a very rich dad. Lord Cartwright had made his money by opening a coal mine. This had grown quickly and now Cartwright Coal Mines employed 500 people, and Lord Cartwright himself owned 25 coal mines in total. He was very rich.

One day Kristy would be in charge of the Cartwright business and so she had been sent to school to prepare her to do the job properly. But Kristy still couldn't work out why she would need to know geography to look after some coal mines. What seemed even more unfair to Kristy was that they had only decided to make her the heir to the lordship a year ago. Up until then it was to be Cameron, Kristy's elder brother, who was to be the next lord. But 18 months ago Cameron had decided to leave. He had packed his things, announced to the family over breakfast that he was going to see the world, and simply walked out. He became a sailor on the first ship that he came to when he reached the harbour, and that was the last Kristy had heard of her brother. She didn't expect to hear from him ever again.

But then she hadn't been home and seen the letter sitting on the hall cupboard with his name on it.

The afternoon dragged on, but eventually the clock struck 4pm and school was over. Kristy collected her books and made her way home. She looked at the blue sky, gazed over the green fields, entered her enormous house and dropped her books in a pile next to the door – servants would clear them away for her. Then she saw it. It was not the letter with her name on that made her heart miss a beat; it was the handwriting on the letter – it was Cameron's. Of this there could be no doubt.

Kristy opened the letter slowly and began to read. The words were simple and to the point, but the handwriting was jerky. It read:

> To my sister Kristy,
> I need your help. I'm being held prisoner on an island called Dax. It is just below the southernmost point of South America. My friend Jason has smuggled this letter out and I've asked him to post it the moment he gets back to England.
> Please come, Cameron.

Up until that moment life had been very ordinary. It seemed that if there was an adventure to be had, Cameron was the one who would have it. Nobody was really surprised when he packed his things and went to sea. He was the courageous one of the family. But now the courageous one was in trouble.

Kristy paced up and down the living room. Her mind was racing. Her brother needed her, but how could she help? She was not good at adventures and was unsure what to do. She wondered whether she should find her father, but he was rarely around these days. She read the letter through again. Her brother needed her. But she would have to give up the comfort of her home – then again, she would get out of school.

Kristy packed a small bag, asked her servant to bring her horse, and set off...

(To be continued...)

2 Delayed

	Programme	Item
Section 1	**Welcome**	
	Rules	
	Prayer	
	Introductory Praise	
	Game 1	Sleeping Lions
	Praise	
	Fun Item 1	
	Game 2	Weapons Of War
	Fun Item 2	
	Bible Text	2 Samuel 11:1
	Announcements	
	Interview	
Section 2	**Worship Time**	
Preaching	**Bible Lesson**	Barak
Time	**Illustration 1**	*Treasure Planet* Video Clip
	Illustration 2	Sleeping Lions
	Illustration 3	"Little Boy Blue"
	Illustration 4	Work! Work! Work!
	Story	The Pirate King (2)
	Prayer	

Sometimes we may have made decisions to go and do something for Jesus, but we get distracted so easily and instead do nothing.

games

Sleeping Lions

PREPARATION	None needed.
PLAYERS	Two per team.
SET-UP	None needed.
OBJECT	The players lie on the floor at A, pretending to be sleeping lions.
WINNING	Leave the players there for the duration of the praise song. The player with the least movement by the end of the praise song wins.

Weapons Of War

PREPARATION	Place at B a number of objects: a shield, a sword, a feather, an arrow, an egg, a ball.
PLAYERS	Three per team.
SET-UP	The players line up at A.
OBJECT	The players in turn run from A to B; at B they collect a weapon of war and return to A.
WINNING	The team with the arrow, the sword and the shield wins.

PreachingTime

BIBLE LESSON BARAK

"What else can I say? There isn't enough time to tell about Gideon, Barak, Samson, Jephthah, David, Samuel, and the prophets." (Hebrews 11:32)

One day, Barak was in a place called Kedesh when Deborah, a servant of God, sent word for him to come and talk with her. When he arrived, she said: "I have a message for you from the Lord God of Israel! You are to get together an army of 10,000 men and lead them to Mount Tabor. The Lord will trick Sisera into coming out to fight you at the Kishon river. Sisera will be leading King Jabin's army as usual, and they will have their chariots, but the Lord has promised to help you defeat them."

"I'm not going unless you go!" Barak told her. Barak knew that God was going to be with him, but still he wouldn't go unless Deborah came. His eyes should have been on what God wanted him to do; he knew he should set off straight away, but he was making excuses. He should have just gone. The job God wanted him to do was very important.

"All right, I'll go!" Deborah replied. "But I'm warning you that the Lord is going to let a woman defeat Sisera, and no one will honour you for winning the battle."

So because Barak didn't go straight away without Deborah and simply trust God, he was to get no honour from the fight. Deborah and Barak left for Kedesh, where Barak called together the troops from Zebulun and Naphtali. Ten thousand soldiers gathered there, and Barak led them out from Kedesh. Deborah went too.

When Sisera learned that Barak had led an army to Mount Tabor, he called his troops together and got all 900 iron chariots ready. Then he led his army away from Harosheth-Ha-Goiim to the Kishon river. Deborah shouted, "Barak, it's time to attack Sisera! Because today the Lord is going to help you defeat him. In fact, the Lord has already gone on ahead to fight for you."

Barak led his 10,000 troops down from Mount Tabor. And during the battle, the Lord confused Sisera, his chariot drivers and his whole army. Everyone was so afraid of Barak and his army; even Sisera jumped down from his chariot and tried to escape. Barak's forces went after Sisera's chariots and army as far as Harosheth-Ha-Goiim. Sisera's entire army was wiped out. Only Sisera escaped. He ran to Heber's camp, because Heber and his family had a peace treaty with the king of Hazor. Sisera went to the tent that belonged to Jael, Heber's wife. She came out to greet him and said, "Come in, sir! Please come on in. Don't be afraid."

After they had gone inside, Sisera lay down, and Jael covered him with a blanket. Sisera was exhausted and soon fell fast asleep. While he slept, Jael killed him. And it turned out exactly as Deborah had said. Because Barak wouldn't go when he was told by God, they still won, but Barak received little honour.

Barak is on our list because he did lead Israel, but he's also there to remind us that when God says "go", we go straight away, we don't get distracted and we don't get lazy. We just go and do what God asks.

Treasure Planet Video Clip

Object needed: *A clip from the video* Treasure Planet.

Show the clip where Jim Hawkins first joins Captain Amelia's ship and is placed in the galley with John Silver.

Jim thought that he would be in charge on the ship. He didn't realise that it wasn't going to be so comfortable and he would have to work. But he wasn't turning back even if it was going to be tough.

Illustration 2

Sleeping Lions

Object needed: *A picture of some lions sleeping or maybe a piece of a natural-history documentary showing a lion hunting.*

How many people say their prayers every day? Not always easy, is it? Sometimes it's hard work.

Today's game of sleeping lions was a lot of fun and some of you didn't move for such a long time. When I watch films of real lions they also seem to spend lots of time sleeping. But not all the time. There are times when these lazy lions will stand up, stretch and hunt. And when they hunt they are anything but sleepy. They are fast, furious and frightening, very frightening.

It's important that they do hunt. They may

want to stay in the sun, they may want to stay where it is comfortable, but if they don't hunt, then they will starve to death. Lying back in the sun may seem like a nice thing to do, but if you're a lion, you can't do it too much.

There is definitely a time for lying in the sun, but there is also a time for saying our prayers, that is, talking to Jesus, and helping others and doing the work we should do. There is a time to work, even when it would be easier to do nothing. There is a time to pray, even when it would easier to go and play.

Illustration 3

"Little Boy Blue"

Object needed: *A copy of the nursery rhyme below on acetate or video projector.*

Little Boy Blue, come blow your horn,
The cow's in the meadow, the sheep's in the corn,
But where is the boy who looks after the sheep?
He's under a haystack fast asleep.

Did any of you know that nursery rhyme? Does anyone want to try and explain what it's about? *(Allow the children to respond.)*

Yes, it's about a boy who goes to sleep instead of looking after the animals. It's just a fun rhyme really, but, in some jobs, if a person goes to sleep when they are supposed to be working, there can be terrible results. When people sleep when they are in charge of big machines, people can die. In former times, signalmen were in charge of controlling the tracks when the trains went past, and if they went to sleep the trains would crash. Terrible things can happen when we want to be relaxing when we should be working.

It is important that we spend some time relaxing. Even God rested on the seventh day when he was creating the world. But when we should be helping others or saying our prayers or doing some work for others, then we should do that and not relax instead.

Work! Work! Work!

Object needed: *Pictures of people at work.*

Some people think that work is a bad thing. Some of you may have heard your mums or dads moan about having to get up in the morning to go to work. Your parents complain about the

ever-increasing housework that you are causing. Some of you moan constantly that you are being forced to do homework. Some of you find praying, talking to God, hard work – me too sometimes.

But our Bible Text today makes it very clear that "No matter how much you want, laziness won't help a bit, but hard work will reward you with more than enough". I think in all situations you'll find that's true. If your parents don't get up to go to work, then nobody is going to pay them and there will be no money for the nice things that you may want. And if your parents decide not to do housework, then your clothes will not get washed and the ironing pile will get bigger and bigger until you end up with nothing to wear!

And if you don't do your homework, then you never learn what you need to learn and reading will be difficult and mathematics will be difficult, and all because you didn't do the work. It may seem as if the easiest thing in the world is to do nothing, but if we do that, we will regret it.

• STORY – The Pirate King (2)

It was such an important task, but suddenly Kristy wasn't sure. She'd stopped her horse outside the school that she hated, but suddenly it didn't look so bad. The thought of never seeing it again made her feel almost sad. But still she kept going.

Then she found herself outside the coal mines, the ones her dad owned – or certainly some of the ones her dad owned. She didn't mind never seeing them again, but Dad? She did feel very worried about Dad. But Cameron needed her. She had to go.

Kristy rode further along the road towards the coast. She passed a funfair in a nearby village

and she knew it would be at her village soon. She passed a whole series of churches with enormous steeples, all of which reminded her of the church in her village. Everywhere she looked there was something that reminded her of her home. But she kept going, because she had to, and to get lazy or turn back was the last thing that would help her brother.

She knew that turning back towards home might seem like a good idea now, but if she did, then in weeks to come she would regret it and Cameron might well be lost for ever. Her brother needed her and she was going to help him. She was making good time and would be able to reach the port very soon. From there, she would be able to get a ship in the right direction, she was sure. She kicked her legs together and the horse started to run faster. The wind blew through her hair. She would try to be at the port before nightfall and on a ship before tomorrow evening. She galloped on.

Cameron lay in the dark. He would be hardly recognisable when Kristy got to him – *if* she got to him. He had assured the Guardians that his sister would come, but they hadn't believed him. They knew how bad people are at finishing what they start and they knew that people will often prefer to stay comfortable than to risk anything for someone else. But Cameron knew Kristy well. If anyone could save him, it would be her. He closed his eyes and in the dark, damp cave he slept.

Far away, his sister rode ever closer, sure now that she was doing the right thing. It might not be the easiest thing and she was sure it wouldn't be the most comfortable thing, but it would be the right thing. The moon was high in the sky, but in the distance Kristy could see the outline of the port. She pulled over to the side of the road and slept under a tree. She would arrive in the morning now. She would find Cameron. She was determined.

(To be continued...)

3 Fatherless

	Programme	Item
Section 1	**Welcome**	
	Rules	
	Prayer	
	Introductory Praise	
	Game 1	Fill The Stores
	Praise	
	Fun Item 1	
	Game 2	Eat The Stores
	Fun Item 2	
	Bible Text	Hebrews 11:32
	Announcements	
	Interview	
Section 2 Preaching Time	**Worship Time**	
	Illustration 1	*Treasure Planet* Video Clip
	Bible Lesson 1	Samson 1
	Bible Lesson 2	Samson 2
	Bible Lesson 3	Samson 3
	Story	The Pirate King (3)
	Prayer	

Overview Samson thought he could do what he wanted. He thought he didn't need to keep his focus on God; God would help him anyway. God loves us, but if we don't keep our focus on God we end up hurt and lost.

games

Preaching Time

BIBLE TEXT

"What else can I say? There isn't enough time to tell about Gideon, Barak, Samson, *Jephthah, David, Samuel, and the prophets." (Hebrews 11:32)*

Game 1

Fill The Stores

PREPARATION	An apple, a banana, some grapes, some cherries and a plate per team.
PLAYERS	Three from each team and a leader.
SET-UP	The fruits are placed at B, the players in relay formation at A.
OBJECT	The first player goes from A to B, collects a piece of fruit and returns to A. When all the fruit is returned, the leader and the team chop up the fruit to construct a face. There are only three minutes allowed.
WINNING	The best face wins.

Game 2

Eat The Stores

PREPARATION	Hopefully you have kept the fruit faces from Game 1.
PLAYERS	A leader per team.
SET-UP	The leader is at A with the fruit face.
OBJECT	To eat the fruit face.
WINNING	The first leader to finish the fruit face completely wins.

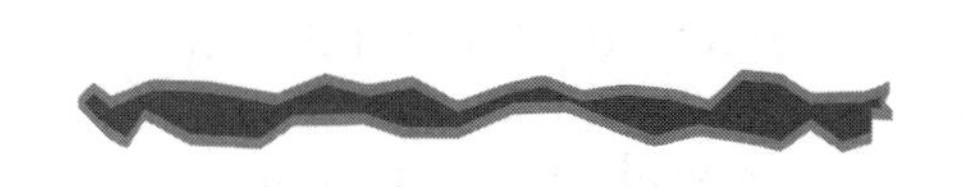

Illustration 1

Treasure Planet Video Clip

Object needed: *A clip from the video* Treasure Planet.

Show the clip where Jim Hawkins is thinking back to the times when his dad was there and walks out – it plays like a flashback music video.

Jim's dad left him when he was very young. Some of you may have dads who have left for one reason or another; others of you may live with your dad only. I have two dads – not two human dads, but a real dad and God, who is also called God the Father. There are some things I can talk to my real dad about, but there is nothing I cannot talk to God about.

Sometimes my dad has let me down; many times I have let my dad down. But God the Father has never let me down, no matter how many times I let him down. God the Father loves us always but he does ask that we keep our eyes on him. Today's Bible character was very special to God, just as you are, but he let God down big time. Let me spend a little bit of time talking to you about God's Incredible Hulk.

BIBLE LESSON 1

Samson 1

Object needed: *A smiling face.*

Samson's birth was a miracle. His mum and dad couldn't have children, then one day an angel appeared to Samson's parents and told them they would have a baby and he would be a Nazirite. A Nazirite was someone who was special to God and who lived by a special set of rules. Samson was not allowed to cut his hair and he was not allowed to drink wine.

Samson was a special child, but no more special than you. Psalm 139 tells me that before you were born God knew exactly how you would look. He watched you growing in your mummy's tummy.

Samson had long hair. He was not allowed to cut his hair. Many people may have made fun of Samson's long hair, but probably only once. For God gave Samson power and he could do amazing things.

On one occasion, a lion had jumped out at Samson but Samson was so strong he tore the lion in half. On another occasion he killed thousands of Philistines with the jawbone of a donkey. On yet another occasion, when the Philistines (God's enemies) had tried to trap him by locking him in a city, Samson had simply pulled the town's gates out of the ground. God's Spirit would come upon Samson and he would do amazing things for God.

It was a great start.

Samson 2

Object needed: *A neutral face.*

There were definitely some interesting things taking place here. You remember the two things that Samson wasn't allowed to do:

1. Drink wine
2. Have his hair cut

You see, keeping these rules showed that he still loved God and was still looking to God for his strength. But the time when he tore the lion in half is interesting. If you or I tore a lion in half we would be telling everyone about it, but not Samson; the Bible says that he didn't tell anyone. This might seem strange until we work out where all this happened. The Bible says the lion attacked him outside Timnah's vineyard. Now does anyone know what we get in vineyards? Yes, wine! Maybe Samson was playing with things he shouldn't be near.

I think he thought he could do whatever he wanted and God would still look after him. This just isn't true.

Samson 3

Object needed: *A sad face and two cards with the words "visionless" and "wounded".*

Now the story gets very sad indeed:

> Some time later, Samson fell in love with a woman named Delilah, who lived in Sorek Valley. The Philistine rulers went to Delilah and said, "Trick Samson into telling you what makes him so strong and what can make him weak. Then we can tie him up so he can't get away. If you find out his secret, we will each give you eleven hundred pieces of silver."
>
> The next time Samson was at Delilah's house, she asked, "Samson, what makes you so strong? How can I tie you up so you can't get away? Come on, you can tell me."
>
> Samson answered, "If someone ties me up with seven new bowstrings that have never been dried, it will make me just as weak as anyone else."
>
> The Philistine rulers gave seven new bowstrings to Delilah. They also told some of their soldiers to go to Delilah's house and hide in the room where Samson and Delilah were. If the bowstrings made Samson weak, they would be able to capture him.
>
> Delilah tied up Samson with the bowstrings and shouted, "Samson, the Philistines are attacking!" (Judges 16:4–9a)

Samson snapped the bowstrings and then he snapped the Philistines! Delilah asked him again what would make him lose his strength.

> "My hair is in seven braids," Samson replied. "If you weave my braids into the threads on a loom and nail the loom to a wall, then I will be as weak as anyone else."
>
> While Samson was asleep, Delilah wove his braids into the threads on a loom and nailed the loom to a wall. Then she shouted, "Samson, the Philistines are attacking!"

Samson woke up and pulled the loom free from its posts in the ground and from the nails in the wall. Then he pulled his hair free from the woven cloth.

"Samson," Delilah said, "you claim to love me, but you don't mean it! You've made me look like a fool three times now, and you still haven't told me why you are so strong." Delilah started nagging and pestering him day after day, until he couldn't stand it any longer.

Finally, Samson told her the truth. "I have belonged to God ever since I was born, so my hair has never been cut. If it were ever cut off, my strength would leave me, and I would be as weak as anyone else."

Delilah realised that he was telling the truth. So she sent someone to tell the Philistine rulers, "Come to my house one more time. Samson has finally told me the truth."

The Philistine rulers went to Delilah's house, and they brought along the silver they had promised her. Delilah had lulled Samson to sleep with his head resting in her lap. She signalled to one of the Philistine men as she began cutting off Samson's seven braids. And by the time she had finished, Samson's strength was gone. Delilah tied him up and shouted, "Samson, the Philistines are attacking!"

Samson woke up and thought, "I'll break loose and escape, just as I always do." He did not realise that the LORD had stopped helping him. (Judges 16:13b–20)

This is one of the saddest verses in the Bible. Samson thought God would be with him, no matter what he did. He thought he could do whatever he liked and God would still be there.

The Philistines grabbed Samson and poked out his eyes. They took him to the prison in Gaza and chained him up. Samson had become *visionless* and *wounded*. He didn't know where he was going and he was hurt. He was lost and hurt.

Display two cards as shown below.

• **Visionless** • **Didn't know where he was going** • **Lost**	• **Wounded** • **Hurt**

Some of you may have felt like this and some of you may be feeling like this now. There is only one answer. Let me show you how the story ends.

> The Philistine rulers threw a big party and sacrificed a lot of animals to their god Dagon... They made fun of Samson for a while, then they told him to stand near the columns that supported the roof. A young man was leading Samson by the hand, and Samson said to him, "I need to lean against something. Take me over to the columns that hold up the roof."
>
> The Philistine rulers were celebrating in a temple packed with people and with three thousand more on the flat roof. They had all been watching Samson and making fun of him.
>
> Samson prayed, "Please remember me, LORD God. The Philistines poked out my eyes, but make me strong one last time, so I can take revenge for at least one of my eyes!" (Judges 16:23–28)

At the very end Samson looked to God. He asked God to help and Samson felt God start to help him again.

> Samson was standing between the two middle columns that held up the roof. He felt around and found one column with his right hand, and the other with his left hand... He pushed against the columns as hard as he could, and the temple collapsed with the Philistine rulers and everyone else still inside. Samson killed more Philistines when he died than he had killed during his entire life. (Judges 16:29–30)

The only answer when we become visionless and wounded is to look again to God and he will strengthen us and help us.

• STORY – The Pirate King (3)

Kristy arrived at the coast. She was going to find her brother and do what she could to rescue him. She wasn't completely sure how she felt about her brother, but he *was* her brother and she felt that she had a responsibility to rescue him. The harbour was a mad world of drunken sailors, men and women trying to sell their day's catch off the back of their boats, people shouting and the overpowering smell of fish.

Kristy had never seen such activity – she had

grown up in the seclusion of the manor house. She had never seen so many people in such a small area. The whole thing seemed so exciting to her. She walked towards what appeared to be a makeshift market. She gazed at one stall full of ornate shells; she marvelled at the collection of pearls of all shapes, sizes and prices on the next. She watched as the various crabs and lobsters crawled over each other in a tank at the next stall, in a desperate attempt not to be plucked out of the water by the old woman who was looking for some dinner for her husband. Kristy walked a little further and found herself enjoying the experience. She was enjoying the sounds, the odd people; she was even getting used to the smell of fish.

She had come to rescue her brother. That was her goal; that's what she was looking towards. But the sights and sounds were so attractive. She thought that maybe staying here overnight wouldn't be a problem. She was fairly sure that one more day wouldn't make much difference to her brother – fairly sure! So she walked into the nearest tavern and asked the barmaid if there was a room she could have for the night. The barmaid took her money and showed her to her room – it wasn't much bigger than a cleaning cupboard but it would do. After all, it was only for one night.

The following day, Kristy got up and wandered downstairs. She ordered breakfast and paid her money. She would be going today so she would need a good breakfast. She finished her breakfast and figured that one more look around outside wouldn't do any harm. After all, she might not be back this way for quite some time.

If anything, the makeshift market had got even bigger. It now included a whole range of clothes that had clearly come from different parts of the world. She looked at some wonderfully coloured carpets with intricate designs. She walked around for many hours until she noticed the sun beginning to set. She rushed back to the inn, ate some dinner and would have been on her way but it was now dark so she decided she would wait one more night...

And so it went on. Every day Kristy found another excuse to stay just one more day. Days turned into weeks, and soon Kristy was out of money. She ordered breakfast one morning and to her horror discovered she couldn't pay for it. The barmaid smiled and looked at Kristy: "You can work here. If you work this morning, then that will cover breakfast and if you work this afternoon, then that should cover your room. If you work this evening, we may even give you some money."

Kristy had forgotten. She had forgotten why she had come here in the first place. She had forgotten her end goal. She had forgotten Cameron... It had happened so easily. She had taken her eyes off the target and so she was in trouble.

Now, every day, Kristy served at tables and wandered around the harbour. Every day she met new people and made new friends. She was enjoying herself. And then one day she walked down for breakfast and saw a family sitting eating their breakfast. They had arrived the night before and they were hungry. They were clearly a mum, a dad and two children – a brother and sister. The girl was about eight and the boy was about ten. They were whispering to each other and giggling about something that only they could see. The parents were telling them off persistently but still they laughed.

Then Kristy's mind began to wander. She remembered the times that she and Cameron had giggled their way through formal dinners. She remembered the secrets they used to share and then, like a bolt of lightning, she remembered why she was there!

She threw down her apron and hurried towards the harbour. Her money was gone and she didn't know how she would pay for her voyage to find her brother, but she was on her way. She marched to the harbour, and at the first ship she climbed on board to talk to the captain. She had remembered why she was there. She had focused again.

(To be continued...)

Whom Do We Trust?

	Programme	Item
Section 1	Welcome	
	Rules	
	Prayer	
	Introductory Praise	
	Game 1	Pirate King (for leader)
	Praise	
	Fun Item 1	
	Game 2	Pirate King (for children)
	Fun Item 2	
	Bible Text	Hebrews 11:32
	Announcements	
	Interview	
Section 2 Preaching Time	Worship Time	
	Bible Lesson	Jephthah
	Illustration 1	*Treasure Planet* Video Clip
	Illustration 2	Trust 1
	Illustration 3	Trust 2
	Story	The Pirate King (4)
	Prayer	

It is often difficult to work out whom to trust and whom we should be holding onto. Some people and things that we think we can rely on often aren't trustworthy.

games

Pirate King (for leader)

PREPARATION	A set of face paints per team and three brushes per team.
PLAYERS	Three players per team and a leader per team.
SET-UP	The players and the leader are at A; the leader is seated facing away from the children. The players have a brush each.
OBJECT	To make the leader look like a "pirate king" in three minutes.
WINNING	The leader who looks most like a "pirate king" wins.

Pirate King (for children)

PREPARATION	A set of face paints per team and a brush per team.
PLAYERS	One player (the leader chooses who) and a leader per team.
SET-UP	The player and the leader are at A; the child is seated facing away from the children. The leader has a brush.
OBJECT	To make the child look like a "pirate king" in three minutes.
WINNING	The child who looks most like a "pirate king" wins.

Preaching Time

BIBLE LESSON JEPHTHAH

"What else can I say? There isn't enough time to tell about Gideon, Barak, Samson, Jephthah, *David, Samuel, and the prophets." (Hebrews 11:32)*

Another one of the characters in Hebrews 11 is someone with a difficult name. His name is Jephthah. He learned whom to trust.

Jephthah was a brave warrior. He trusted his father but was soon to learn not to do that when he was forced to leave the clan he belonged to. He trusted his brothers but was soon to learn not to do that when they forced him to leave the house because he was only a stepbrother – he had a different mother from the rest.

> Jephthah went to the country of Tob, where he was joined by a number of men and they became outlaws.
>
> But the leaders of Gilead went to Jephthah and said, "Please come back to Gilead! If you lead our army, we will be able to fight off the Ammonites."
>
> "Didn't you hate me?" Jephthah replied. "Weren't you the ones who forced me to leave my family? You're coming to me now, just because you're in trouble."
>
> "But we do want you to come back," the leaders said. "And if you lead us in battle against the Ammonites, we will make you the ruler of Gilead."
>
> "All right," Jephthah said. "If I go back with you and the LORD lets me defeat the Ammonites, will you really make me your ruler?"
>
> "You have our word," the leaders answered. "And the LORD is a witness to what we have said."
>
> So Jephthah went back to Mizpah with the leaders of Gilead. The people of Gilead gathered at the place of worship and made Jephthah their ruler. Jephthah also made promises to them. (Judges 11:4–11)

Jephthah was a brave warrior. He trusted the Lord his God and was soon to discover that God can always be trusted and would never let him down.

Then the LORD's Spirit took control of Jephthah, and Jephthah went through Gilead and Manasseh, raising an army. Finally, he arrived at Mizpah in Gilead, where he promised the LORD, "If you will let me defeat the Ammonites and come home safely, I will sacrifice to you whoever comes out to meet me first."

From Mizpah, Jephthah attacked the Ammonites, and the LORD helped him defeat them.

Jephthah and his army destroyed the twenty towns between Aroer and Minnith, and others as far as Abel-Keramim. After that, the Ammonites could not invade Israel any more. (Judges 11:29–33)

Treasure Planet Video Clip

Object needed: *A clip from the video* Treasure Planet.

Show the clip where Jim Hawkins is on the ship in the storm and the rope is cut.

The captain thought she could trust Jim Hawkins, and she was right. She might have thought that he didn't secure the ropes properly but she was wrong; Jim could be trusted.

The captain thought she could trust Spider, and she was very wrong. She might have thought he was simply doing his job, but he had cut the rope and killed an innocent man.

Whom can we trust and whom can we not trust? It's very difficult.

Illustration 2

Trust

Object needed: *A rope.*

When I was your age, I lived in a house that had a hill behind it, a really steep hill. At the bottom of this steep hill was a pile of nettles and then a river. At the top of the hill was a huge tree.

My friends and I had learned a wonderful game. We had managed to get a rope around the top of the tree and now you could run off the edge of the hill, swing on the rope in this huge circle and land on the opposite side of the hill. At the centre you would be about 20 metres away from the ground and it was very exciting.

I loved it. In fact I loved it so much that I got up early one Saturday morning so that I could get to the hill before my friends came, so I could get lots of goes by myself. It was all working really well; I was getting lots of goes. I was swinging one way and then the other. I was performing twists and turns and landing backwards; I was having a great time.

And then it went wrong. I took a big run, I twisted in mid-air, I was over the huge drop and cheering as I swung around, and then just before I was coming back in to land, the rope snapped...

I tumbled down the hill, through the nettles and into the river. I was bruised, I was covered in nettle stings and I was soaking wet. I had to walk home and sit in a bath with lots of special cream to try to stop the nettle stings hurting. As if that wasn't bad enough, my friends wouldn't talk to me because they blamed me for breaking the swing.

I had trusted in the rope and it had let me down. There have been lots of things over the years that I have trusted in that have let me down. A colour TV that I wanted to watch the final of the FA Cup on went wrong. A computer crashed, losing me loads of work. A car broke down on the way to a major meeting... Lots of things have let me down, but worse than being let down by things is being let down by people.

Trust 2

Object needed: *Four ropes reaching up to four pictures: one reaching up to a picture of parents; another reaching up to a picture of some children, labelled "friends"; another to a picture of a boyfriend and girlfriend; and one to a sign saying "God". Secure only the rope reaching up to the word "God".*

So whom can we trust? This is very difficult.

Our parents are usually to be trusted all the time. It's great to have good parents. But not everyone does. Sometimes parents get divorced; they can still be great parents, but we may feel they have broken our trust. Sometimes, for whatever reason, parents let us down.

Our friends can be much more unreliable. They promise to call for you and forget, they promise to be kind and then say nasty things about you, they promise to be trusted and then they steal your boyfriend! It's good to have friends we can trust, but often they let us down.

Boyfriends and girlfriends are what people seem to get upset about most of all. Some think their boyfriend can be trusted and then he lets them down, and others think that their girlfriend would never do anything unkind and then she decides to go out with someone else! Boyfriends and girlfriends are fine (as long as you're 25 of course!) but they can't always be trusted.

And finally, God. Well, there's not much to say. He is always there. He never lets us down. He can always be trusted. He always keeps his promises. It is good to have someone we can always trust, no matter what.

● STORY – The Pirate King (4)

The first captain wanted 50 gold coins and Kristy had no money. She stood on the edge of the harbour wondering which ship could take her to her destination. She thought she had better ask another captain. But the next was going the wrong way, and the next wanted large amounts of gold and the next wanted even more, and the next wasn't setting off for another month. Finally Kristy came to the last ship in the harbour and she walked on board. The captain watched her as she walked towards him. He bowed low as she arrived, smiled and said: "Mademoiselle, how can I be of service?"

Kristy was taken aback. The captain had only one eye and very little hair. He looked as if he

hadn't washed for months, but still, he was being kind. Kristy mumbled: "I need to get to a small island just off the coast of South America, called Dax."

The captain nodded. "Yes, that's the way we are going."

Kristy was shocked. "Are you sure?"

The captain called his men together: "Isn't it right, lads, that we is going to an island just off the coast of South America?" The men, who all looked even more unwashed than the captain, nodded.

"Then how much?" Kristy enquired.

"Oh, no charge," said the captain with a smile. "We were going that way anyway."

So the deal was done and the ship set off. Kristy was even provided with her own quarters. She slept well and when she got up in the morning the ship was far out to sea and making good time, by the looks of things. She could no longer see land in any direction.

"How long before we get there?" she enquired of a very tattooed sailor.

"Not long now!" He almost laughed the answer.

Kristy spent the day watching the seamen work. They seemed to be fixing some nets – very large nets at that. She figured they must be fishermen. She watched as some dolphins played near the side of the ship. She enjoyed the breeze blowing against her face. But then, when night-time came, Kristy was a little more suspicious. She gazed up at the night sky and, although she hadn't paid too much attention to her lessons about constellations and star patterns, she knew enough to realise she was going the wrong way.

She ran to tell the captain, but he smiled and told her she was mistaken. When she insisted, the scene changed somewhat. Out of nowhere three sailors arrived, carrying chains. They began to wrap them around her. The captain nodded, "Yes, you are correct, Mademoiselle; we are not going to no South American island. We is on our way to do some fishing. Shark fishing. But we didn't have any bait. Nothing to attract the sharks. Until now. You'll be good shark bait, I'm sure. Lock her in the brig, lads. We'll fish tomorrow."

Kristy couldn't believe how stupid she had been. She had trusted someone she knew nothing about. She had trusted someone who had let her down. And it looked as if she had trusted someone who was intent on killing her.

She lay awake wondering what it would be like to be eaten alive by sharks. She wouldn't have to wait long. At first light she was carried to the edge of the deck and her chains were removed. A rope was tied to her ankles and she was very unceremoniously thrown into the sea. The rope was dragging her through the water and the spray from the waves was almost blinding her. But through her blinking eyes she saw them approaching: lots and lots of pointed fins above the water, coming closer to her. She began to kick and scream. She knew this was the wrong thing to do, but there was no way she could be calm. Then she saw one of the sharks coming closer and closer. It opened its huge mouth and snapped it closed. But where it had closed its mouth Kristy had gone – leaving the shark's jaws empty.

It all happened so fast. The shark had approached, there had been a huge bang followed by several more bangs in quick succession, and then a rope was wrapped around her and she had found herself soaring into the air. Then she landed on her back on board a ship – but certainly not the ship she had just left. She looked around at many smiling faces, much younger faces. A very unusual man looked down at her. He was the very epitome of what she had imagined a pirate to look like – he had one leg, a hook as one of his hands, and a patch over one eye. She looked up and, sure enough, flying overhead was a flag bearing the notorious skull and crossbones – matched by the skull and crossbones on the pirate's hat.

Getting to her feet, Kristy could see the other ship. It was burning. There were huge holes in its side and it was sinking so, so quickly. The crew were splashing around in the water and being picked off one by one by the feasting sharks.

The pirate reached out his hand to Kristy and she shook it. "Hi," he began, "my name is Sir Alexander Bartholomew James, but for short they simply call me the Pirate King!"

(To be continued...)

5 Learning

	Programme	Item
Section 1	**Welcome**	
	Rules	
	Prayer	
	Introductory Praise	
	Game 1	Learning
	Praise	
	Fun Item 1	
	Game 2	More Learning
	Fun Item 2	
	Bible Text	Hebrews 11:32
	Announcements	
	Interview	
Section 2	**Worship Time**	
Preaching	**Bible Lesson**	Samuel
Time	**Illustration 1**	*Treasure Planet* Video Clip
	Illustration 2	We Have To Learn
	Illustration 3	The Soldier
	Story	The Pirate King (5)
	Prayer	

We need to learn maths and English and geography and a whole load of other stuff, and we also need to learn to listen to God.

games

Game 1

Learning

PREPARATION Cards showing the numbers 7, 8, 9, 10 and the symbols +, –, x, per team.

PLAYERS Three per team.

SET-UP The cards bearing the numbers and symbols are placed at B. The players are in relay formation at A.

OBJECT The players in relay formation (the second player doesn't go until the first comes back) go from A, collect a number or symbol and then return. When all the symbols and numbers are collected they are arranged so that the answer is 91.

WINNING The first team to make the equation wins.

Game 2

More Learning

PREPARATION Cards bearing the words and phrases "and Hampshire", "In", "ever happen", "hurricanes hardly", "Hertford, Hereford" per team.

PLAYERS Three per team.

SET-UP The cards bearing the words and phrases are placed at B. The players in relay formation at A.

OBJECT The players in relay formation (the second player doesn't go until the first comes back) go from A, collect a word or phrase and then return. When all the words are collected they are arranged to make a well-known saying.

WINNING The first team to construct the saying wins.

BIBLE LESSON SAMUEL

"What else can I say? There isn't enough time to tell about Gideon, Barak, Samson, Jephthah, David, Samuel, *and the prophets." (Hebrews 11:32)*

We're going to jump over one of our Hebrews 11 people today. We'll come back to David next time, but we'll take a quick look at Samuel now.

Samuel was to grow up to be a very famous prophet – someone who could hear what God was saying and who would go and tell others. He would tell kings what God wanted them to know. But our story starts long before this.

One evening, Samuel, who was still a boy at this point, was lying in his bed. He was trying to sleep when he heard a voice. He rushed into Eli's room (Samuel lived with Eli the priest, who by then was getting very old) and said, "Eli, did you call me?"

Eli said no and sent him back to his bed.

Several minutes later, Samuel heard another voice and ran to tell Eli. Again Eli said, "Go back to bed, you're hearing things." The third time Samuel came, Eli knew it might just be God. He told Samuel to answer: "Speak, Lord, for your servant hears."

When the voice came, Samuel answered as he was told. God began to speak to Samuel. Samuel learned to listen to God when he was just a boy – amazing really.

We need to learn maths and English and geography and a whole load of other stuff, and we also need to learn to listen to God.

Treasure Planet Video Clip

Object needed: *A clip from the video* Treasure Planet.

Show the clip where Jim Hawkins is on the makeshift windsurfer, saving everyone at the end of the movie.

This is one of my favourite parts of the movie: the big climax where Jim saves the day. The interesting thing is this. Jim can fly like this because he learned to do it when he was young. The things we learn when we are young will help us as we grow older.

We Have To Learn

Object needed: *None needed, although you may choose some of the items listed below.*

There are some things we learn as we grow up. I learned how to feed myself fairly early on, a little later I learned how to use my potty, and a while after that I graduated to the toilet. I learned to read and write and I learned how to tie my laces and zip up my jacket.

I learned a pile of stuff in school and I learned some more stuff after I left school. In fact I learn every day. But along the way I also learned some other stuff. I learned how important it is to read my Bible. I learned what God did for me and how Jesus died on the cross and rose from the dead. I learned how to listen to God. I learned how to understand what God wanted me to do.

These are things we can learn as we grow up. We don't have to wait until we're old. We can learn to talk to God now.

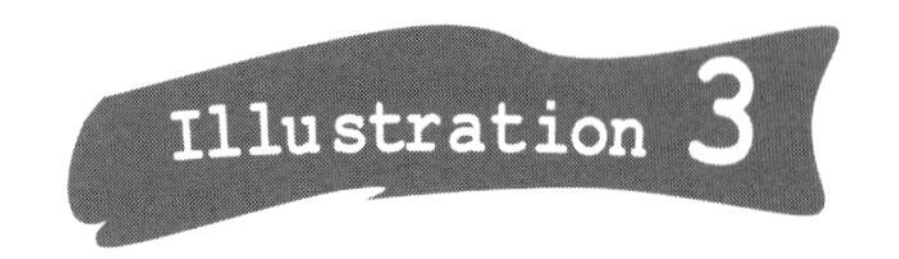

The Soldier

Object needed: *A picture of a soldier.*

Imagine a soldier walking onto the battlefield. He is wearing his uniform, but that's all he knows how to do. He knows how to button up his uniform. He doesn't know how to use his gun, or how to take orders. He doesn't know how to march or even what the enemy looks like. Nobody has taught him how to keep his head low when he's under fire.

This soldier is not really going to last very long, is he? This soldier is going to find himself very dead, very quickly. We have to learn things before we end up in difficult situations. We need to learn to listen to God and to pray before the hard times come, and hard times *will* come. We need to build this stuff into our lives now, and then we will have someone to turn to when things go wrong: a God who will never let us down.

• STORY – The Pirate King (5)

"So what brings you to these waters? And how did you get mixed up with those misfits?" asked the Pirate King, gesturing to the sailors who were rapidly becoming shark food. Kristy was in shock, but with stammering sentences she managed to recount how she had received her brother's letter and was doing her best to try to get to the island to rescue him.

"You are in luck," said the Pirate King. "We have been busy this month and have a very large amount of treasure that we need to deposit on another island not far from there. We will take you." And so they set off for a far and distant island. The Pirate King, such a strange-looking individual, stood at the front of the ship gazing constantly through his telescope until several weeks later he announced: "Land ahoy!" And they were there. The Pirate King ordered several of his men to row Kristy to the shore and then return.

So she found herself on this strange island. Before her was an enormous cliff face. There was no way off this beach but to climb, but as she walked closer to the cliff she could tell that she would never be able to climb up there. Then she noticed that the cliff wasn't right; she couldn't put her finger on what wasn't right, but she was sure that something wasn't. Then she began to remember her geology lessons. She remembered how the older rock would be at the bottom – and that was what was wrong. This rock in front of her wasn't the same as the rest.

She walked forward and looked closer. She leaned against it – and it moved! It wasn't rock at all! She almost fell through and found herself in a dark cave – well, certainly darker, but not as dark as she would have expected, because three large, blazing torches hung on the walls.

Kristy allowed her eyes to adjust and then she looked around. There was something written on the wall. It said:

> When you position the light
> and the triangle is revealed,
> then look to the right
> and you can proceed.

Kristy looked at the lights a little more closely; there were numbers written around them in a circle. She wobbled the first light but it would not move; it was positioned at number 50.

She looked at the second light and it too was fixed. She tried to move it but it wouldn't budge; it was fixed at position 65. She touched the third light and it moved freely. She sat down staring at the three torches. How was she going to proceed? Then it came to her, Professor Sanderson's voice echoed in her mind: "The angles of a triangle add up to 180 degrees."

Surely it couldn't be this simple! The first light was at 65, the second was at 50, so to make it add up to 180 this third light must be positioned at 65. She moved the third light to the number 65. Suddenly there was a door on her right side. She was sure it hadn't been there before, or perhaps, as she now realised, the light was now shining on it, making it visible. She pushed the door and it swung open. She walked through.

She was still in the caves, but there was now a bridge ahead of her, and beneath the bridge was an enormous drop – she couldn't see the bottom. She approached the bridge and then she saw him, or her, or it, or whatever it was. It was a strange creature indeed. It had a caterpillar's body and two heads. The heads seemed to be in conversation with each other and then, as they saw Kristy approaching, they stopped talking and stared. They looked at Kristy as if she were their next meal arriving. And Kristy was in no doubt that they were thinking just that. When she came close enough, she stopped.

"I would like to cross over, please," she began. "Do you think that would be OK?"

The heads exchanged looks and then smiled at each other. They spoke together: "We would like very much for you to try to cross our bridge, we really would. We would like you very much to cross. For we are hungry and we have eaten nothing but fish for so long. We are not permitted to eat the other one, the boy, but nobody has said that we cannot eat the girl."

They stared at Kristy and she was sure she saw one of them lick its lips. Her mind was racing. They had spoken of a boy; she was sure they meant her brother. She spoke again: "Is there any way I may pass without being eaten?"

They looked at each other again and seemed to frown. "Yes!" They began to talk together again. "But we do not like it. Still, we have no choice. The guardians have commanded that we must ask a question. If the question is answered incorrectly or the question is not answered, then we may eat you. If you answer correctly, then you must be allowed to pass."

Kristy was seriously considering running for it but she knew she would not get far. So she said: "OK. Ask me the question."

The heads looked at each other and then together they began to ask: "What is the name of our third uncle on our mother's side?" Kristy was panic-stricken – she could never answer that! But she didn't have to. A voice came out of nowhere; it spoke as one voice but sounded like a choir. It said: "You know the rules, Smag. Ask a real question or she must be allowed to pass."

The creature looked dejected but with a sigh asked: "What did the Greeks use to enter the city to rescue Helen of Troy?" Kristy couldn't believe it. She wished she had listened a little better in that subject, and then eventually it came to her.

"A Trojan horse, yes, a TROJAN HORSE!"

The creature looked dejected but it moved aside. Kristy was so glad she had remembered what she'd learnt when she was younger. She walked across the bridge and into the final room. And there, lying on the floor, was Cameron. He looked a little rough. He certainly looked thinner, but her brother was alive. She moved towards him. He looked up and stared.

"You got my message! Thank you for coming, Kristy! Thank you so much." Kristy took one step towards him – and then they appeared: hundreds and hundreds of pairs of eyes appearing in the darkness...

(To be continued...)

6 Treasure

	Programme	Item
Section 1	Welcome	
	Rules	
	Prayer	
	Introductory Praise	
	Game 1	Treasure-map Jigsaw
	Praise	
	Fun Item 1	
	Game 2	Fill The Chest
	Fun Item 2	
	Bible Text	Hebrews 11:32
	Announcements	
	Interview	
Section 2	Worship Time	
Preaching	Bible Lesson	David
Time	Illustration 1	*Treasure Planet* Video Clip
	Illustration 2	The Sinking Boat
	Illustration 3	Value
	Story	The Pirate King (6)
	Prayer	

Overview There is nothing more valuable in all of creation than humankind. God sent his only Son to die for humankind. Jesus wept over humankind. The Bible even tells us that God loves us in exactly the same way that he loves Jesus. We are God's treasure.

Game 1

Treasure-map Jigsaw

PREPARATION	Copy the treasure map in Appendix 4 onto a piece of card per team. Then cut the card into seven pieces.
PLAYERS	Three per team.
SET-UP	The jigsaw pieces are placed at B. The players line up at A in relay formation.
OBJECT	The players run from A to B in relay order. They collect a jigsaw piece and return. When all the pieces are collected the jigsaw is constructed.
WINNING	The first team with a constructed jigsaw wins.

Fill The Chest

PREPARATION	Lots and lots of coloured stones in a box at A. An empty box per team at B.
PLAYERS	Three from each team.
SET-UP	Three players in standard relay pattern at point A.
OBJECT	The first person runs from A to a point about two metres before B – mark the point with a masking-tape line – carrying a coloured stone. They then throw the stone into their box.
WINNING	The team with the most stones in the box wins.

Preaching Time

BIBLE LESSON **DAVID**

"What else can I say? There isn't enough time to tell about Gideon, Barak, Samson, Jephthah, David, *Samuel, and the prophets." (Hebrews 11:32)*

David was an exceptional person. He was chosen by Samuel (whom we talked about last time) to be king. He stood up against Goliath and defeated him. He became an outlaw because King Saul wanted to kill him, but still he did the right thing.

Eventually David became king. He could have had anything he wanted. He could have asked for money or huge houses or anything you could imagine. Instead, David asked God for one thing; he said: "God, this is what I ask, this is what I seek: that I might be in your temple to worship you all the days of my life."

What an amazing thing. The most important thing to David was to be close to God. We sometimes forget which things are most valuable.

Treasure Planet Video Clip

Object needed: *A clip from the video* Treasure Planet.

Show the clip where John Silver chooses to let the treasure go in order to save Jim Hawkins.

This is a very interesting clip. John Silver had spent his entire life trying to get to Treasure Planet and his dream was of getting rich there. Now he was prepared to let it all go for the sake of a person he had known for only a short time.

But John Silver knew that a life is worth more than any amount of treasure. In fact, a life is God's greatest treasure.

The Sinking Boat

Object needed: *A picture of a houseboat.*

Mr Harris lived on a boat with his son, Thomas. There were lots of things Mr Harris liked but only a few he treasured. Every so often, he would take some of his treasured possessions out of his old wooden chest.

The chest contained a very old family Bible in which were written the names of his family going back nearly 1,000 years. In the chest were also two golden coins that were very old, and a medal, a very special medal, which his father had won in the last war.

Thomas would look at the items and then he would ask his usual question: "Dad, if our boat sank, what treasure would you save?"

Mr Harris would smile and answer, "Well, the greatest treasure of them all, of course." But when Thomas would ask which one that was, Mr Harris would simply smile and say nothing.

One night a huge storm started and, sure enough, the boat started to sink. Mr Harris wasted no time in grabbing his greatest treasure and rushing to the lifeboat. When he reached the shore he turned to see his chest, his medal, his coins and his family Bible sinking into the ocean.

But there, sitting beside him on the lifeboat, was his greatest treasure – an eight-year-old boy named Thomas.

Real treasures are rarely *things*. God's greatest treasure is *us*.

Value

Object needed: *A video clip of the crucifixion – consider using* The Miracle Maker*; a chocolate bar; a can of pop; a games console.*

The more something is worth, the more you are willing to pay for it.

This is a chocolate bar. It's worth about 30p, so you'd be willing to pay 30p for it.

This is a can of pop. It's worth about 50p, so you'd be willing to pay 50p for it.

This is a games console. It's worth about £150, so you'd be willing to pay £150 for it.

Some things are harder to put prices on. There's a story in the old part of the Bible about a man who worked for fourteen years so that he could marry the woman he loved.

How much would a person be worth? Now Jesus was prepared to do this...

Show the video clip.

The Bible says this: "With his blood Jesus purchased people for God." You were worth so much that Jesus was willing to die for you. God's greatest treasure is you.

● STORY – The Pirate King (6)

Kristy took one step towards him and then they appeared: hundreds and hundreds of pairs of eyes appearing in the darkness. Then the eyes became hoods. And the hoods became people – well, certainly people-shapes. Kristy couldn't help feeling that they might be more than people. Their eyes shone out of the hoods as they all stood before her. The smallest of them was well over two metres tall. They looked at Kristy and then at Cameron.

"So someone did come. We did not expect

they would. We allowed Cameron to send the letter but we did not expect anyone to come." These words appeared in Kristy's mind but she hadn't seen any lips moving. For that matter she was sure she hadn't heard any sounds with her ears.

"This man came to take our treasure. But we can never let the treasure leave; it is not for humans. He pleaded with us to spare his life. We told him that if someone was prepared to risk everything for him, then we would let him go. We did not believe that humans would risk all to save one of their own kind. We thought humans cared only for themselves and not for others. We did not believe that you knew the value of life."

Kristy didn't know what to say, so she said nothing. She remembered how she had nearly not bothered at all; she remembered how she was so distracted by the excitement of the market, but in the end she had come. She had eventually remembered how rescuing another person was the only important thing.

Then they were gone; the people vanished. Kristy grabbed her brother and they ran for the exit, but they were horror-stricken at the sight that greeted them. Now there was not just one horrible two-headed creature, but the whole cave was full of them. They were hideous creatures with wide-open mouths. Then one of them spoke. It was the same one that had let them in and asked them the question. The creature spoke slowly and was obviously taking pleasure in the words: "The guardians said we had to let you in. But not out. I think it is dinner time now. I don't think there is anyone to help you now."

"There is always us, of course." A voice came from nowhere. The creatures turned. And there he stood, sword drawn, his men behind him: the Pirate King.

The creatures charged forward. The Pirate King chuckled out loud and then walked towards them. There was a lot of squealing and crashing and slashing of swords. Then it was all over. The last few creatures ran quickly past Kristy and Cameron into the passageways and were gone.

There he stood, having hardly broken into a sweat: the Pirate King. He smiled, the gaps in his teeth showing: "I thought you might need a lift home," he began, "but we're always happy to have a fight." Kristy smiled. She ran forward and hugged the Pirate King. He was taken aback. Hugs were something, probably the only thing, he wasn't able to cope with.

And so they set sail and several days later they arrived back in England. Cameron never stopped saying thank you. But Kristy smiled and simply said: "I would have done anything to get out of going to school."

They laughed!

ONE-OFF LESSONS

One-off Lesson: George

	Programme	Item
Section 1	Welcome	
	Rules	
	Prayer	
	Introductory Praise	
	Game 1	Music
	Praise	
	Fun Item 1	
	Game 2	
	Fun Item 2	
	Bible Text	Proverbs 24:10
	Announcements	
	Interview	
Section 2 Preaching Time	Worship Time	
	Bible Lesson	David at Ziklag
	Illustration 1	*There are no Illustrations needed for this lesson.*
	Illustration 2	*The Bible Lesson and the Story are both quite*
	Illustration 3	*substantial. They will fill the time allocated.*
	Story	George
	Prayer	

"Sometimes you just have to keep going." This must be my most-used lesson in travelling – you may have heard it. I have primarily used it for adults, but children need to hear this too.

games

Game 1

Music

PREPARATION	A tape with 20 current songs. Play 30 seconds of each song.
PLAYERS	Everyone.
SET-UP	A tape recorder.
OBJECT	The song is played and the first hand up gets asked the title and the group. If they are right, the team gets the point; if not, someone else is asked. If the song finishes and nobody has answered you keep going to the next song.
WINNING	The team that gets the most songs correct wins.

Game 2

The first game will take up all the allocated game time for this lesson.

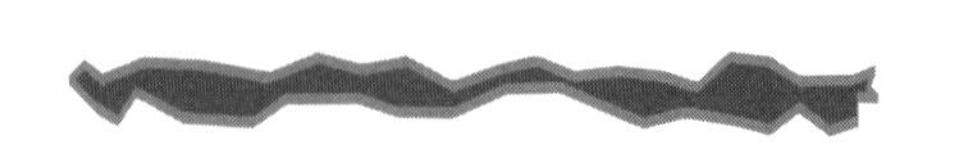

PreachingTime

BIBLE LESSON DAVID AT ZIKLAG

"Don't give up and be helpless in times of trouble." (Proverbs 24:10)

David had been journeying long and hard. He had led his men valiantly. He had lived with incredible standards of integrity and righteousness. He had always done the right thing. He was now returning to camp, hoping to come back to his wife and children and enjoy a time of rest and relaxation before continuing. Then suddenly, as he rode into camp, he saw smoke billowing high into the air. Ziklag was on fire. His possessions were in flames. As he came closer, the enormity of the situation hit him. Not only were all his possessions on fire, but his wife and children and everything he and his men owned were gone.

And, as if the situation couldn't get any worse, his friends, those he had helped, those he had encouraged when they were downcast and depressed, those he had carried when they couldn't support themselves – those selfsame men now wanted to kill him; they wanted to stone their leader to death.

David was facing one of his hardest times. Several weeks after this, David would ride triumphantly into Jerusalem and would be crowned king. He would prove to be the greatest king Israel would ever have (apart from King Jesus himself). But before he got to Jerusalem, he had to get through Ziklag.

Ziklag is David's final test before kingship. If he passes this test, he will walk on into triumph and glory; if he fails, the shepherd boy will at best return to his sheep; at worst he will die.

David had been through many tests that prepared him for Ziklag. At the time, the other tests must have seemed difficult, but they all prepared the man of God for the next rung of the ladder. So let's see what we can learn from David:

1. He had an open and honest relationship with God.
2. He knew about the power of praise.
3. He knew how to draw power from God.

(You may want to expand on each of the above three points.)

And because David knew about these things, he gathered his men and went and found those who had attacked his village. He brought back his wife and children and possessions. Several weeks later, David was king. He did not give up; he kept going.

● STORY – George

George was born in the state of Georgia in the United States of America. His parents lived on a plantation. The house they rented belonged to a very wealthy man indeed and they worked for that man and he paid them for their work. They in turn paid rent to that man to live in the house. It was hard work, up every morning at sunrise, out into the fields to plant or to dig or to gather in the crops. They worked through until sunset and returned home to make dinner. George's mother and father both worked in the fields and, come harvest time, George would help out as well. They didn't mind working because the owner of the land paid them quite well; not brilliantly, but well enough to pay rent, buy food and clothes and sometimes even to buy chocolate.

It hadn't always been this way. George's grandfather had worked the same land but as a slave. He was treated very poorly and was forced to work very hard with no pay at all.

George's mother and father couldn't read. But George knew that if he wanted to do what was in his heart to do, then he would have to learn to read. He began to teach himself and, with just a little help from the rich man's daughter, who went to a nearby school, he learned to read. But he wanted to do more than read; he wanted to go to Princeton University – a very famous college. He wanted to train to become a lawyer. But Princeton cost many thousands of dollars to attend even then, and George's mum and dad would never have enough money to send him.

George's mum and dad tried to convince him that it was impossible, but he refused to believe them. He was determined. He knew he would never get enough money to go to Princeton by staying on the plantation so he headed for the city and eventually got a job as a porter on a train. He would carry suitcases on and off the train, collect tickets, show people to their seats – he would do anything to earn money to pay for his fees when he eventually got to Princeton.

One of the things he would do to try to earn a little more money was to stay up into the early hours of the morning, cleaning and polishing people's shoes. He would knock on the doors of the passengers – for George worked on a long-distance train with bedrooms built in – and ask if they needed their shoes polishing. He would then work late into the night polishing shoes. 1am, 2am, 3am, 4am... he would be up cleaning and polishing shoes. It may sound an easy job but scraping doggy do-do off shoes into the middle of the night was not George's idea of fun. Still, he wanted to go to university, and nothing was going to stop him. And, at 7 o'clock every morning, he would get up and begin his portering work. He worked very hard.

Mr Spencer was a businessman. He travelled the train very often. But on this particular night he had a lot on his mind – he'd just started a business deal in Chicago and was on his way to New York to complete another deal. His mind was working very quickly that night. It was 2 o'clock in the morning and he couldn't sleep. He decided to go for a walk. He was making his way up the train when he saw a light on in the engine room. He walked up and looked in. There, sitting on the floor, was George, surrounded by hundreds of pairs of shoes.

He looked up as Mr Spencer walked in and said: "Good evening, sir, or should I say, good morning. What brings you up here?"

Mr Spencer explained that he couldn't sleep. He then enquired what George was doing and, more to the point, why? George made Mr Spencer a milky drink and began to explain how he was working so very hard to go to Princeton to train to be a lawyer. Mr Spencer listened intently before he returned to his carriage to go to sleep. That was the last George saw of Mr Spencer.

George worked for another year on that train until eventually he had enough money to pay for the first term's fees at Princeton. There was no way he could get all the money at once, but he had enough for the first term. He made an appointment with the headmaster of Princeton College and went to see him.

Most people would have given up many years earlier. Many would never have started. But George knew what he wanted to do and he wasn't going to let anyone stop him. It might have seemed impossible but here he was in the office of the headmaster of Princeton University.

"You've sent me some money, George," the headmaster began, "but I can't take it."

George began to shake. Had he worked so hard and so long yet still he wouldn't be allowed to enter the college? He tried to explain: "Mr Headmaster, I know it's not enough for three years. I know it's not enough for one year, but if you could just let me pay for the first term, then I will go away and earn enough money for the second term and come back again, and then go and earn enough for the third. But please let me start, I've worked so hard... "

The headmaster smiled: "George, I didn't mean you couldn't attend. I meant I couldn't take your money. A year ago a man called Mr Spencer walked into this office and handed me enough money for you to stay in college for three years – until the end of the course – but he said this to me; he said that you were only to have the money if you actually came."

Many people think coming to God is impossible. They think that they will never make it, that they will never be good enough, or righteous enough. They are absolutely right. In our own strength we cannot come to God. But in the same way that George could never enter Princeton without the help of a man with great resources, we too have a great benefactor. He has available to him the entire resources of heaven. He came, he lived among us, he died on a cross to make heaven accessible to you and me, to make God accessible to you and me. We could not do it, so he did it for us. We could never be good enough, but when we give our lives to Jesus it is as if we are wrapped in Jesus, and when God looks at us, he sees Jesus. We are clothed in righteousness.

Boys and girls, if you are willing you can approach God today through Jesus. God is willing. There will be a time for prayer afterwards.

So George began his course and four years later he became a lawyer. Some time after that he became a high court judge, one of the first black men in the USA to do so. He succeeded because he tried.

One-off Lesson: The Scottish Preacher

	Programme	Item
Section 1	**Welcome**	
	Rules	
	Prayer	
	Introductory Praise	
	Game 1	Baton Relay Race (for boys)
	Praise	
	Fun Item 1	
	Game 2	Baton Relay Race (for girls)
	Fun Item 2	
	Bible Text	1 Kings 2:2–3
	Announcements	
	Interview	
Section 2 Preaching Time	**Worship Time**	
	Bible Lesson	David Dies
	Illustration 1	Magazine Rack
	Illustration 2	Life
	Illustration 3	Pass The Baton
	Story	The Scottish Preacher
	Prayer	

It is not just about how well we serve Jesus; it is also about helping others to serve Jesus.

games

Baton Relay Race (for boys)

PREPARATION	A baton or something similar per team.
PLAYERS	Six per team and a leader.
SET-UP	The players line up at A.
OBJECT	The first person runs from A to B and back, holding the baton. On their return they pass the baton to the next player.
WINNING	The first team to complete the race wins.

Baton Relay Race (for girls)

PREPARATION	A baton or something similar per team.
PLAYERS	Six per team and a leader.
SET-UP	The players line up at A.
OBJECT	The first person runs from A to B and back, holding the baton. On their return they pass the baton to the next player.
WINNING	The first team to complete the race wins.

BIBLE LESSON **DAVID DIES**

"My son, I will soon die, as everyone must. But I want you to be strong and brave. Do what the Lord your God commands and follow his teachings." (1 Kings 2:2–3)

David was an amazing king. He ruled in a place called Israel thousands of years ago. He was the best king they would ever have before King Jesus was born. But, not long before David died, he told his son Solomon:

> My son, I will soon die, as everyone must. But I want you to be strong and brave. Do what the LORD your God commands and follow his teachings. Obey everything written in the Law of Moses. Then you will be a success, no matter what you do or where you go. You and your descendants must always faithfully obey the LORD. If you do, he will keep the solemn promise he made to me that someone from our family will always be king of Israel.

David had done some amazing things; he was a shepherd who had become king. As a young man he had killed a giant named Goliath; later he was forced to be an outlaw. But David always did the right thing. He could have lost it all at Ziklag but instead he went on to be a great king. All that was very important, but for David something else was important too, and that was ensuring that, after he was gone, what he had started would continue.

David was about to die, but Solomon would continue what he had started. It is important that our work doesn't die when we are gone. If God is involved in the things we do, then they will last.

Illustration 1

Magazine Rack

Object needed: *A magazine rack.*

When I was at school I used to go to woodwork. I was hopeless at it and I never really tried too hard. Everything I made fell apart. Whenever I had to saw in a straight line I would not concentrate properly and it would end up wobbly. Whenever I would try to use the drill I would start talking to someone else and the holes would be too big.

One day I had to make a magazine rack. I was going to take it home and give it to my mum for Christmas. But as usual I really didn't build it very well. I made the holes too big and cut the wood the wrong shape and screwed it together wrongly. I hadn't really made something that I could be proud of. I hadn't given it proper time or attention.

Lots of people live their lives like this. They never do things properly or honestly. They never work hard at doing things right. They end up with a life they can't be proud of.

I wrapped my magazine rack in gift paper and gave it to my mum for Christmas. She opened it and, although it looked a little ugly, she smiled and said thank you. Then she tried to put a magazine in it. It was OK. Then she tried another. It was still OK. Then she tried a third and the whole thing fell apart.

We need to build our woodwork properly. But, more importantly, we need to build our lives well.

Illustration 2

Life

Object needed: *The following on acetate:*

This is a wonderful formula for living our lives well. But look where it starts: doing what's right. This is the most important part. If we do what's right, then we will live fulfilled and we will die happy.

Illustration 3

Pass The Baton

Object needed: *A picture of a relay runner.*

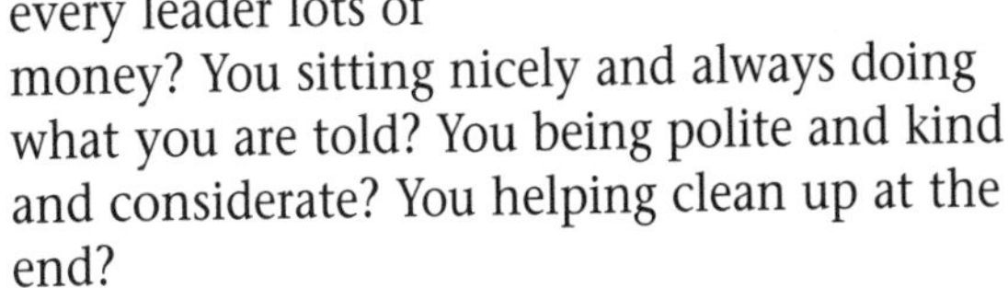

What would make me successful? What would make this children's club successful? What would make these leaders incredibly happy?

You bringing every leader lots of money? You sitting nicely and always doing what you are told? You being polite and kind and considerate? You helping clean up at the end?

These are all good things, but there is something that would make me and your leaders feel even more successful: if you would listen to what is said and start to do what we are talking about; if you got older and became a leader in our children's club; if you did just what the leaders do here, and said to God: "God, I want to help others by telling them about you, just like these leaders do."

You see, ultimate success is when you manage to pass on to someone else the job that you were doing. This means to show others how to show others Jesus.

• STORY – The Scottish Preacher

In a small church in Scotland in the 1800s the elders of the church gathered for a special meeting. The subject under consideration was the future of their minister. He was getting quite old and the only work of any significance he had undertaken in the last year was to run a Sunday school in which a nine-year-old boy had made a decision to serve Jesus. It didn't take the elders long to reach their decision. The minister was asked to step down.

They did not understand the significance of that little Sunday school and the impact that little boy would have. They thought the man in charge was a waste of money and they were looking for value for money. They didn't understand that it isn't about how much we do; it's about how much we help others do. It's no good if we start, but there's nobody to carry on.

The little boy grew up. His name was Bob. When Bob was older he would speak in universities up and down the country about what God wanted people to do. Bob's full name was Robert Moffatt. He told the people he spoke to: "There is a land in the north of Africa that has never been reached with the good news about Jesus. I saw the smoke of a thousand villages that have never heard the gospel. Who will go?"

A young man in the audience answered in his heart, "I will go". And he did. His name was David Livingstone. Africa owes much to David Livingstone. He was one of the first people to tell them about the love of God.

But it all started with a Scottish minister who did nothing of apparent significance that year, only leading a nine-year-old child to Christ! If only those men in his church had known how important his work was, they would have paid him twice as much money.

SEASONAL SPECIALS

Christmas Special: Christmas Firsts

	Programme	Item
Section 1	**Welcome**	
	Rules	
	Prayer	
	Introductory Praise	
	Game 1	Christmas Pudding Mix
	Praise	
	Fun Item 1	
	Game 2	Christmas Pudding Roll
	Fun Item 2	
	Bible Text	Isaiah 9:6
	Announcements	
	Interview	
Section 2 Preaching Time	**Worship Time**	
	Bible Lesson	Luke 1
	Illustration 1	The First Santa
	Illustration 2	The First Christmas Card
	Illustration 3	The First Christmas Tree
	Story	The First Christmas
	Prayer	

Overview There is only one historical basis for the celebration of Christmas: the birth of Jesus Christ. A lot of things have attached themselves to this one historical fact, but they all happened a long time after that major historic event. This lesson tries to strip away the things that surround the story from the central issue. However, remember to tread gently around the Santa Claus theme.

games

Christmas Pudding Mix

PREPARATION The ingredients for Christmas pudding at A and a bowl and spoon at B.

PLAYERS As many players as you have ingredients at A and one player at B.

SET-UP The players line up at A. The bowl is at B with the extra player.

OBJECT The first player runs from A to B carrying an ingredient. They then return to A; the next person then goes with the next ingredient. The player at B is doing the mixing.

WINNING The first team back wins the first set of points. However, there is a second set of points up for grabs. The puddings are now cooked (there should be enough time) and at the end of the session an independent judge tries a piece of each pudding. The best pudding gets the second set of points.

Christmas Pudding Roll

PREPARATION A Christmas pudding (very well baked – to concrete point!) per team.

PLAYERS Five per team.

SET-UP The players line up in relay formation at A with the puddings.

OBJECT Five of the players line up in relay formation at A. The players push the pudding from A to B and back using their noses.

WINNING The first team back wins.

BIBLE LESSON **LUKE 1**

"For to us a child is born, to us a son is given, and the government will be on his shoulders. And he will be called Wonderful Counsellor, Mighty God, Everlasting Father, Prince of Peace." (Isaiah 9:6)

The First Santa

Object needed: *A Santa hat.*

The original Santa Claus was the bishop of Myra in Asia in the fourth century. He was one of the most overworked saints ever. One of the legends about him suggests that he was a shy man who liked to give presents away anonymously to the poor. So, one day, he climbed onto the roof of a house and dropped a purse of money down the chimney of a family of needy girls. The purse landed in one of their stockings, which were hanging to dry near the fire.

Illustration 2

The First Christmas Card

Object needed: *A Christmas card.*

Christmas cards can be fun to get, but a nightmare to remember to write. I usually send them only to the people who send one to me first, and even then I usually upset someone by forgetting them.

The first Christmas card was made in 1843 by Sir Henry Cole. The card was sent to his friend and showed a picture of a family celebrating Christmas. These days, literally millions of cards will pass through the hands of the general post office. Some of them may even get delivered – you never know!

The First Christmas Tree

Object needed: *A Christmas tree.*

Christmas is never really complete without the Christmas tree. Putting it up, decorating it and putting the presents underneath are all exciting events. It is all made more exciting when Dad is shouting swear words because the lights don't work, your brothers and sisters are throwing baubles about, and the finale is saved for Christmas Day when the entire things falls on top of Granny.

The origin of the first tree is a bit more sinister. A missionary in the eighth century went to Germany to teach the Christian faith. On one occasion he found a group of people under an oak tree, preparing to sacrifice a child to the tree gods. The missionary rescued the child and chopped down the tree finding a small fir in its roots. He called it the "Tree of the Christ-Child". Another tradition was born.

In 1540 Martin Luther chopped down an evergreen tree and took it home to remind him that life continued through the winter. He attached some small candles to it. Then in the mid-19th century Prince Albert, a German who was married to Queen Victoria, introduced the custom to England. The ultimate Granny-squashing device was born.

• STORY – The First Christmas

Jane Ray has illustrated the nativity in her book The Story of Christmas. *It is worth showing some of the pictures as you tell the story.*

In the days of Herod the king, in the town of Nazareth, there lived a young woman named Mary. She was going to marry a carpenter, whose name was Joseph. Now the angel Gabriel was sent from God to Nazareth, to the house where Mary lived. And the angel said, "Hello, Mary! Blessed are you among women, for God has chosen you to be the mother of his Son. You shall give birth to a baby boy, and he shall be called Jesus."

And Mary said, "Let what you have said be done." And the angel left.

Now, while Mary was waiting for her child to be born, an order went out for every person to return to the town of his birth, so that a count could be made of all the people in the land. And Joseph and Mary left Nazareth together to go to Bethlehem, where Joseph was born.

When they reached Bethlehem, Mary knew it was time for the baby to be born. But the town was filled with people and there was no room for them at the inn. So the innkeeper led them to his stable, and there Mary gave birth to her son, and wrapped him in swaddling clothes. She laid him in a manger, with the ox and the ass standing by.

Now there were some shepherds in the fields nearby, keeping watch over their flocks by night. And the angel of the Lord appeared before them, and the glory of the Lord shone around. The shepherds crouched, trembling, among their sheep, but the angel said to them: "Don't be afraid, I bring you good news! Today in Bethlehem a child is born and he is Christ the Lord. This is a sign to you that you will find the baby wrapped in swaddling clothes, lying in a manger."

And a lot of other angels appeared and began praising God and singing, "Glory to God in the highest and peace on earth, goodwill to all men." The shepherds left their flocks and hurried to the stable and when they found Mary and Joseph and the baby, lying in the manger, they knelt before him and worshipped him. Then they returned home, praising God for all that they had seen, and all the people who heard them hastened to Bethlehem to see the baby for themselves.

There came also three wise men from the east, who had seen a bright light in the skies. Bearing gifts, they travelled far across seas and mountains, until they reached the city of Jerusalem. "Where is the baby who is born to be king?" they asked. "We have seen his star in the east, and have come to worship."

Now King Herod was troubled when he heard of this other King, more powerful than himself. And he sent for the wise men, saying: "Go and search for the child and return once you have found him, so that I too may come and worship him." But the king meant to kill Jesus.

And the star shone bright in the skies, guiding the wise men onwards, till it led them to

Bethlehem, and the stable where the baby lay. And when they found the baby with Mary, his mother, the wise men laid their gifts before him and worshipped him. Then they opened up their treasures for the baby – gold, and frankincense, and myrrh.

But being warned by God in a dream not to return to King Herod, they departed to their own country by another way.

And in time Joseph took Mary and the baby Jesus home to Nazareth, and the baby grew tall and strong: and the grace of God was upon him.

Easter Special: Three Trees

	Programme	Item
Section 1	**Welcome**	
	Rules	
	Prayer	
	Introductory Praise	
	Game 1	Egg Catch
	Praise	
	Fun Item 1	
	Game 2	Egg Find
	Fun Item 2	
	Bible Text	1 Corinthians 1:27
	Announcements	
	Interview	
Section 2	**Worship Time**	
Preaching	**Bible Lesson**	
Time	**Story**	Three Trees
	Prayer	

Overview One day a farmer plants three very special seeds. Three trees grow tall and strong. Every day they discuss what they want to be when they are eventually chopped down. They all have big ambitions. But the fulfilment of those ambitions is far beyond their wildest dreams.

Egg Catch

PREPARATION You will need an egg per team.

PLAYERS Two players per team.

SET-UP Players line up, one metre apart, facing each other.

OBJECT The first player throws the egg to the second. If the second player catches the egg, he (or she) takes a step backwards. If the second player drops the egg a marker is placed at the furthest point he or she reached. After catching the egg he or she throws it back to the first person.

The teams throw in turn.

WINNING The team that reaches the greatest distance apart wins.

Egg Find

PREPARATION Thirty eggs (cream eggs will do just fine).

PLAYERS Five from each team.

SET-UP Five players in standard relay pattern at point A. The eggs are hidden so that the teams can tell where they are, but the players cannot.

OBJECT The first person runs from A, finds an egg and returns. The second player then runs. This continues until one of the team has ten eggs.

WINNING The first team with ten eggs and every player sitting down wins.

"But God chose the foolish things of this world to put the wise to shame. He chose the weak things of this world to put the powerful to shame." (1 Corinthians 1:27)

● STORY – Three Trees

Once a farmer went out to sow three special seeds. He prepared the ground and planted them in just the right place. He watered them and the sun shone on them. He watered them again. The sun shone on them again. They began to grow. He watered some more. The sun shone some more. And they grew and grew and grew and grew until they were three of the tallest trees in the area.

Every day the trees would have discussions with each other. They would talk about the way the sun shone; they would talk about the squirrels who ran up and down their branches; they would talk about the way the wind blew so strong sometimes. But always they would come back to the same subject. They would ask each other: "What do you want to be when you are eventually chopped down and made into something by the carpenter?" The trees thought very hard about the question. Maybe they could be a skateboard, or a doll's house, or maybe a great big chair. They thought long and hard until each of them had made up their minds.

"I'd like to be a bed for a king," said the first tree.

"I'd like to be a ship for a king," said the second.

"I'd like to be a signpost to show people which way to go," said the third.

Many years went past. The trees talked about many other things but always they thought about the thing that they wanted to be. Then one day, over 40 years after the seeds were first planted, the carpenter came to chop down the trees. He took his axe and chopped down the first tree.

The carpenter took the tree away and began to work. He sawed and hammered and hammered and sawed. He took out his chisel and mallet and chopped away some of the edges. He took out his sandpaper and took off the rough edges. There it was. It was finished.

The tree was so excited: "I'm going to be a bed for a king!" Then he looked in the mirror. What he saw made the tree very sad. He wasn't a bed for a king but a smelly old feeding trough for animals. The carpenter took him and placed him in a stable. The tree felt very sad indeed.

The carpenter took the second tree away and began to work. He sawed and hammered and hammered and sawed. He took out his chisel and mallet and chopped away some of the edges. He took out his sandpaper and took off the rough edges. There it was. It was finished.

The tree was so excited: "I'm going to be a ship for a king!" Then he looked in the mirror. What he saw made the tree very sad. He wasn't a ship for a king but a smelly old fishing boat. Some fishermen came and took him away. Every day they would set out to sea. They'd fill their nets with fish and then empty them into the boat. The tree was very sad indeed.

The carpenter took the third tree away and began to work. He sawed and hammered and hammered and sawed. He took out his chisel and mallet and chopped away some of the edges. He took out his sandpaper and took off the rough edges. There it was. It was finished.

The tree was so excited: "I'm going to be a signpost for people everywhere!" Then he looked in the mirror. What he saw made the tree very sad. He wasn't a signpost for people everywhere but a lump of wood. He felt the saddest of all the trees.

And that's where they stayed: one feeding trough, one fishing boat and one lump of wood, which the carpenter eventually gave to some soldiers. That could be the end. And a very sad ending it would be. But it's not.

One day God decided to send Jesus into the world. Jesus was born in a stable. There was no bed so he was placed in a feeding trough for animals. When he was older, so many people wanted to hear him speak one day on a beach that he was forced to move further and further backwards almost into the sea. Then he saw it: a fishing boat. He climbed on board and spoke to the people from there. When Jesus' time on this earth was nearly finished he died on a cross – nothing more than a lump of wood – for the wrong things we had all done. And three days later, he rose from the grave.

The trees' ambitions were fulfilled in the strangest ways. The tree that wanted to be a bed for a king became a bed for the King of all kings, King Jesus. The tree that wanted to be a ship for a king became a ship for the King of all kings, King Jesus. And the tree that wanted to show all people which way to go became the tree that was to show all people the way to heaven. He became a signpost to heaven: the cross.

Those three trees were the happiest trees in the entire world. They not only became what they wanted to be, they became what God wanted them to be. And all because of King Jesus.

APPENDIX 1
Handouts

Sample letter for schools

ST MARY'S, MYTOWN
Church Office, Church Green Road,
Bletchley, Milton Keynes
01908 000000
mark-griffiths@newchurch.com

Monday 17 January 2005

Dear Headteacher / Assembly Co-ordinator,

Re: Assemblies For Primary Schools

The last academic year was interesting, to say the least. We have taken nearly 100 assemblies a term, taken several harvest presentations for parents, several carol concerts for parents and old folk, and a number of those ever-interesting Ofsted assemblies – we now have over 20 Ofsted assemblies completed. So, here is the first assembly series of the new academic year:

JANUARY – BECAUSE HE TRIED
People thought it was impossible to run a four-minute mile until Roger Bannister did it; then many others ran it in under four minutes. People thought Everest couldn't be climbed until Edmund Hillary climbed it; then many others climbed it. Sometimes when we think something is impossible we never actually try. The mountain's too big; the distance is too great... Sometimes when we try, we discover that things open up in front of us, just because we tried. This is the story of George and his determination to become a lawyer even though he and his family have never left the farm.

FEBRUARY – GREEN NOSES
A return to Max Lucado's Punchinello stories – you may remember the first story, "You are Special". If not, this isn't a problem; the stories are independent. The Wemmicks have all started painting their noses green so that they can be like the other Wemmicks. Individuality is the main theme of this assembly.

MARCH – THREE TREES
This assembly has been used in many places by many different people, but it is still very popular. One day a farmer plants three very special seeds. Three trees grow tall and strong. Every day they discuss what they want to be when they are eventually chopped down. They all have big ambitions. But the fulfilment of those ambitions is beyond their wildest dreams. The Easter story is woven into this assembly.

Booking assemblies for the next three months is a simple process of picking up the phone between 9am and 12noon each day and working out three suitable dates with our administrator. If you are part of a combined school I can come in twice or we can do back-to-back assemblies; the choice is yours. There is no charge for this service; it is very much a part of our vision to be a positive part of our community. I will also endeavour over the next couple of months to visit each of the schools within the parish to see if we can be of further service as a church.

Mark Griffiths

Sample leaflet to advertise your children's club

THE DREAM factory

Games • Quizzes • Bouncy Castle • Computer Games • Basketball • Art and Craft • Talk Time • Bible Lessons • Outings • Pool and Snooker • Face-painting • Stories • Café Area

Every Saturday 10am to 12 noon
St John's Church
Mychurch Road, My Town
For those aged 5 to 11 years

Admission only £1
Further information on 0111 111 1111

Sample handout for home visits

My Kids Club COLOURING COMPETITION

To be returned on Friday evening at the start of children's club

APPENDIX 2
The Curriculum In Various Contexts

The following is an example of how the curriculum can be "remixed" for use in special events or children's camps.

Fatherless

	Programme	Item	Timings
Welcome	**Welcome**		2 minutes
	Rules		3 minutes
Prayer	**Prayer**		3 minutes
Praise	**Introductory Praise**		5 minutes
	Fun Item(s)		4 minutes
	Praise		5 minutes
	Story	The Pirate King (Part 3)	10 minutes
	Worship		5 minutes
Preaching		Samson	15 minutes
Time	**You will need:**		
	1. A picture of the Incredible Hulk		
	2. A picture of a happy face		
	3. A picture of a neutral face		
	4. A picture of a sad face		
	5. Two cards with the words "visionless" and "wounded" on them		
Response	**Response**		3 minutes
Handouts	**Handouts**		3 minutes
	Farewells		2 minutes

Samson thought he could do what he wanted. He thought he didn't need to keep his focus on God; God would help him anyway. God loves us, but if we don't keep our focus on God we end up hurt and lost.

WELCOME

RULES

PRAYER

Father, open our hearts today.
Allow us to hear what you want to say.
Speak to those who believe in you and love you,
But also speak to those who don't know you exist.
Show us today the importance of keeping our eyes on you.
In Jesus' name we ask these things,
Amen.

PRAISE

FUN ITEM(S)

PRAISE

STORY – The Pirate King (Part 3)

Kristy arrived at the coast. She was going to find her brother and do what she could to rescue him. She wasn't completely sure how she felt about her brother, but he *was* her brother and she felt that she had a responsibility to rescue him. The harbour was a mad world of drunken sailors, men and women trying to sell their day's catch off the back of their boats, people shouting and the overpowering smell of fish.

Kristy had never seen such activity – she had grown up in the seclusion of the manor house. She had never seen so many people in such a small area. The whole thing seemed so exciting to her. She walked towards what appeared to be a makeshift market. She gazed at one stall full of ornate shells; she marvelled at the collection of pearls of all shapes, sizes and prices on the next. She watched as the various crabs and lobsters crawled over each other in a tank at the next stall, in a desperate attempt not to be plucked out of the water by the old woman who was looking for some dinner for her husband.

Kristy walked a little further and found herself enjoying the experience. She was enjoying the sounds, the odd people; she was even getting used to the smell of fish.

She had come to rescue her brother. That was her goal; that's what she was looking towards. But the sights and sounds were so attractive. She thought that maybe staying here overnight wouldn't be a problem. She was fairly sure that one more day wouldn't make much difference to her brother – fairly sure! So she walked into the nearest tavern and asked the barmaid if there was a room she could have for the night. The barmaid took her money and showed her to her room – it wasn't much bigger than a cleaning cupboard but it would do. After all, it was only for one night.

The following day, Kristy got up and wandered downstairs. She ordered breakfast and paid her money. She would be going today so she would need a good breakfast. She finished her breakfast and figured that one more look around outside wouldn't do any harm. After all, she might not be back this way for quite some time.

If anything, the makeshift market had got even bigger. It now included a whole range of clothes that had clearly come from different parts of the world. She looked at some wonderfully coloured carpets with intricate designs. She walked around for many hours until she noticed the sun beginning to set. She rushed back to the inn, ate some dinner and would have been on her way but it was now dark, so she decided she would wait one more night...

And so it went on. Every day Kristy found another excuse to stay just one more day. Days turned into weeks, and soon Kristy was out of money. She ordered breakfast one morning and to her horror discovered she couldn't pay for it. The barmaid smiled and looked at Kristy: "You can work here. If you work this morning, then that will cover breakfast and if you work this afternoon, then that should cover your room. If you work this evening, we may even give you some money."

Kristy had forgotten. She had forgotten why she had come here in the first place. She had forgotten her end goal. She had forgotten Cameron... It had happened so easily. She had taken her eyes off the target and so she was in trouble.

Now, every day, Kristy served at tables and wandered around the harbour. Every day she met new people and made new friends. She was enjoying herself. And then one day she walked down for breakfast and saw a family sitting eating breakfast. They had arrived the night before and they were hungry. They were clearly a mum, a dad and two children – a brother and sister. The girl was about eight and the boy was about ten. They were whispering to each other and giggling about something that only they could see. The parents were telling them off persistently but still they laughed.

Then Kristy's mind began to wander. She remembered the times when she and Cameron had giggled their way through formal dinners. She remembered the secrets they used to share and then, like a bolt of lightning, she remembered why she was there!

She threw down her apron and hurried towards the harbour. Her money was gone and she didn't know how she would pay for her voyage to find her brother, but she was on her way. She marched to the harbour, and at the first ship she climbed on board to talk to the captain. She had remembered why she was there. She had focused again.

(To be continued...)

• WORSHIP

• PREACHING TIME

Display the picture of the Incredible Hulk.

Today we are going to talk about God's Incredible Hulk. He never turned green but he was incredibly strong. His name was Samson and here's what happened...

Display the picture of the smiling face.

Samson's birth was a miracle. His mum and dad couldn't have children, then one day an angel appeared to Samson's parents and told them they would have a baby and he would be a Nazirite. A Nazirite was someone who was special to God and who lived by a special set of rules. Samson was not allowed to cut his hair and he was not allowed to drink wine.

Samson was a special child, but no more special than you. Psalm 139 tells me that before you were born God knew exactly how you would look. He watched you growing in your mummy's tummy.

Samson had long hair. He was not allowed to cut his hair. Many people may have made fun of Samson's long hair, but probably only once. For God gave Samson power and he could do amazing things.

On one occasion, a lion had jumped out at Samson but Samson was so strong he tore the lion in half. On another occasion, he killed thousands of Philistines with the jawbone of a donkey. On yet another occasion, when the Philistines (God's enemies) had tried to trap him by locking him in a city, Samson had simply pulled the town's gates out of the ground. God's Spirit would come upon Samson and he would do amazing things for God.

It was a great start.

Display the picture of the neutral face.

There were definitely some interesting things taking place here. You remember the two things that Samson wasn't allowed to do:

1. Drink wine
2. Have his hair cut

You see, keeping these rules showed that he still loved God and was still looking to God for his strength. But the time when he tore the lion in half is interesting. If you or I tore a lion in half we would be telling everyone about it, but not Samson; the Bible says that he didn't tell anyone. This might seem strange until we work out where all this happened. The Bible says the lion attacked him outside Timnah's vineyard. Now does anyone know what we get in vineyards? Yes, wine! Maybe Samson was playing with things he shouldn't be near.

I think he thought he could do whatever he wanted and God would still look after him. This just isn't true.

Display the picture of the sad face.

Now the story gets very sad indeed:

> Some time later, Samson fell in love with a woman named Delilah, who lived in Sorek Valley. The Philistine rulers went to Delilah and said, "Trick Samson into telling you what makes him so strong and what can make him weak.

Then we can tie him up so he can't get away. If you find out his secret, we will each give you eleven hundred pieces of silver."

The next time Samson was at Delilah's house, she asked, "Samson, what makes you so strong? How can I tie you up so you can't get away? Come on, you can tell me."

Samson answered, "If someone ties me up with seven new bowstrings that have never been dried, it will make me just as weak as anyone else."

The Philistine rulers gave seven new bowstrings to Delilah. They also told some of their soldiers to go to Delilah's house and hide in the room where Samson and Delilah were. If the bowstrings made Samson weak, they would be able to capture him.

Delilah tied up Samson with the bowstrings and shouted, "Samson, the Philistines are attacking!" (Judges 16:4–9a)

Samson snapped the bowstrings and then he snapped the Philistines! Delilah asked him again what would make him lose his strength.

"My hair is in seven braids," Samson replied. "If you weave my braids into the threads on a loom and nail the loom to a wall, then I will be as weak as anyone else."

While Samson was asleep, Delilah wove his braids into the threads on a loom and nailed the loom to a wall. Then she shouted, "Samson, the Philistines are attacking!"

Samson woke up and pulled the loom free from its posts in the ground and from the nails in the wall. Then he pulled his hair free from the woven cloth.

"Samson," Delilah said, "you claim to love me, but you don't mean it! You've made me look like a fool three times now, and you still haven't told me why you are so strong." Delilah started nagging and pestering him day after day, until he couldn't stand it any longer.

Finally, Samson told her the truth. "I have belonged to God ever since I was born, so my hair has never been cut. If it were ever cut off, my strength would leave me, and I would be as weak as anyone else."

Delilah realised that he was telling the truth. So she sent someone to tell the Philistine rulers, "Come to my house one more time. Samson has finally told me the truth."

The Philistine rulers went to Delilah's house, and they brought along the silver they had promised her. Delilah had lulled Samson to sleep with his head resting in her lap. She signalled to one of the Philistine men as she began cutting off Samson's seven braids. And by the time she was finished, Samson's strength was gone. Delilah tied him up and shouted, "Samson, the Philistines are attacking!"

Samson woke up and thought, "I'll break loose and escape, just as I always do." He did not realise that the LORD had stopped helping him. (Judges 16:13b–20)

This is one of the saddest verses in the Bible. Samson thought God would be with him, no matter what he did. He thought he could do whatever he liked and God would still be there.

The Philistines grabbed Samson and poked out his eyes. They took him to the prison in Gaza and chained him up. Samson had become *visionless* and *wounded.* He didn't know where he was going and he was hurt. He was lost and hurt.

Display two cards as shown below.

- **Visionless**
- **Didn't know where he was going**
- **Lost**

- **Wounded**
- **Hurt**

Some of you may have felt like this and some of you may be feeling like this now. There is only one answer. Let me show you how the story ends.

The Philistine rulers threw a big party and sacrificed a lot of animals to their god Dagon... They made fun of Samson for a while, then they told him to stand near the columns that supported the roof. A young man was leading Samson by the hand, and Samson said to him, "I need to lean against something. Take me over to the columns that hold up the roof."

The Philistine rulers were celebrating in a temple packed with people and with three thousand more on the flat roof. They had all been watching Samson and making fun of him.

Samson prayed, "Please remember me, LORD God. The Philistines poked out my eyes, but make me strong one last time, so I can take revenge for at least one of my eyes!" (Judges 16:23–28)

At the very end Samson looked to God. He asked God to help and Samson felt God start to help him again.

> Samson was standing between the two middle columns that held up the roof. He felt around and found one column with his right hand, and the other with his left hand. He pushed against the columns as hard as he could, and the temple collapsed with the Philistine rulers and everyone else still inside. Samson killed more Philistines when he died than he had killed during his entire life. (Judges 16:29–30)

The only answer when we become visionless and wounded is to look again to God and he will strengthen us and help us.

RESPONSE

There may be those here today who understand the last two words that describe Samson at the end: "visionless" – he didn't know where he was going – he felt lost. And "wounded" – he felt hurt. But if you feel lost or hurt there is a God who wants you to look to him again. And he promises to bind up broken hearts and show you the way to go.

If it is appropriate, ask the children who want to be prayed for to come forward – or stand up, or raise a hand – then members of the team should pray for them where they are.

HANDOUTS

FAREWELLS

APPENDIX 3
Bible Texts

"No one can come to me, unless the Father who sent me makes them want to come."

John 6:44

"God cares for you, so turn all
your worries over to him."

1 Peter 5:7

"You did not choose me (God). I (God) chose you and sent you out to produce fruit, the sort of fruit that will last."

John 15:16

"You will be rewarded when the time is right, if you don't give up."

Galatians 6:9

"And so, if we have God's Son, we have this life. But if we don't have the Son, we don't have this life."

1 John 5:12

“Jabez was a man who got his name because of the pain he caused his mother…”

1 Chronicles 4:10

"But he was still the most
respected son in his family."

1 Chronicles 4:9

“One day he prayed to [. . .] God, ‘Please bless me and give me a lot of land.’ ”

1 Chronicles 4:9

“ ‘Be with me so I will be safe from harm.’ ”

1 Chronicles 4:10

"And God did just what Jabez had asked."

1 Chronicles 4:10

"Faith that doesn't lead us to do good deeds is all alone and dead!"

James 2:17

“Do something to show that you have really given up your sins.”

Matthew 3:8

“Suppose one of you wants to build a tower. What is the first thing you will do? Won’t you sit down and figure out how much it will cost and if you have enough money to pay for it?”

Luke 14:28

"I will know that you are working together and that you are struggling side by side to get others to believe the good news."

Philippians 1:27

"And endurance builds character, which gives us a hope..."

Romans 5:4

"So we must get rid of everything that slows us down, especially the sin that just won't let go. And we must be determined to run the race that is ahead of us."

Hebrews 12:1

“[You] will learn that I am the Lord. No other gods are real.”

Isaiah 45:6

"In the beginning God created
the heavens and the earth."

Genesis 1:1

"The Word became a human being and lived here with us. We saw his true glory, the glory of the only Son of the Father. From him all the kindness and all the truth of God have come down to us."

John 1:14

“The greatest way to show love for friends is to die for them.”

John 15:13

"... and then they will hand him over to foreigners who will make fun of him. They will beat him and nail him to a cross. But on the third day he will rise from death."

Matthew 20:19

"I don't need to write to you about the time or date when all this will happen. You know that the Lord's return will be as a thief coming at night."

1 Thessalonians 5:1–2

"But the Holy Spirit will come upon you and give you power. Then you will tell everyone about me..."

Acts 1:8

“I will build my church, and death itself will not have any power over it.”

Matthew 16:18

“Increase in number there; do not decrease.”

Jeremiah 29:6

“When you walk through fire
you won’t be burnt.”

Isaiah 43:2

"For you will receive power when the Holy Spirit comes upon you; and you will be my witnesses in Jerusalem and in all Judea and Samaria, and to the ends of the earth."

Acts 1:8

“I forget what is behind, and I struggle for what is ahead.”

Philippians 3:13

"I press on towards the goal
to win the prize for which God
has called me."

Philippians 3:14

“Go to the people of all nations and make them my disciples.”

Matthew 28:18

"Making the most of every opportunity, because the days are evil..."

Ephesians 5:16

"But God showed how much he loved us by having Christ die for us, even though we were sinful."

Romans 5:8

"People judge others by what they look like, but I (God) judge people by what is in their hearts."

1 Samuel 16:7

"They will also heal sick people by placing their hands on them."

Mark 16:18

"Now the time has come for me to die. My life is like a drink offering being poured out on the altar. I have fought well. I have finished the race, and I have been faithful."

2 Timothy 4:6–7

"At that time Moses was born, and he was no ordinary child."

Acts 7:20

"And the fire will test the quality of each person's work."

1 Corinthians 3:13

“God replied: ‘Don’t come any closer… the ground where you are standing is holy.’ ”

Exodus 3:5

"I praise you because I am fearfully and wonderfully made."

Psalm 139:14

"Because the one who is in you is greater than the one who is in the world."

1 John 4:4

"If you think you are standing firm, be careful that you don't fall!"

1 Corinthians 10:12

"But God does not take away life; instead, he devises ways so that a banished person may not remain estranged from him."

2 Samuel 14:14

"What else can I say? There isn't enough time to tell about Gideon, Barak, Samson, Jephthah, David, Samuel, and the prophets."

Hebrews 11:32

“Don’t give up and be
helpless in times of trouble.”

Proverbs 24:10

"My son, I will soon die, as everyone must. But I want you to be strong and brave. Do what the Lord your God commands and follow his teachings."

1 Kings 2:2–3

"For to us a child is born, to us a son is given, and the government will be on his shoulders. And he will be called Wonderful Counsellor, Mighty God, Everlasting Father, Prince of Peace."

Isaiah 9:6

"But God chose the foolish things of this world to put the wise to shame. He chose the weak things of this world to put the powerful to shame."

1 Corinthians 1:27

APPENDIX 4
Visual Aids

Hudson Taylor's Time Line

1832	Hudson Taylor Born
1851	Hudson begins medical studies in Hull
1852	Hudson continues medical training in London
1853	Hudson sets sail for China (1st Visit)
1854	Hudson arrives in China
1856	Peter dies by drowning
1857	Nyi becomes a Christian
1858	Hudson marries Maria
1859	First child born
1860	Hudson is very ill; he and Maria return home
1862	Qualified as a doctor
1862	Second child born
1864	Third child born
1865	Fourth child born
1865	CIM started
1866	Hudson returns to China (2nd Visit)
1868	Fifth child born
1870	Sixth child born

1870	The new baby and Hudson's wife dies
1871	Hudson marries his second wife, Jennie
1875–86	Hudson journeys back and forth from China
1887–	Hudson journeys through Europe, Australia and North America
1898	Many missionaries beheaded
1903	Jennie dies
1905	Hudson Taylor dies and is buried in China alongside his first wife, Maria

KAZAKHSTAN
RUSSIA
MONGOLIA
CHINA
INDIA

UNITED KINGDOM

APPENDIX 5
Useful Contacts

LEGAL ISSUES AND CHILD PROTECTION

Legislation surrounding children's clubs and the very serious issues associated with child protection are outside the remit of this book. The rules change with infuriating frequency and the procedure to ensure your club/project has the proper policies in place can be a minefield. The best I can do is point you in the direction of the experts.

For all you need to know about writing a clear child protection policy, contact:

Churches' Child Protection Advisory Service
PO Box 133
Swanley
Kent
BR8 7UQ

Tel: (0845) 120 45 50

Also, it is certainly worthwhile owning a copy of: *A Policy on Child Protection: A Policy Document of the House of Bishops*, published by SPCK. This is worth having, whatever your denominational affiliation.

For help on other legal issues, including police checks, contact:

Criminal Records Bureau
Disclosure Services
PO Box 110
Liverpool
L69 3EF

Tel: (0870) 90 90 844

For help with data protection issues, contact:

Information Services
Information Commissioner's office
Wycliffe House
Water Lane
Wilmslow
SK9 5AF

Tel: (01625) 545 745

APPENDIX 6
Recommended Resources

Recommended Resources

MUSIC

Children of the Cross, Jim Bailey (Kingsway)
God's Gang, Jim Bailey (Kingsway)
King of Heaven, Doug Horley (Kingsway)
Shout to the Lord Kids 1 & 2, North Point Church (Integrity)
Fandabidozzie, Doug Horley (Kingsway)
Whoopah Wahey!, Doug Horley (Kingsway)
Lovely Jubbly, Doug Horley (Kingsway)
Ishmael's Collections, Ishmael (Kingsway)
Soul Survivor Collections, Compilation (Survivor Records)
Extreme Worship, Jim Bailey (Kingsway)
Every Move I Make, Promiseland (Willow Creek)

MATERIAL FOR SCHOOLS

52 Ideas for Junior Classroom Assemblies, Chris Chesterton & Pat Gutteridge (Monarch)
52 Ideas for Infant School Assemblies, Chris Chesterton & Elaine Buckley (Monarch)
The Lion Storyteller Bible (Lion Publishing)

BOOKS

77 Talks for 21st Century Kids, Chris Chesterton (Monarch)
77 Talks for Cyberspace Kids, Chris Chesterton & David T. Ward (Monarch)
Fusion, Mark Griffiths (Monarch)
Impact, Mark Griffiths (Monarch)
Don't Tell Cute Stories – Change Lives, Mark Griffiths (Monarch)
Reclaiming a Generation, Ishmael (Kingsway)
Devil Take the Youngest, Winkie Pratney (Bethany House)
Fire on the Horizon, Winkie Pratney (Renew Books, Gospel Light)
Streets of Pain, Bill Wilson (Word)
The Tide is Running Out, Peter Brierley (Christian Research)
Children's Ministry, Lawrence O. Richards (Zondervan)
The Prayer of Jabez for Kids, Bruce Wilkinson (Thomas Nelson)
Come Holy Spirit, David Pytches (Hodder & Stoughton)

MATERIAL FOR SMALL GROUPS

History Makers, Andy & Catherine Kennedy (Spring Harvest)
Children in the Bible, Andy & Catherine Kennedy (Spring Harvest)

HOLIDAY CLUB MATERIAL

Kim's Quest, Mark Griffiths (Monarch)

VIDEOS

The Veggie Tales Series, Big Idea Production (distr. Word)
The Testament Series (Bible Society)
The Miracle Maker (Bible Society)

RECOMMENDED WEBSITES FOR RESOURCE MATERIAL

www.kingdomcreative.co.uk
www.duggiedugdug.co.uk
www.ishmael.org.uk
www.kidzblitz.com
www.tricksfortruth.com
www.armslength.com

PUPPETS AND GENERAL

For a spectacular range of puppets, visit www.armslength.com or www.tricksfortruth.com

SUMMER CAMPS

For information on interdenominational summer camps for children, check out www.treasurekids.co.uk, www.pathfinder.com or www.new-wine.org

SHORT-TERM MISSION

King's Kids offer short-term mission opportunities for children and can be contacted via the Youth With A Mission website www.kingskidsengland.co.uk

CONTACT

If you would like Mark Griffiths to come and talk to your children's leaders or you have any observations on this book, please contact me on markgriff@lineone.net